VOICE OF REGION

THE LONG JOURNEY TO SENATE REFORM IN CANADA

RANDALL WHITE

DUNDURN PRESS
Toronto & Oxford
1990

Copyediting: Judith Turnbull and Patti Giovannini
Design and Production: Andy Tong
Printing and Binding: Gagné Printing Ltd., Louiseville, Quebec, Canada

The writing of this manuscript and the publication of this book were made possible by support from several sources. The publisher wishes to acknowledge the generous assistance and ongoing support of The Canada Council, The Book Publishing Industry Development Programme of the Department of Communications, and The Ontario Arts Council.

J. Kirk Howard, Publisher

Canadian Cataloguing in Publication Data

White, Randall.
  Voice of region

Includes bibliographical references.
ISBN 1-55002-054-4 (pbk.)

1. Canada. Parliament. Senate - Reform.
2. Regionalism - Canada - History. 3. Canada.
Parliament. Senate - History. I. Title.

JL157.1990.W48 1990   328.71'071   C89-095248-5

Dundurn Press Limited
2181 Queen Street East, Suite 301
Toronto, Canada
M4E 1E5

Dundurn Distribution Limited
73 Lime Walk
Headington, Oxford
England
0X3 7AD

VOICE
OF
REGION
THE LONG JOURNEY TO
SENATE REFORM IN CANADA

RANDALL WHITE

Current Issues in Historical Perspective: Number Two

CONTENTS

Part Four: Beyond Survival

Conclusion

Appendices: Three Proposals for a Reformed Senate

PREFACE AND ACKNOWLEDGEMENTS

This book is the second volume in the Dundurn Press series: **Current Issues in Historical Perspective.**

The narrow premise of the series is that, particularly in late twentieth century Canada, it is often hard to grasp the significance of current political debate, without some concrete awareness of how at least the broadest issues have evolved historically. This is especially true for a number of key Canadian constitutional issues, and Senate reform is certainly one of them.

The late twentieth century Hungarian-born American historian John Lukacs has summarized a wider premise: In our time, "reality has become dependent less on those who cry 'Wolf!' than on those who see that the emperor has no clothes, indeed, that he is not a human figure at all; and that the inevitable element in the reality of that kind of seeing is a knowledge — or at least a consciousness — of history."

Within the customary limitations of time and space, I have tried to tell a complete story. I hope that some readers will be interested enough to pursue it from start to finish. Others, however, will be more interested in only some parts of the story, and I have tried to make the book equally useful for them.

I think the book is, in the first place, written to people in Ontario, whom I know best, and who may not be as familiar with the argument as people in other parts of the country. The book equally aspires, however, to make contact with the much wider Canadian audience, from *Ocean to Ocean* (to borrow the title of a book by the late nineteenth century Nova Scotian, George Monro Grant). In this setting, what follows can no doubt be classed as one version of an Ontario pro-Senate reform view of its subject.

Saying this of course implies nothing about pretending or presuming to speak for Ontario. Even the current premier has recently stressed that only the regional electorate has this right and privilege. I simply mean to recognize and make clear where the book is coming from, on an issue where this does make a difference. According to the current premier of Prince Edward Island, the "reality of Canada is that the perspective changes depending on where you are."

Some both inside and outside Ontario may feel that an Ontario pro-Senate reform view of the long journey to Senate reform in Canada (to paraphrase the title of another book: Gabriel Sagard's *The Long Journey to the Country of the Hurons*, first published in French in the seventeenth century) is a contradiction in terms. They have forgotten Oliver Mowat, premier of Ontario without interruption from 1872 to 1896, and a proponent of an elected Senate for the Canadian Confederation at the Quebec Conference of 1864. It may or may not be equally intriguing that Oliver Mowat was a Liberal premier of Ontario, in a venerable Central Canadian Grit tradition.

I should also make clear that the book is not a short history of the Canadian Senate. It is a short account of the historical background to the current debate on Senate reform in Canada.

This debate is not fundamentally about how a particular branch of the machinery of government at Ottawa has evolved over time. It is about how Canadian national political institutions have — and have not — responded to the particular varieties of regionalism in the Confederation, and especially to the regionalism of Western and Atlantic Canada.

Thus the book has as much to do with the history of Canadian regionalism as with the history of the Canadian Senate. It is tilted more toward Atlantic and Western Canada than toward Ontario and Quebec. It is especially tilted toward Western Canada, since that is where concern for Senate reform has been most intense, in our own time and for much of the rest of the twentieth century.

Similarly, when it does directly address the Senate or the Canadian upper or second chamber of government as an institution, the book deals only with the federal Senate in Ottawa. It takes no serious account of the history of the pre-Confederation provincial Legislative Councils, which were, in one formal sense, the initial models for the federal Senate of Canada. In some provinces, these institutions continued for some time after Confederation. Ontario was not one of them, and the book's Ontario origins may be reflected here as well. On the other hand, none of the provincial Legislative Councils has survived down to the present, and their history has no logical relationship to the current debate on Senate reform.

The book is based on research in various kinds of historical and contemporary political literature, and related primary data. A select bibliography at the end suggests my debts in this context. Unless otherwise noted, the sources for all data given in tables and the text are Statistics Canada and Canada's chief federal electoral officer.

The concept for the book was suggested by Kirk Howard at Dundurn Press. I am particularly indebted to him and to Jeanne MacDonald, and to Ian Low, Andy Tong, and Rashid Farah, for many forms of highly valued aid and support.

Boyd Holmes has subjected the style and substance of the original manuscript to an apt and stimulating critique. Ron Stagg of the History Department at Ryerson Polytechnical Institute has saved me from some mistakes in historical detail, and made many helpful and telling suggestions about the text. Patti Giovannini and Judith Turnbull have carefully guided the manuscript through its final stages.

I am also indebted to officials of the following organizations, who kindly responded to queries relating to the later parts of the book: the Department of Federal and Intergovernmental Affairs, Alberta; the Office of the Premier, Federal-Provincial/International Relations, British Columbia; the Secretary to Cabinet for Intergovernmental Relations, Manitoba; the Department of Intergovernmental Affairs, New Brunswick; the Intergovernmental Affairs Secretariat, Newfoundland and Labrador; the Executive Council Secretariat, Intergovernmental Affairs, Northwest Territories; the Office of Special Advisor on Constitutional and Intergovernmental Affairs, Nova Scotia; the Ministry of Intergovernmental Affairs, Ontario; the Executive Council Office, Prince Edward Island; the Executive Council Office, Yukon Territory; the Secretary Canadian Intergovernmental Conferences, and the Secretary to the Cabinet for Federal-Provincial Relations, both in Ottawa. Finally, I owe a note of thanks to Tom Hogue and Andrew Coyne for some very recent documentation on Senate reform in Canada.

R.W.
Toronto, December, 1989.

INTRODUCTION

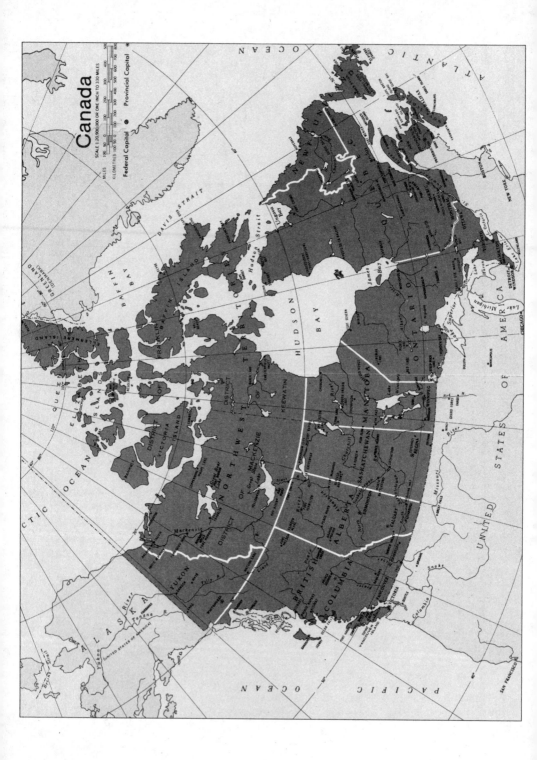

Canada

1
THE CANADIAN QUESTION IN THE 1990s

When the political scientist Donald Smiley published a provocative study of Canadian federalism in 1972, he observed that the "completion of this short book has been delayed by two periods in which I ceased work because of the judgement that the federation would not last as long as it would take to finish the manuscript." In 1983 James Lee, then premier of Prince Edward Island, similarly confessed that the "mood of the times has been characterized by extreme pessimism with regard to a future for Canada."

In September 1989 Pierre Laurin, Quebec general manager for Merrill Lynch Canada, told the federal Progressive Conservative caucus from Quebec that "Canada today is in serious danger of breaking apart .... The danger is far greater than it was during the 1980 referendum or during the October Crisis of 1970." In October 1989 John Godfrey, editor of *The Financial Post* in Toronto, reported "an ominous feeling that the country is falling apart."

Such feelings have a long history. Goldwin Smith, an eminent expatriate intellectual from the United Kingdom, first raised "the Canadian question" in 1891. Then as now, it involved sometimes emotional debate about relations between Canada and the United States. It was complicated by often choleric controversy over the future of what Smith called the "French province" of Quebec, and the place of the French language in Canada outside Quebec.

The Canadian question in the 1990s also subsumes two other fundamental issues, unknown to practical politics in the late nineteenth century. One involves the future of the country's Indian, Inuit, and Métis peoples in the twenty-first century. The other takes up what a still relevant book of the 1920s christened the "unreformed Senate of Canada."

The second of these newer issues is the subject of the present book. In the 1990s, however, it is impossible to ponder the future of the Canadian Senate realistically without addressing its wider political and constitutional context. The book begins and ends with meditations on how Senate reform relates to the larger Canadian question, in its late twentieth century incarnation.

If nothing else, trying to answer the question keeps Canada in business. This is probably as worthwhile a national quest as any other country can lay claim to in our time. And it has its fair share of implications for the wider concerns of humanity in the age of the global village. As in the past, ultimate habits of moderation and compromise are likely to remain a crucial part of the Canadian future. But, to borrow a phrase from the novelist Anthony Burgess, in the 1990s the disparate Canadian body politic is also flirting with the rash act of "taking Canada seriously."

Canada and the United States

It is Canada's fate to be a part of North America north of the Rio Grande and the Gulf of Mexico, without being part of the United States of America. This is a fate assigned by history. On democratic assumptions each generation is at least theoretically free to make history as it pleases. Yet for more than 200 years people who have called themselves Canadians have recurrently decided to keep faith with the particular destiny handed down by the past. Opinion polls in the late twentieth century make clear that the great majority of Canadians, in all regions of the country, continue to oppose any form of political union with the United States.

At the same time, Canadian opinion has always been more divided on the issue of economic relations between the two countries. The first formal free trade agreement between what are now Canada and the United States predates the Canadian Confederation of the late 1860s and early 1870s (and the American Civil War). In the late 1980s the pressures of a newly emerging global economy, reflected in plans for an unprecedented economic integration of Western Europe by 1992, led to a new Canada-U.S. Free Trade Agreement in North America. The agreement has a 10-year implementation period that began in 1989. It can be cancelled by either party on six months notice.

At the edge of the 1990s, the future of the Canada-U.S. Free Trade Agreement is far from clear. Brian Mulroney's Progressive Conservative Party won a majority of House of Commons seats in the November 1988 Canadian federal election, in which "Mulroney's trade agreement" was the central issue. But the federal Liberals and New Democrats, who opposed the agreement, won 52% of the popular vote. Staunch opponents of the deal during the election campaign have continued their opposition even after its implementation. By the late fall of 1989, opinion polls had still not registered majority support among all the people of Canada.

A rather too strong Canadian dollar throughout the agreement's first year of implementation can be blamed for dampening initial positive effects anticipated by strong supporters of Canada-U.S. free trade. In October 1989 the Ottawa lawyer and political observer Arthur Drache argued that "it seems to most observers that at least up to now, the much-touted benefits which were to accrue to Canadian business from free trade have yet to become apparent." At about the same time, *Business Week* in the U.S. reported:

> So far, Mulroney has failed to convince many Canadians that free trade is a good thing .... Many Canadians believe that freer competition will lead to a harsher society .... Since winning the election a year ago with only 43% of the popular vote, Mulroney's approval rating has sunk to 27%. If he can't do a better job of selling his trade and fiscal reforms, Canadians will have no qualms about registering their displeasure come next election.

Yet, whatever may become of the particular trade agreement negotiated by Brian Mulroney's government, in one way or another Canada and the United States are bound to maintain the increasingly close economic ties that have developed over the past half century and more. Discussion has begun as well on some form of new trade agreement between the United States and Mexico, in which Canada may or may not be involved. (Even without an agreement, as the chief executive of Cementos Mexicanos, Lorenzo Zambrano, has recently explained, the "economic border between Mexico and the United States has disappeared.") In the fall of 1989 Canada at last decided to join the international arm of the Western Hemisphere known as the Organization of American States.

At bottom, what is happening flows from changes in the global economy that virtually all parts of the world must somehow accommodate. In turn, these changes raise new challenges for Canada's national political institutions. And one of these challenges is to at last reform the Senate of Canada.

The University of Calgary political scientist Ted Morton has summarized the argument: "As Canada enters the new era of free trade with the U.S., it needs a strong and effective national government to protect its interests." Alas, Canada's present national government is rooted strictly in the elected House of Commons at Ottawa. The "House of Commons, based on the 'representation by population' formula, is dominated by Ontario and Quebec." The Confederation does have a Senate, meant to bolster national representation from Atlantic and Western Canada. But this is merely an appointed body — a "political nullity" in Morton's language. The "antidote for this problem is Senate reform: elected, effective, and a more equal delegation from each province."

In the late twentieth century, Canada's need to address the continuing evolution of the Canada-U.S. economic relationship from a position of strength is a key reason for including Senate reform in any answer to the Canadian question that Canadians might contrive.

The Distinct Society in Quebec

The evolution of the now vanished British Empire has bequeathed three new transcontinental federations outside the Old World heartland of English-speaking culture: the United States, Canada, and Australia. Canada is the only one of the three that does not have an elected (and an equal and effective) Senate to represent regional interests in national political institutions.

One reason for this is that the first people who called themselves Canadians spoke French. Even today Canada, unlike Australia or the United States, is a French-speaking as well as an English-speaking country, with the great majority of its French-speaking citizens living in the province of Quebec. Historically, many French Canadians have viewed the kind of elected Senate that both Australia and the United States have as a threat to the survival of the French fact in the wider Canadian democracy.

13

History, however, evolves. Sometimes it even progresses. In the past generation both the role of Quebec and the French fact in Canada have been objects of agonized debate and impassioned political action. Real progress was made in the 1970s and 1980s. But as the 1990s begin, some key aspects of the issue remain unresolved. Though the future of Quebec and French Canada is far from the only element in the Canadian question of the 1990s, it remains extremely important.

In principle, there are only two ways of accommodating Morton's approach to Senate reform with a vigorous national commitment to the French fact in Canada. Either vastly much larger numbers of Canadians from the Atlantic to the Pacific must speak both French and English than is now the case, or the province of Quebec must be recognized as a "distinct society" within Canada, as provided in the 1987 Meech Lake Accord.

Senator Keith Davey has described Canada's "Senate Chamber" in Ottawa as "a majestic place .... Set against basic red coloring (in the House of Commons it is green), the elegant stone and wood carvings of saints, explorers, generals and their symbols are beautiful. The Senate is adorned with six huge paintings of World War I events, from a collection presented to Canada by Lord Beaverbrook. The magnificent vaulted ceiling consists of glass sections outlined in gold leaf. Its two massive bronze chandeliers each weigh about two tons." In the eyes of late twentieth century advocates of major Senate reform, this is too majestic a setting for a national "political nullity."

The more than two decades of national efforts to promote French and English bilingualism in Canada outside Quebec have had more success than they are credited with. Nonetheless, in practice, the constitutional recognition of Quebec as a distinct society is still the only realistic antidote to Quebec's traditional fears about the implications of Senate reform for the continued flourishing of Canada's historic French culture.

A few vocal advocates of major Senate reform have not altogether grasped this point, either because they do not care deeply enough about the fate of Canada's French fact or because they have not thought the matter through. But the most aggressive, serious, and politically influential Senate reformers do understand what is at stake.

This explains the staunch defence of the Meech Lake Accord put up by Alberta's intergovernmental affairs minister, Jim Horsman, in a speech to the Toronto corporate elite early in 1989. Much later in the year, the Vancouver businessman Gordon Gibson, co-author of an important 1981 report advocating an elected Canadian Senate, declared that the "only successful solution" to Canada's constitutional dilemmas in the 1990s "will surely retain a full 'distinct society' for Quebec, and a new central institution like the 'triple E' Senate for outer Canada."

Awkward questions can be raised about the implications of a "full" (or officially unilingual French) distinct society, inside Quebec, for the future of the French language in Canada outside Quebec. The editors of *The Financial Post* also made a fundamental point in the fall of 1989, when they stressed that it is no longer acceptable for those who cannot speak both of Canada's official languages to aspire seriously to the office of prime minister of Canada. This

> has nothing to do with "forcing" unilingual Canadians to be bilingual. It has everything to do with communicating to both official-language groups, and, in so doing, to help bring these groups closer together. Awareness of that should be a further encouragement to those who aspire to national leadership to acquire a facility in both languages.

Yet in the 1990s Canada has exhausted the potential of "let's pretend" solutions to its constitutional dilemmas (as in "Let's pretend that at some unknown point in some distant future the vast majority of us, in all parts of the country, actually will speak both official languages"). Quite rightly, such solutions do not fool les Québécois. Moreover, even with the best of intentions, public policies which pretend that Canada outside Quebec — and, to a lesser extent, outside New Brunswick — actually is a functioning bilingual society, ultimately constitute an anti-democratic attack on the historic culture and heritage of English-speaking Canada.

In the same spirit, if English-speaking Canada in the late twentieth century is to agree both to a distinct society in an officially unilingual French Quebec and to an officially bilingual federal prime minister and senior public service in Ottawa, then French-speaking Canada must agree to some version of an elected, effective, and "more equal" federal Senate. To say that Canada cannot have such a Senate because Quebec will never agree is equivalent to saying that Quebec cannot have a distinct society because Canada will never agree. The practical implication of both propositions is a long period of Canadian constitutional deadlock, or worse.

There are those who believe that accepting this kind of deadlock is the best option for Canada in the 1990s. But Canada has other problems at the edge of the twenty-first century — including, as matters stand, the 10-year implementation period of the Canada-U.S. Free Trade Agreement. Is it at all realistic to believe that the country could actually surmount these other problems in an extended state of constitutional deadlock?

Indians, Inuit, and Métis

History is a complicated business. Attempts to resolve the problems of the present by appealing to the facts of the past create unanticipated challenges for the future. Historically, it is less than correct to say that the French and the English are the two "founding peoples" of modern Canada. Preston Manning, leader of the new federal Reform Party based in Western Canada, has explained: "We challenged the other guys. You go and take your policies into the Cree and Chipewayan lands and tell them you're the founding people and see if you get out alive."

In strict etymological terms "Canada," unlike "America," is actually an Indian word (though it is Iroquoian rather than Cree or Chipewayan). The culture that took the historic Canadian fur trade to the Rocky Mountains was not French, but "French and Indian." The culture that took the Canadian fur trade from the Atlantic to the Pacific, a full generation before the fur trade in the northern United States, was French and English and Indian (and, for that matter, German, "American," Jewish, and African as well).

Here, as elsewhere, "let's pretend" solutions have been exhausted. Modern Canada has not been notably more just or generous to its more ancient Indian, Inuit, and Métis peoples than the United States, Australia, or New Zealand have been to their aboriginal populations, to say nothing of Mexico and various countries in Central and South America.

Yet there is a muted Canadian tradition of honouring the Indians and the Métis for their historic roles in the fur trade, which played a more central part in early Canadian than in early American history. And it is a fact that the rights of "the Indian, Inuit, and Métis peoples of Canada" have at least a small place in the renewed Canadian Constitution of 1982.

Much more remains to be done. Canada's Indian, Inuit, and Métis population today is larger than the individual populations of a number of the smaller provinces in the Confederation. If all provinces are to be more or less equal, and Quebec is to be a distinct society, then even the present population weight of the aboriginal peoples cries out for its own form of constitutional recognition. This too must be part of what it means to keep faith with the particular fate that history has assigned to Canada.

Of equal importance, this most ancient element of Canada's past foreshadowed a significant element of its future. The Canada that is moving into the twenty-first century, like the Canada of the multiracial fur trade in the seventeenth, eighteenth, and early nineteenth centuries, is not just a white man's country. As early as the 1860s, there were those who had intimations of what this would eventually mean . During the debates in the assembly of the old United Province of Canada on the projected union of the British North American colonies, in February 1865, Henri Joly de Lotbinière declared:

> I propose the adoption of the rainbow as our emblem. By the endless variety of its tints the rainbow will give an excellent idea of the diversity of races, religions, sentiments and interests of the different parts of the Confederation.

(Subsequently, Joly de Lotbinière went on to serve briefly as premier of Quebec in 1878 and 1879, as minister of inland revenue in Wilfrid Laurier's federal government at Ottawa from 1896 to 1900, and as lieutenant-governor of British Columbia from 1900 to 1906.)

Taking Canada's Indian, Inuit, and Métis heritage seriously has other implications. Simple linear or universalist interpretations of Canadian constitutionalism, that take the 1982 Charter of Rights and Freedoms as the highest and most fundamental value of the new Confederation, cannot do full justice to Canada's real historical experience. If Canada is to hinge its twenty-first century constitutional existence on no more than an abstract bill of rights, in the universalist tradition of the American and French revolutions, it might just as well join the United States at last.

A Canada determined to keep faith with its history will value some principles espoused by the 1960s Red Tory political thinker George Grant. It "is true that no particularism can adequately incarnate the good." But it is "also true that only through some particular roots, however partial, can human beings first grasp what is good." And it "is the juice of such roots which for most men sustain their partaking in a more universal good."

In this spirit, plans for Senate reform that are authentically rooted in Canada's own experience will make some modest bow to the Indian, Inuit, and Métis issue in the larger Canadian question. This points to uncharted and even exotic rivers ahead. But then, in the age of glasnost and perestroika, a united Western Europe, a Hungarian republic, the Japanese miracle, and the Pacific Rim, so does much else that seems about to happen in the world at large.

The Long Journey to Senate Reform

The Canada-U.S. Free Trade Agreement provides a key reason for finally taking action on the unreformed Senate of Canada. Canada's particular history, and the particular form of the Canadian question in the 1990s, means that Canada's version of an elected Senate cannot be altogether the same as the versions adopted by Australia and the United States. But in reference to the Canadian question, Senate reform is also an issue in its own right.

The motivating force behind the issue is the history of Canadian regionalism. According to a recent item in the *British Journal of Canadian Studies*, "Regionalism remains a persistent theme within the study of Canada; indeed Canada is perhaps best known for its regional diversity and its perennial concern for national unity and identity." The evolving history of Canadian regionalism suggests answers to such questions as why Canada does not yet have an elected Senate at least similar in principle to those of Australia and the United States, and why it will need one in the twenty-first century.

This book sets out a brief and necessarily rather broad account of this history, as background to the current political debate on Senate reform in Canada. In the process, it sketches the historical Canadian debate on Senate reform that stretches back to the 1870s.

The book finally comes to focus on the specific "Triple E" reform proposals, first published in 1985 by the Alberta Legislative Assembly. Since the early 1970s, an assortment of alternative proposals have been advanced by other public and private organizations. The book enumerates these and briefly discusses the most important of them, with special emphasis on the 1984 joint committee report of the federal Senate and House of Commons in Ottawa.

In the last half of the 1980s, the Alberta Triple E proposals were endorsed in principle by the premiers of all four provinces of Western Canada. Similarly, while the premiers of the four provinces of Atlantic Canada expressed somewhat more varied views, in all parts of the country Alberta's proposals had the unique virtue of crystallizing the essential terms of the Senate debate.

Without any doubt, any major Senate reform that actually takes place will depart from Alberta's particular model, perhaps in dramatic ways. This book itself has critical things to say about certain aspects of Alberta's proposals. Yet in the world of practical politics, Alberta must be credited with taking the lead on the issue.

Its leadership has had shaky moments. But it has shown coherence and commitment as well. Witty things can be said about the more visceral motivations of some Alberta Senate reformers. But the concrete details of Senate reform are complicated. Extended discussions of complicated proposals that have not won serious political support in any quarter serve no practical purpose. In the end, it makes most analytic sense to focus the book on Alberta's Triple E model.

No student of how modern democracy actually works will be surprised to discover that in Alberta, as elsewhere, the late twentieth century debate on Senate reform has been led by political elites. Yet the Canadian people at large have also been caught up in the debate. According to an April 1989 Gallup Poll, majorities in all regions except Quebec support the principle of an elected Senate. Even in Quebec there is more support for an elected Senate than either for abolishing of or maintaining the existing Senate. There is also apparently more support for an elected Senate in Ontario than in Atlantic Canada, despite what is often said about Ontario's narrow self-interest in the subject.

GALLUP POLL, APRIL 1989

"Which of these things would you like to see done about the Canadian Senate?"

Region			%	
	Don't Know	Abolish Senate	Continue Appointed Senate	Elect Senate
Prairies	11	14	11	64
British Columbia	11	20	13	57
Ontario	14	14	17	55
Atlantic	10	22	18	51
Quebec	26	26	12	35
ALL CANADA	**16**	**19**	**14**	**51**

(Percentages may not add exactly to 100, due to rounding.)

All this adds up to a greater degree of popular support for an elected Senate than Brian Mulroney's free trade agreement with the United States currently enjoys. Even without such an institution, however, the real mechanics of democracy in Canada require more than a simple majority of the national popular vote. After the First Ministers' Conference of November 1989, journalistic pundits and academic analysts shared strong feelings that the prospects for significant Senate reform during the 1990s are in fact remarkably dim. According to Robert McKenzie, a usually astute English Canadian commentator on Quebec politics, "Imagining that Quebec will accept a Triple E Senate," in return for the 1987 Meech Lake Accord in its present form, "is the political equivalent of buying high-priced Florida marshland by mail."

Such feelings have no place in the text that lies ahead. Nevertheless, any realistic historical perspective must acknowledge that a workable approach to Canadian Senate reform, with practical support in all regions, requires a great deal of discussion and debate. Even on the most optimistic assumptions, this will take time.

Thus, putting something about Senate reform in a parallel political agreement to the Meech Lake Accord, (something that might serve as a beginning for the talks on Senate reform to start in November 1990) could be an act of nation-building statesmanship. Such a clause could not contain much more than a few general principles, and perhaps some commitments about processes of negotiation and ratification. Much remains to be done before there can be concrete proposals for anyone to vote on.

Yet, whatever may happen to the Meech Lake Accord, this book shares Gordon Gibson's conviction that, in the end, some version of a constitutionally entrenched distinct society for Quebec, together with an elected, effective, and more equal federal Senate for Atlantic and Western Canada, will be at the centre of the most realistic and durable answer to the Canadian question for the twenty-first century.

In expressing his conviction, Gibson also issued "a modest call for a bit of dialogue on what is the usefulness of Canada anyway." What follows aspires to stand as a modest contribution to this bit of dialogue. It shares as well Gibson's conviction that "the magic of Canada does not reside in Ottawa .... The magic of Canada resides in Canadians, all across the country." And, however Canadians all across the country finally decide to answer the Canadian question in the 1990s, the sun will "still shine and children smile."

2
THE DEEPEST ROOTS

The Canadian Confederation established in the late 1860s and early 1870s does have an institution known as a Senate. The Canadian Senate is one of the two houses of the federal Parliament at Ottawa. Except for the initiation of so-called money bills, and (since 1982) the ratification of constitutional amendments, its powers are formally equal to those of the Canadian House of Commons. Anything within the legislative authority of the federal government at Ottawa that is to become the law of the land must be passed by majorities of the members in both the Senate and the House of Commons.

The declared original purposes of the Canadian Senate are in some ways similar to those of the senates in the federal systems of the United States and Australia. The Senate of Canada is at least theoretically meant to represent the interests of disparate geographic regions, as opposed to the interests of the majority of the national population, in the national institutions of a political federation that embraces an unusually large geographic territory.

After its creation in 1867, however, the Canadian Senate rather quickly became (as perhaps had been intended) the political nullity that Ted Morton at the University of Calgary, and many others, have bemoaned in the late twentieth century. It departed fundamentally from the model that now prevails in both Australia and the United States, and it has been a recurrent object of popular contempt and ridicule for more than 100 years.

The reasons for all this flow from the somewhat unusual history of Canadian regionalism. The most familiar elements in this history date from the later part of the nineteenth century, but to grasp why the Canadian Confederation started out with the peculiar kind of Senate that it did, requires an awareness of what happened in the preceding two and a half centuries. Here lie the deepest roots of the distinctive Canadian variety of regionalism that animates the 1990s debate on Canadian Senate reform.

Canada's Primeval Regionalism

Geography is the fundamental point of departure for any discussion of regionalism, in Canada or any other place. And part of the particular significance of regionalism in Canada stems from the simple fact that Canada is, geographically, the second largest country in the world today. (The largest is the U.S.S.R. The other eight of the 10 largest are, in descending order: China, the U.S.A., Brazil, Australia, India, Argentina, Sudan, and Algeria.)

Beyond Canada's sheer size, geography divides the country into a variety of physiographic regions. Canada is still only thinly populated, and its population is concentrated in a comparatively few southerly locations, close to the border with the United States. Scatterings of people, however, live in even the most remote parts of the county's vast expanse. Among the most settled, most southerly regions, there are marked geographic variations.

This primary physical diversity does not coincide neatly with what the Constitution Act, 1867 (formerly the British North America Act, 1867) describes as "the Four Divisions of Canada,"(Western Canada, Ontario, Quebec, and Atlantic Canada) which are represented in the present Canadian Senate. For instance, *The Illustrated Natural History of Canada,* a multi- volume popular series first published in 1970, divides the country into eight distinctive physical regions: the Arctic Coast, the Pacific Coast, the Mountain Barrier, the Western Plains, the Canadian Shield, the Great Lakes, the St. Lawrence Valley, and the Atlantic Coast.

Similarly, Canada's physical diversity does not coincide neatly with the 10 provinces and two territories into which the country is divided politically. Yet, ultimately, political, cultural, social, and economic varieties of regionalism in Canada are all rooted in geographic diversity. Acid rain, the ozone layer, the greenhouse effect, or even a new ice age may eventually alter the nature of this diversity. But they will not alter the connection between physical geography and the regionalism of human societies. In Canada, as elsewhere, regionalism in this sense is an abiding human condition.

Thus, right at the beginning of what we now call Canadian history, in the sixteenth and seventeenth centuries, the geographic regions of Canada were starkly if not exactly reflected in the regionalism of the Indians of Canada. This was far from clear to the first Europeans who came to the place. Yet it had notable implications for their long-term future.

Though Canada is itself an Indian word, the white man did not know the full variety of the country's Indian inhabitants until 1793, when Alexander Mackenzie, sometime partner of the North West Company, became, with the help of Indian guides, the first person of European origin to travel across the North American continent. Some Inuit in the far north did not see their first white people until the twentieth century.

Similarly, there was no comprehensive study of Canadian Indians until Diamond Jenness published *The Indians of Canada* in 1932. Jenness was a white anthropologist who migrated to Canada from New Zealand. He was a man of his time, and in many respects his book has been superseded by more recent scholarship. It is still instructive, however, to note how he divided Canada's first peoples into seven main groups, each associated with a particular "cultural area" or "physiographic region":

(1) the **Algonkian tribes of the eastern woodlands;**

(2) the **Iroquoians** in the St. Lawrence Valley and the lower Great Lakes — or what would subsequently be called Central Canada;

(3) the **Plains tribes** in what *The Illustrated Natural History* calls "the Western Plains of Canada"

(4) the **tribes of the Pacific coast**, where "early navigators ... compared the forts, carved house-posts, whale-bone clubs, and cedarbark beaters of British Columbia with the forts, house-posts, and clubs of far-off New Zealand and the tapa-cloth beaters of central Polynesia";

(5) the **tribes of the Cordillera** or Mountain Barrier;

(6) the **tribes of the Mackenzie and Yukon basins** in what are now the northern parts of the Western Canadian provinces, and the western Northwest Territories and the Yukon;

(7) the **Inuit** (or "Eskimo" to Jenness) — not Indians at all, but a distinct people, who had migrated from Asia much more recently than the peoples to the south and were uniquely adapted to survival in the far northern Arctic, at a minimum level of technology.

Jenness stressed as well that even before the arrival of Europeans in the New World the "conditions of life" were "easiest" in two of these seven regions. The first was the region of the Iroquoians in the St. Lawrence Valley and the lower Great Lakes — the location of modern Toronto and Montreal. The second was the region of the tribes of the Pacific Coast — the location of

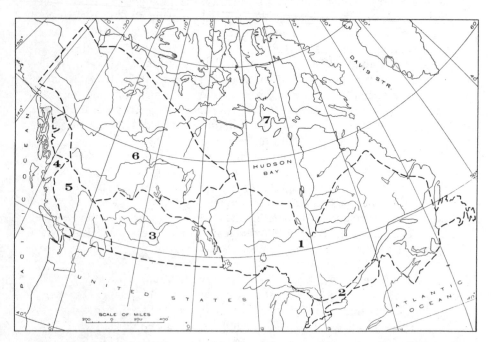

Diamond Jenness's 1930s map of Indian "physiographic regions" or "cultural areas" in Canada.

modern Vancouver. It cannot be entirely accidental that these same two regions are also home to the three largest metropolitan areas in the Canada of the late twentieth century. We have not altogether escaped the geographic constraints that shaped the lives of Canada's original founding peoples.

Diverse Destiny: Goldwin Smith and Harold Innis

Modern anthropologists, and others, sometimes note that it is hard to superimpose the boundary between Canada and the United States (or, for that matter, between the United States and Mexico) on any more general North American map of Indian cultural areas on the eve of European contact. In the same spirit, according to a long, much disputed tradition, Canada is not just a country of several diverse geographic regions. These regions are also, in the language of the late twentieth century Canadian historian Carl Berger, "northern projections of American ones."

The most eminent historical exponent of this tradition in English-speaking Canada was the highbrow journalist Goldwin Smith. Locally known in his day as "the sage of the Grange" (after the house where he lived and worked, now part of the Art Gallery of Ontario), Smith was a former Regius Professor of History at Oxford University in England. Family tragedy in the old country prompted him to settle at Toronto in the early 1870s, while still in his 40s. Here, until his death in 1910, he developed a second career as a controversial English Canadian advocate of Old World intellectual life, adapted to the late nineteenth century North American ideals of democracy and the family farm.

Whatever else, Goldwin Smith was an intelligent man. There are obvious factual bases for the extreme Canadian continentalist tradition he promoted, especially in regard to the more densely settled, most southerly parts of the country. Atlantic Canada is in many respects a northern projection of New England. Quebec is a northern projection of New England and New York, and Ontario of New York and the American Midwest. The western plains of Canada are an unmistakeable projection of the western plains of the United States. And when Vancouver today boasts that it is "the second largest port on the West Coast," it means the West Coast of both Canada and the United States. (The largest port is Long Beach, California.)

To elevate this aspect of Canada's geographic diversity to some first principle, however, is to misconstrue the real world of Canadian regionalism, in a fundamental way. Such an approach would equally misconstrue regionalism in North America at large. The main countries of the modern continent are Canada, the United States, and Mexico. No doubt Canada shares a fate suggested by the Mexican President Porfirio Diaz almost a century ago: "Poor Mexico, so far from God, and so close to the United States." Yet there are now long uncontested lines of national division in North America, and they reflect north-south, not east-west contours of cleavage.

Two decades after Goldwin Smith's death, Harold Innis provided an explanation for this element of Canadian regionalism when he published *The*

Fur Trade in Canada: An Introduction to Canadian Economic History (in 1930, two years before the appearance of Diamond Jenness's pioneering book on the Indians of Canada).

In the 1960s Innis was described by a wit in the modern United Kingdom as "Canada's first and perhaps only genuine intellectual." He was born in 1894 into the same southwestern Ontario dry agrarian culture that produced the iconoclastic economist John Kenneth Galbraith, who won fame and at least a modest fortune in the United States. Despite similar beckoning southern breezes, Innis remained in Canada. He died in Toronto in 1952, having lived just long enough to leave some sensible marks on the early career of Marshall McLuhan. In between, he was wounded in Europe during the First World War, taught at a rural public school in Alberta, studied at McMaster University (then in Toronto) and the University of Chicago, and married a girl from Wilmette, Illinois. Then he wrote *The Fur Trade*, became head of the Department of Political Economy at the University of Toronto, did work for the provincial government of Nova Scotia, and served as president of the American Economic Association. He blossomed most completely as an early pioneer in the study of the world history of communications media, his best-known book in the field being *The Bias of Communication*.

In some respects, Innis's vision of the Canadian fur trade obscured the east-west diversity of the first Canadian resource economy. But it did capture much at the bottom of a countervailing regional urge to unity in what he liked to call the "northern half of North America." In his conclusion to *The Fur Trade in Canada*, he articulated a nativist perception of the modern Canadian Confederation that Goldwin Smith was never quite able to grasp with enthusiasm. As the civilization of Europe spread across the New World, North America north of the Rio Grande

> became divided into three areas: (1) to the north in what is now the Dominion of Canada, producing furs, (2) to the south in what were during the Civil War the secession states, producing cotton, and (3) in the centre the widely diversified economic territory including the New England states and the coal and iron areas of the middle west demanding raw materials and a market.

According to this view, two key geographic features separated what is now Canada from the United States. One was the vast rocky wilderness of the Canadian Shield, an immense repository of natural resources, fundamentally unsuited to mass European settlement. ("We are only beginning to realize the central position of the Canadian Shield," Innis wrote in 1930.) The other was "the extensive waterways which characterize the northern part of North America." These geographic features helped prolong linkages between the developing Canadian economy and the global ambitions of Western Europe. Within Canada itself, they fostered an east-west transcontinental economy, with its "centre" in the lower St. Lawrence Valley and a "periphery" or "hinterland" in the Great Lakes region and then on the plains and in the mountains of the Canadian West.

The French and Indian Romance, the Cod Fisheries, and the Hudson's Bay Company

Real history is always more complicated than any single conception can accommodate. Both Goldwin Smith's and Harold Innis's visions of Canada's economic geography can be seen in the early history of European contact with the most northern part of North America.

To start with, Canadian history in its narrowest and most nominally authentic sense began in the 1530s, when Jacques Cartier sailed up the St. Lawrence River and learned the word Canada from the mysterious St. Lawrence Iroquoians. It set down roots in the early seventeenth century, when Samuel de Champlain, "the Father of Canada or New France," established Quebec City in 1608. As the seventeenth century progressed, a French-speaking society that called itself "Canadien" gradually took shape in the lower St. Lawrence Valley, with Montreal (founded in 1642) as its most westerly urban centre.

By the early eighteenth century this society of the lower St. Lawrence was defined by quasi-feudal seigneuries and habitant farms, laid out in narrow, vertical strips along the liquid highway of "the River of Canada." It was a place where the traditional life of the Indians, though still much admired, had clearly been superseded by the life of a French Catholic colony, before the French Revolution.

This colony provided a base, however, for the much more expansive French and Indian fur trade, in the Indian "upper country" to the west. As early as 1615 Champlain himself had journeyed westward, via the Indian transportation technology of the canoe and portage, to visit the country of the Huron in what is now central Ontario. In the late seventeenth and early eighteenth centuries trading outposts were established at such places as Cataraqui (present-day Kingston), Detroit, Kaministiquia (Thunder Bay), and (toward the middle of the eighteenth century) Toronto — hinterland centres where European manufactured goods were exchanged for Indian fur resources. The vast loneliness of the northwestern wilderness interior encouraged miscegenation among Europeans and Indians, giving rise to the unique culture of the Canadian Métis. The most adventurous French and Indian traders pressed still further west along the extensive northern waterways. By the 1740s Pierre Gaultier de Varennes et de La Vérendrye and his Indian guides had reached the Rocky Mountains.

All this is at the centre of Innis's depiction of the early Canadian fur trade. Yet, as early as the 1670s and 1680s, René Robert Cavalier Sieur de La Salle had begun to follow waterways that led from the St. Lawrence River and the

Great Lakes to the southwestern interior of the continent. He followed the Mississippi River to the Gulf of Mexico and claimed Louisiana for the King of France.

The historical sources suggest some confusion about the exact boundary between Canada and Louisiana. The status of the "Illinois Country," home to the wilderness beginnings of what would later become Chicago and St. Louis, is a notable case in point. New Orleans on the Gulf of Mexico, founded in 1718, was the capital of French Louisiana but even French Canadians never believed that it was a part of Canada.

Even before he founded Quebec City in 1608, Champlain had arrived on what is now the Canadian Atlantic Coast, in 1604. This marked the beginnings of another French (and Indian) culture in North America in an area that would come to be known as Acadia. Broadly, it covered the modern provinces of Nova Scotia, New Brunswick, and Prince Edward Island. Acadia became another place that did not see itself as a part of the Canada in the St. Lawrence Valley, with its northwestern Indian upper country to the west of Montreal.

Acadia was on the northern frontier of the British Protestant colonies of New England, which began in the 1620s and 1630s. It was claimed by the King of England as Nova Scotia (New Scotland in Latin), and it became a site for recurrent French and English (and Indian) conflict in the later seventeenth and early eighteenth centuries. By the Treaty of Utrecht in 1713 the King of France recognized the claims of the King of England to much of the territory involved.

In the 1750s British imperial officialdom deported large numbers of French-speaking "Acadiens" to Louisiana. Many subsequently returned to the new British province of Nova Scotia. Others became the "Cajuns" of the modern U.S. state of Louisiana. At the same time, Nova Scotia attracted English-speaking migrants from Protestant New England. They became the so-called "neutral Yankees of Nova Scotia," on the first of recurrent northern thrusts of the Anglo-American settlement frontier that would follow Canadian history all the way to "the last Best West" of North America in the early twentieth century.

———————

Innis's Canadian fur trade started on the Atlantic Coast in the late fifteenth and early sixteenth centuries and reached the Pacific Coast in the late eighteenth and early nineteenth centuries. Some of his followers (historian Donald Creighton is the foremost example) saw the fur trade as a unique key to the structure of the first Canadian resource economy and as a singular guide to subsequent Canadian political and economic development. Innis himself, however, came to stress the diversity of the first resource economy and the resulting "necessity of tolerance in approaching the complex difficulties which accompany the divergent points of view" in twentieth century Canada.

In 1940, a decade after the publication of his book on the fur trade, Innis published *The Cod Fisheries: The History of an International Economy*. This took up the "task of indicating the significance of the fishing industry" on what is now Canada's Atlantic Coast. The region involved included the old French Acadia that had gradually evolved into the British Nova Scotia in the first half of the eighteenth century, the northern British colonies of New England, and the far northern British fishing colony of Newfoundland, another object of French-English rivalry in the seventeenth century and a place where French fishermen would enjoy treaty rights granted by the British from 1713 to 1904.

Transient Portuguese, Spanish, French, and English fishermen were part of the North Atlantic cod fisheries, along with settled French and British colonists in the New World. While the history of the fur trade drew attention to "the centralizing tendencies of the St. Lawrence" in the first Canadian resource economy, the history of the cod fisheries showed that "fishing from numerous ports of an extended coast line made for decentralization."

Innis's earlier work on the fur trade had implied other limitations on the centralizing tendencies of the St. Lawrence, and on the concept of the French and Indian wilderness romance as the unique forerunner of the Canada that would finally greet the twentieth century. In the middle of the seventeenth century two dissident St. Lawrence traders, Pierre-Esprit Radisson and Médard Chouart des Groseilliers, had travelled to London, England, to seek financial backing for a rival northwestern fur trade, linked with Western Europe via the sub-Arctic coastline of Hudson Bay.

This led to the establishment of the English Hudson's Bay Company in 1670. All the territory drained by Hudson Bay was named Prince Rupert's Land and claimed for the King of England. The late seventeenth and early eighteenth centuries were marked by recurrent struggles over the Hudson Bay fur trade, between the French with their Indian allies, and the English with theirs. The Treaty of Utrecht in 1713, by which the King of France acknowledged the claims of the King of England to Prince Rupert's Land ended this chapter of conflict, but down to the first quarter of the nineteenth century, the Hudson's Bay Company would compete with the Canadian fur trade centred in Montreal for the wilderness resources and Indian consumer markets in the northwestern interior.

Summing up very briefly, in the earliest history of what is now called Canada there was both Goldwin Smith's east-west diversity and north-south unity, and Harold Innis's east-west unity and north-south diversity. There was also diversity within Innis's unity. There were both French and English influences, and the Indians and the Métis were still close to the centre of events. ("We have not yet realized," Innis wrote in 1930, "that the Indian and his culture were fundamental to the growth of Canadian institutions.") Europeans had some slight familiarity with the geography west of the Great Lakes as far as the Rocky Mountains, but not beyond.

Put another way, by the middle of the eighteenth century it was already possible to talk about several varieties of regionalism. Within the universe of French imperial ambition in North America, there was the regionalism of

29

Canada, Acadia, and Louisiana. In the most northern part of North America, there was the regionalism of the fur trade and the cod fisheries. On the Atlantic Coast, there was the regionalism of French Acadia and British Nova Scotia and Newfoundland (and this was mixed in with European religious tensions between Catholics and Protestants). Within Canada there was the regionalism of the French Catholic agricultural and commercial centre in the lower St. Lawrence Valley and of the French and Indian fur trade resource hinterland west of Montreal (with cultural tensions among Europeans, Indians, and Métis). Within the northwestern hinterland there was the regionalism of the English Hudson's Bay Company, and the French Canadian fur trade based in Montreal.

La Conquête and the American War of Independence

In the second half of the eighteenth century, all these northern North American varieties of regionalism were stirred up in a fresh way by two dramatic military conflicts. These conflicts created new circumstances that would eventually lead to the Canadian Confederation of the late 1860s and early 1870s.

In the language of those who were already calling themselves Canadians, the first conflict was la Conquête — the final conquest of the French empire in America by the British Empire. In the already much more populous British colonies to the south, it was known as the French and Indian War. In Europe it was perceived as part of the global struggle among rival imperial powers known as the Seven Years War. It began in the middle of the 1750s and ended with the Peace of Paris in 1763. At the Peace of Paris, Canada and virtually all of what remained of French Acadia after the 1713 Treaty of Utrecht became part of the British Empire.

The second conflict was the American War of Independence — the ultimately successful revolt of the British Thirteen Colonies against the King of England. This war began in the middle of the 1770s and ended with the Peace of Versailles in 1783. The colonial revolutionaries, who were far from unanimously supported by the mass of the population in the Thirteen Colonies, received important strategic aid from the King of France. The final result of their struggle was the creation of the United States of America.

The role of the most northern part of North America in these events was full of historic irony, defeats within victories, and victories within defeats.

To start with, the Peace of Paris in 1763 was immediately followed by the Indian uprising known as the Conspiracy of Pontiac, based around the old French and Indian fur-trading outpost at Detroit. This amounted to an Indian protest against the potential destruction of the old French and Indian fur trade empire on the heels of the French defeat in America. Pontiac himself, war chief of an Algonkian nation called the Ottawa, described what took place as a "beaver war." In the words of modern American historian Howard Peckham, it was "the most formidable Indian resistance the English-speaking people had yet faced, or ever would face, on this continent."

The uprising prompted the British Royal Proclamation of 1763, which declared the western interior of North America an Indian Territory and, in effect, gave the protection of the British Empire to the Canadian fur trade in the Great Lakes region.

The Royal Proclamation also reorganized the old French Canada of the St. Lawrence Valley into the new British province of Quebec. The original intention was that French Canadians would be gradually absorbed into the English-speaking mainstream of the other British colonies in North America, much as was already happening in the old French Acadia and new British Nova Scotia. Within a decade, however, this intention had been abandoned.

There were only some 60,000 French Canadians living in the St. Lawrence Valley in the middle of the eighteenth century, compared with as many as one million British colonists to the south. But this was still much larger than the French population of old Acadia. As the Thirteen Colonies grew increasingly restive, British imperial officials thought it wise to secure practical support from the people of old French Canada. The result was the Quebec Act of 1774, which reinstated the quasi-feudal French Catholic social institutions and civil law of French Canada. The French Canadians would remain subjects of the British Empire, but they would keep their own language and distinctive culture.

The Quebec Act also extended the boundaries of the British-governed fur-trading French society of the St. Lawrence Valley into the Indian Territory of 1763, to include much of what is now Ontario and the U.S. Midwest. This appealed to new English-speaking merchants in Quebec City and Montreal, who were busy taking over the management of the Canadian fur trade from French officials who had retreated across the Atlantic Ocean after 1763.

The ultimate consequence was that, despite appeals from Benjamin Franklin and a brief American patriot invasion and occupation of Montreal in 1775–76, the Canada of the St. Lawrence Valley and the Great Lakes did not join the American War of Independence.

For more complicated reasons, the old French Acadia that had become British Nova Scotia did not side with the Thirteen Colonies either. Indifference among a small, diverse, and scattered population remote from the centre of conflict played a part in Nova Scotia's decision. So did the interests of new Halifax merchants, who valued the global reach of the British imperial trading system and the connections of the cod fisheries with the Old World. More ancient traditions of Acadian neutrality, flowing from a strategically vulnerable geographic location, were important as well.

In the end the King of France helped the former New World subjects of the King of England to found a new independent United States of America. At the Peace of Paris in 1763, the old French Louisiana had been assigned to Spain. Napoleon would subsequently recover the territory for France, just in time to sell it to the still youthful United States in 1803. But in the American War of Independence the King of England had helped the former New World subjects of the King of France in Canada and Acadia to remain aloof from the new Anglo-American republic.

For a generation after the war, the British Empire would protect the old French and Indian fur trade in the Great Lakes from the worst ravages of the Anglo-American settlement frontier. The most northern part of North America would remain distinct from the territory to the south, as it had been in the preceding century and a half.

The North West Company and the Struggle for the Border of British North America

While the Quebec Act helped save the French Catholic culture of the lower St. Lawrence Valley from the fate that would eventually overtake French culture in Louisiana, French Canadians after la Conquête were still treated as "a conquered people."

Similarly, although the French and Indian fur trade survived and many French Canadians continued to be part of it, starting in the 1760s, however, its financing and higher management were taken over by a diverse assortment of English-speaking people who settled in Quebec City and Montreal. Some came from the United Kingdom, some from the old British colonies to the south. Many were Scottish, some English, some Irish, some Jewish, and a few of German descent.

By the end of the American War of Independence, the most influential among these new "British" managers who socialized at the Beaver Club in Montreal, had come together to form the North West Company. During the next generation it became, in Innis's language, "the first organization to operate on a continental scale in North America" and a "forerunner" of the Canadian Confederation.

The North West Company picked up where La Vérendrye had left off, at the Rocky Mountains in the 1740s. With Alexander Mackenzie's journey of 1793, it reached the Pacific Ocean — a full generation before its few American competitors to the south. Like its own Montreal-based French forerunners, it competed with the Hudson's Bay Company in the far northwest until 1821, when the two companies finally merged, under the latter's name.

This dramatic westward expansion of the new Canadian fur trade shaped the definition of the boundary between Canada and the United States. According to Goldwin Smith's continentalist tradition, there is virtually no geographic logic to this boundary. But, in the spirit of Harold Innis, present-day geologists draw an unambiguous east-west line across North America to mark the "maximum extent of glaciation", in the land-forming processes of the primeval past.

Territory north of this glaciation line roughly corresponds to what were the best fur-producing areas of North America. It includes ground fought for by the French and Indians in the middle of the eighteenth century, lakes and forests considered part of the British province of Quebec just before the American War of Independence, and land claimed by the westward-moving British fur merchants of Montreal in the early nineteenth century. At several strategic points, the line stretches considerably further south than the bound-

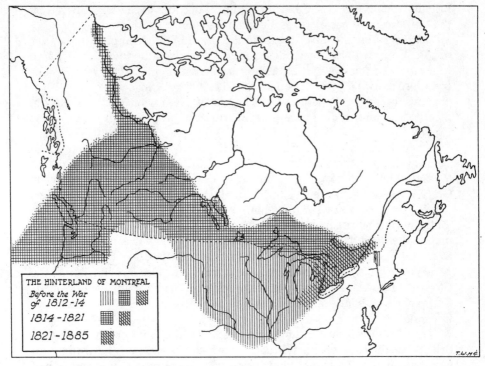

"The hinterland of Montreal," from Arthur Lower's *Colony to Nation: A History of Canada* (1946).

ary between the United States and modern Canada (officially known from the late 1780s until the early 1870s as "British North America").

This official boundary was gradually negotiated by British imperial and American republican officials from the late eighteenth to the mid-nineteenth centuries. The process started with the drawing of a line through the middle of the Great Lakes at the end of the American War of Independence in 1783. It was given momentum by Jay's Treaty of 1794, which confirmed this line and established precedents of compromise for an ultimately unsatisfactory resolution of the boundary between modern Maine and New Brunswick in 1842.

In an earlier era, it was often a northern nativist complaint that British policy routinely sacrificed early French, Indian and Métis as well as Acadian interests, to the larger objective of promoting good relations between the British Empire and its wayward children in the new Republic. On the other hand, with an eye on the experience of Mexico, defenders of imperial policy can argue that without the strong arm of the Empire even greater Canadian sacrifices would have been inevitable. The youthful frontier republic made an aggressive bid to annex ground north of the Great Lakes in the War of 1812–14, but seasoned imperial redcoats helped ensure that the northern

British provinces of "the Canadas" did not succumb to the fate suffered by the Mexican province of Texas, less than a generation later.

At the same time, like Canada under the old French empire, in the War of 1812 Canada under the British Empire was also allied with fur-trading Indians — in this case inspired by the Shawnee chief Tecumseh, a self-confessed spiritual heir of Pontiac in the 1760s. The official seal of the British province of Upper Canada, which fought off the major Yankee invasion, included a calumet or peace pipe in tribute to "the Indian allies of the Crown."

In 1818, as part of an effort to resolve the westward extension of the kinds of conflicts that had led to the War of 1812, officials of the Empire and the Republic agreed on the boundary of British North America, from the Great Lakes west to the Rocky Mountains. It would be the invisible line marked on the map by the forty-ninth parallel of latitude. Such spokesmen for the northern British fur merchants as the legendary northwest wilderness map-maker David Thompson complained that the line was too far north — to no ultimate avail. With the Treaty of Oregon in 1846, the forty-ninth parallel was extended all the way west to the Pacific Ocean, even though the Canadian fur trade had earlier beaten back John Jacob Astor's American Fur Company well south of the line, in the modern states of Washington and Oregon.

By the middle of the nineteenth century, the southern boundary of British North America was virtually complete. Despite all the varieties of regionalism that had put down roots in the preceding two and a half centuries, and the regionalism of the Indians from long before, the geographic framework for modern Canada was in place. For Goldwin Smith, it was merely an artifact of the diplomacy of the British Empire. But for Harold Innis, "La Vérendrye had laid down the boundary of Canada in the search for the better beaver of the northern areas."

3
EARLY ENGLISH CANADA

Within emerging new boundaries, by the early nineteenth century the Canada that Cartier, Champlain, and the Indians first crystallized in the sixteenth and seventeenth centuries had, at least survived into the eighteenth century.

The ancient Canada that would survive on into the nineteenth and twentieth centuries, however, was not strictly the homogeneous, French-speaking Catholic society, most deeply rooted in the St. Lawrence Valley. It was, to borrow from the writings of Pierre Trudeau, the "polyethnic" French, Indian, and Métis wilderness romance that reached deep into the northwest as far as the Rocky Mountains, and had eastern connections with French-speaking Acadia, where intermarriage with the Algonkian nations of the Micmac and Malecite was a minor regional tradition.

The price of survival was to expand the original French and Indian diversity. Neither la Conquête nor the American War of Independence would finally extinguish the most ancient beginnings of modern Canada's diverse destiny. But both would influence and change this destiny profoundly.

In the nineteenth century Canada would absorb new elements of both British and American varieties of English-speaking Protestant and Catholic culture, and, eventually, the cultures of the Pacific Coast Indians, the tribes of the Yukon and Mackenzie basins, and even the Inuit. By the late nineteenth century, some form of English-speaking culture would be the choice of the majority in a growing population, everywhere except on the banks of the lower St. Lawrence River. By the start of the twentieth century, both the French and the Indians would become besieged minorities in their native land. Yet they would not disappear. French Canadians dedicated themselves to "la survivance" (a cause still celebrated by the motto "Je me souviens" that appears on Quebec automobile licence plates).

The processes through which all this gradually took shape hold obvious precedents for most of the regionalist pressures that stalk present-day Canada. They hold the origins of most of the conflicts that lie at the bottom of the case for Senate reform in the 1990s. And they hold the seeds of the countervailing urge for Canadian unity in the the twenty-first century.

The cutting edge was the growth and development of modern English-speaking Canada. Its earliest beginnings can clearly be traced to the Atlantic coast of Newfoundland in the sixteenth century and to the old Northwest territories (or Prince Rupert's Land) of the Hudson's Bay Company in the seventeenth century. Yet, English-speaking people who actually called themselves "Canadians" did not appear until the late eighteenth century. It is also an awkward but simple fact that these English Canadians first settled in what is now Ontario — province of opportunity and opportunism alike.

Their appearance can be traced back to the end of the American War of Independence, in 1783. But the historical dynamics of the case are complicated. Here as elsewhere, Canada would become most notable for its unusual diversity.

Old Acadia and the British Northwest

In the 1780s as many as 40,000 American Loyalists moved into what remained of British North America after the War of Independence. They believed, more or less, that what became the United States of America ought to have stayed in the British Empire. Their broadly conservative Anglo-American instincts would eventually blend, somewhat uneasily, with parallel impulses among strong French Canadian supporters of the Roman Catholic Church — great beacon to French Canada. One result would be the much-observed (and sometimes exaggerated) "small-c conservatism" of some parts of modern Canada's English and French elite cultures.

The vast majority of the American Loyalists of the 1780s, however, moved not into the old French Canada, but into the old French Acadia, on the Atlantic Coast. To help accommodate them, British imperial officialdom created the province of New Brunswick out of the western section of Nova Scotia, in 1784. (Intriguingly enough, New Brunswick, the most thoroughly "Loyalist province" of the modern Confederation, would also become the most successful refuge of the remaining French-speaking Acadians.)

Some American Loyalists moved to what remained of Nova Scotia and to Cape Breton Island, also separated from Nova Scotia at that time but then rejoined in 1820. A few moved to Prince Edward Island. This province had been French, as Ile St-Jean, until the Seven Years War. It was established as a separate British province, known as St. John's Island, in 1769. Its name was changed to Prince Edward Island in 1799.

Strong political convictions aside, the Atlantic American Loyalists were successors to the neutral Yankees of Nova Scotia, of the generation before. They brought the social and economic mores of the New England frontier. They were not "British" in the same sense as the Scottish Highlanders who would join them in the New World, or even as the Irish and English fishermen who had earlier taken hold of Newfoundland. On the other hand, the Atlantic Loyalists were resolutely "British North American."

By the late 1830s Nova Scotia had spawned Thomas Chandler Haliburton, the first thoroughly interesting indigenous literary voice in what we now call English Canada. Yet Haliburton himself was no Canadian, in any modern sense of the word. Like his near contemporary, Halifax-born Samuel Cunard, he would die in the United Kingdom. His peripatetic fictional Yankee trader, Sam Slick, is said to have begun a native North American tradition of English-speaking humour later perfected by Mark Twain. In the nineteenth century, the people of the British North American Atlantic provinces would actively disavow the label "Canadian" until the 1870s. Even after this, attachments to the word would remain profoundly qualified by

36

strong Atlantic regional and imperial sentiments, well into the twentieth century, and in Newfoundland, longer still.

Something not altogether similar can be said about the handfuls of English-speaking British North American subjects in the vast, northwestern territories of the Hudson's Bay Company. In 1821, when it merged with the North West Company, the company itself began a very gradual process of Canadianization. That process would not end until 1970, however, when the company's head offices were finally moved to Canada from the United Kingdom.

Among rival English-speaking partisans of both companies, or even of smaller, rival northwest enterprises, "Canadian" first referred to the French-speaking fur trade operatives still in their midst. These Canadians had much more in common with the Métis and the Indians. Their late nineteenth century folk hero would be the Métis prophet Louis Riel. Even when they spoke English as well as French, they were quite unlike the crusty migrants from the Orkney Islands and other parts of the British Isles (and the old Thirteen Colonies), who managed the wild fur trade outposts of the early nineteenth century British Northwest.

In the end, even many Orkneymen were drawn into the older Canadian polyethnic romance, or, in the imperial lexicon, "went native." By the middle of the nineteenth century, some exclusively English-speaking people, who had in fact begun to call themselves Canadians, had begun to arrive in what is now Western Canada. As early as 1793, Alexander Mackenzie wrote "from Canada by land", on a rock at the edge of Bella Coola inlet on the Pacific Ocean.

Yet George Vancouver, naval captain of the British Empire, arrived on the coast of modern British Columbia by sea only a month after Mackenzie. Captain Vancouver knew nothing of Canada. He had just before been surveying the coasts of Australia and New Zealand in the South Pacific. Similarly, the first attempt at English-speaking agricultural settlement in what is now Manitoba, at the time of the War of 1812 was masterminded by the British philanthropist Lord Selkirk. His settlers were a handful of indigent Scottish and Irish labourers, displaced by the early progress of the industrial revolution across the ocean. The first organized scheme for English-speaking settlement in what is now British Columbia was initiated on Vancouver Island in 1849 by the Hudson's Bay Company, still far more British than English Canadian.

The Two Canadas

For better or for worse, the historic advance guard of English Canada in the nineteenth century would arise in the central interior of British North America. After the War of Independence some American Loyalists moved north into the old French Canada. A few thousand settled in the St. Lawrence Valley. They joined the British merchants of Montreal and Quebec City, as ancestors of the modern English-speaking minority in the predominantly French-speaking province of Quebec.

Of much greater consequence for the future, some 6,000 Loyalists settled west of the Ottawa River, especially along the upper St. Lawrence, which led through cascading white water rapids to the eastern end of Lake Ontario. Here, in the old upper country region north of the Great Lakes, Indians still accounted for the vast majority of the population. Mere handfuls of French Canadians were concentrated in the vicinity of Detroit, to a lesser extent at Niagara, and to a lesser extent still at Toronto and Cataraqui (Kingston).

To accommodate the new English-speaking arrivals west of the Ottawa River, in 1791 British officialdom divided the old 1774 province of Quebec — with its southwestern extension lopped off by the 1783 boundary settlement — into two parts. Except for a new elected assembly, Lower Canada, to the east of the Ottawa, largely retained the French Catholic institutions of the Quebec Act, though these were presided over by a fundamentally British governing class and a British-dominated economic elite. Upper Canada, to the west, acquired new English and even Protestant institutions, on the Anglo-American colonial model that still survived in the Atlantic provinces.

The late eighteenth century "British Constitution" imported into the old French Canada (by the imperial Constitutional Act, 1791) saw itself as a benign blend of monarchic, aristocratic, and democratic elements. Yet the particular variation that the "parent state" bequeathed to Upper Canada had pronounced monarchic and aristocratic overtones.

This variation reflected an imperial aspiration to restrain tendencies toward what were seen as the colonial democratic excesses of the old Thirteen Colonies. It created an instant Tory ruling oligarchy in the new northern wilderness province of Upper Canada — a more passionate and strident version of the similar British colonial oligarchies that had more gently set down roots in old French Acadia and Newfoundland. Some of the Upper Canadian oligarchs came from the United Kingdom. But John Beverley Robinson, the most noble and high-minded of them all, was the descendant of American Loyalist refugees from the planter aristocracy in the "Old Dominion" of Virginia.

The full-blown dream of a new Anglo feudal grandeur in the wilderness north of the Great Lakes, however, would be short-lived. From the early 1790s down to the War of 1812, another wave of English-speaking settlement would quickly swell the Upper Canadian population to close to 100,000 people. This migration was sometimes slyly labelled "late Loyalist" in the conservative English Canadian historiography of an earlier era. Yet, for the most part, it was only a northern extension of the same push of the Anglo-American frontier that was unleashed by the War of Independence and that settled western New York and Pennsylvania and, eventually, Ohio, Indiana, Michigan, and Illinois.

Most of these new arrivals had more in common with the earlier neutral Yankees of Nova Scotia than with the American Loyalists of the 1780s. They brought into Upper Canada the "agrarian cupidity," and growing agrarian democratic enthusiasms of the nineteenth century northern family-farm frontier in English-speaking North America. Some among them believed that the American Republic would soon annex the British province of Upper Canada.

The War of 1812 decided that the northern half of North America would pursue its own diverse destiny — in the much later words of the loyal Anglo-Iroquoian poetess Pauline Johnson, "in Canada, under the British flag." Yet, as in the late eighteenth century, Canadian history in the early nineteenth century was streaked with ironies, defeats within victories, and victories within defeats. The old Empire stopped the new Republic from moving north, militarily and politically, but it did not stop the English-speaking family-farm society of the North American frontier from displacing the earlier culture of the fur traders and the Indian allies of the Crown.

Moreover, the deepest instincts of the North American frontier in the continental interior could be neither thoroughly "British" nor altogether "Tory." Even in the northern wilderness, the new midwestern frontier culture bred a new nativist aspiration, at the same time as it wrote off the old native culture of the Indians. When the smoke of battle had lifted, some residents of Upper Canada had at last begun to think of themselves as "Canadians" — New World English-speaking brothers and sisters, of a sort, to the much longer established French-speaking "Canadiens" to the east.

By the 1820s some among both kinds of Canadian New World natives had begun to grow restless under the too-restraining hands of the British Tory oligarchs who, thanks to the aid of the Indians and the Empire, had triumphed in the War of 1812.

The French and English Struggle for Colonial Democracy

By the 1820s the influence of the North American frontier in Upper Canada was itself being leavened by a new wave of immigration from the United Kingdom across the ocean. This would swell the Upper Canadian population to a million people by the middle of the nineteenth century, surpassing the predominantly French-speaking population of Lower Canada, to say nothing of the British Atlantic provinces or of the still fundamentally wild fur trade frontier of the British Northwest.

Yet even many of the new immigrants from the United Kingdom were fleeing the social, political, and economic restraints of oligarchs in the Old World. One among their number, the Scottish "Firebrand", William Lyon Mackenzie, led the Upper Canadian Rebellion of 1837 — in effect, a North American frontier protest against the reign of the oligarchs in British North America. ("Up then, brave Canadians," Mackenzie urged: "Get ready your rifles, and make short work of it .... Our enemies ... are in terror and dismay; they know their wickedness and dread our vengeance .... Woe be to those who oppose us, for 'in God is our trust'.")

In keeping with the emergent moderating forces, only a few newly conscious English Canadians actually got their rifles ready for Mackenzie's rebellion. But subsequent events showed that many more sympathized with his democratic cause. And the Upper Canadian Rebellion of 1837 was accompanied — in fact, preceded and succeeded — by the somewhat more violent and fiercely supported Lower Canadian Rebellion of 1837–38.

Louis Joseph Papineau, the son of a seigneur, led the Lower Canadian Rebellion. Like Mackenzie's uprising, Papineau's was partly inspired by what the French aristocrat from across the ocean, Alexis de Tocqueville, had only recently immortalized as *Democracy in America*. It also reflected a radical, assertion of French Canadian identity, which had smoldered for some three-quarters of a century under the regime of la Conquête.

Both French and English rebellions were put down by the Tory oligarchs and the armed force of the Empire; and by the studied neutrality of the still quite youthful government of the American Republic, some of whose less prudent citizens, however, had rushed to the aid of the Canadian rebels. But the rebellions nonetheless convinced British officials that change was required in the government of "the two Canadas."

The Empire decided (much too late, as it happened) to reverse the principles of the 1774 Quebec Act and make an effort to anglicize French Canada. To this end, in 1841 Upper and Lower Canada — the precursors of modern Ontario and Quebec — were joined together, under a single version of the British Constitution, in the United Province of Canada. Further, the United Kingdom, increasingly beset by political and economic agitation at home, was now prepared to make some concessions to the principle of popular rule in its British North American colonies.

At this point, Canada's diverse destiny took the crucial leap of faith that would lock in its modern future. More moderate and pragmatic colleagues of Papineau and Mackenzie, co-led by Louis Hippolyte LaFontaine of Montreal and Robert Baldwin of Toronto, joined to form a French and English Reform alliance in the elected assembly of the United Province of Canada, which expressed the democratic element in the colonial constitution.

This alliance decisively frustrated the imperial ambition of at last anglicizing the French Canadians. Of at least equal importance, in March 1848, just over half a dozen years after the United Province was established, the appointed British governor, Lord Elgin, conceded control of Canada's domestic affairs to LaFontaine and Baldwin's French and English Reform alliance. The fundamental principle was that the alliance clearly commanded a majority of seats in the elected assembly. This amounted to a partial, colonial version of what would later become British parliamentary democracy in the United Kingdom itself, though in British North America at the time, it was more prosaically known as "responsible government."

Universal male suffrage as opposed to male suffrage dependent on ownership of property would not arrive until the late nineteenth century. Voting rights for adult females, as in both the United States and the United Kingdom, would wait until the second decade of the twentieth century. The voting rights of Indians who chose to remain on one of the reserves, which were beginning to dot the landscape in the more developed parts of British North America, would be restricted until after the Second World War.

The wider Canadian Confederation would not secure unambiguous authority over its foreign as well as its domestic affairs until 1931 or, at best,

1926. The highest Canadian court of appeal would remain in the United Kingdom until 1949. And the final, formal elements of British control over the Canadian Constitution would not disappear until 1982. Nonetheless, by 1848 — the abortive "year of revolution" in continental Europe — at least the bare beginnings of what we would now call a modern, democratic Canada had fallen into place. Collectively, its people spoke both English and French (though very few anglophones also spoke French, and many francophones still spoke no English). Without being altogether clear on the matter, it had collectively picked up the torch lit by Cartier, Champlain, and the Indians of Canada, in the sixteenth and seventeenth centuries.

Regional Variations on the Atlantic Coast

To the east, the British subjects of what by 1820 had become the four modern Atlantic provinces, were still almost two generations away — and those in Newfoundland much longer — from even beginning to consider themselves "Canadians." They nonetheless watched events in the Canadas with a degree of interest. There had been vague stirrings along the New Brunswick border in 1837. But, for all practical purposes, the new British gentlemen of old French Acadia spurned even the modest political excesses indulged in by their fellow British subjects in the Great Lakes area and the St. Lawrence Valley.

In 1839 Thomas Chandler Haliburton of Nova Scotia published, in the United Kingdom and the United States, a tract on the Canadian rebellions, somewhat disparagingly entitled *The Bubbles of Canada*. Despite a few cursory references to Mackenzie, the tract concentrated on Papineau. Like many of his fellow, and now overwhelmingly English-speaking, British Atlantic compatriots Haliburton viewed "Canada" as essentially a place of French-speaking people. As an unfortunate result of the 1774 Quebec Act, "Canada became a Gallic and not a British colony."

Yet since the 1790s there had been, in fact, two Canadas. By the middle of the nineteenth century, they would have, together, a population of close to two million people, compared with only about a third that amount in all four Atlantic provinces. In the two decades following the 1841 act of Canadian union, the old Upper Canada's population would increase by 200%, Lower Canada's by some 130%, and the British North American Maritimes' by only 65%. By the 1850s the population of the predominantly English-speaking Upper Canada (or Canada West) was larger than that of the predominantly French-speaking Lower Canada (or Canada East).

Haliburton was a shrewd enough observer to sense the thrust of the developments that lay ahead. Even in 1839 he understood that, in the British North America of the mid- to late nineteenth century, the "fate of Canada will determine that of all the other colonies." Haliburton himself was a loyal British North American Tory and a happy subject of the cosmopolitan Empire. For him, the "advocate of the ballot box and extended suffrage is not the man to govern a colony." His native province, however, was home to the neutral Yankees as well as to refugees from the same Old World Scotland that had bred William Lyon Mackenzie. As in the more central provinces, their contentment with the rule of the British Empire did not extend to the reign of even a more gentlemanly version of the Tory oligarchs.

By the 1830s many of the disparate and factious Reformers of Nova Scotia, the most populous of the Atlantic provinces, had found a spiritual master in the Halifax journalist, politician, "ladies' man," and connoisseur of "low company," Joseph Howe. After some difficult beginnings, in 1828 Howe took over an established local paper known as the *Novascotian*, which made his reputation. His modern biographer, Murray Beck, has described him as a "Conservative Reformer." Circumstances and convictions finally pushed him in more liberal directions, but he began his career as a close friend of Haliburton, whose Sam Slick adventures he first published.

A moderate, pro-British, Nova Scotian patriot first and foremost, Howe rebuffed a plea for support from Lower Canadian radicals in the mid-1830s. Though he would eventually fight a gentle duel with a Tory opponent over political issues, he took pride in Nova Scotia's refusal to stoop to any serious political violence. He nonetheless inspired a spirited struggle in the province's colonial elected assembly, broadly parallel to the struggle that LaFontaine and Baldwin waged further west. In February 1848 "responsible government" was conceded in Nova Scotia — almost exactly one month before the formal triumph of the French and English Reform alliance in the United Province of Canada. In this respect at least, the heartland of the Maritimes (or "Lower Provinces," as they were often known at the time) more than kept pace with the mid-nineteenth century burst of growth and change in British North America.

Howe's struggle also set precedents for colonial democracy in the other Atlantic provinces. By the middle of the 1850s, the United Kingdom had conceded responsible government in Prince Edward Island, New Brunswick, and Newfoundland.

In the British Northwest, still presided over by the Hudson's Bay Company, and still predominantly populated by Indians, political development remained in a more strictly colonial stage. (The Crown Colony of British Columbia was established in 1858, and in 1859 the company's fiefdom of Vancouver Island was converted to a Crown colony as well. In 1866 Vancouver Island was annexed to British Columbia, but the resulting precursor of the modern Canadian province would still not have responsible government until it joined Confederation in 1871.)

By the middle of the 1850s, however, there were early beginnings of a modern democratic people — or several modern democratic peoples — in at least all the more developed regions of British North America, from the Great Lakes east to the Atlantic Coast.

The Second Resource Economy and the Earliest New Industrialism

Mixed in with the political changes in mid-nineteenth century British North America was a diverse assortment of changes in the colonial economic base

Joseph Howe: "the tribune of Nova Scotia" — journalist, ladies' man, first publisher of Thomas Chandler Haliburton's adventures of Sam Slick, and leader of the mid-nineteenth century struggle for colonial democracy (or "responsible government") in what is now Atlantic Canada.

—now overwhelmingly under the command, even on the banks of the lower St. Lawrence River, of English-speaking people.

After the War of 1812 the first Canadian resource economy of the fur trade had begun its retreat into the far northwest. The trend culminated with the merger of the North West and Hudson's Bay companies in 1821. The fur trade's ocean-going links with the markets and manufacturers of Europe became increasingly focused on Hudson Bay, not the St. Lawrence River.

The old fur trade business establishments on the St. Lawrence became the more complex establishments of the "British Canadian merchants of Montreal." They diversified out of furs and into the second resource economy of lumber and wheat—more suited to the expanding English-speaking settlement frontier in the central interior of British North America. They also diversified into the business of high finance, setting up regional branches of firms headquartered in London, England. The Bank of Montreal, founded on the profits of the fur trade, was chartered in 1822.

By the early 1840s the British merchants of Montreal formed an English-speaking economic elite in French-speaking Lower Canada, with interests in the newly developing regions of both Upper Canada and the American Midwest. By the late 1840s they presided over a complete Great Lakes–St. Lawrence canal system, which adapted the ancient canoe and portage Indian waterways of the old upper country fur trade to more modern forms of commerce.

The first resource economy of the cod fisheries continued to thrive, to a somewhat lesser extent, on the Atlantic Coast. Here too, however, there was diversification into lumbering (especially in New Brunswick) and coal (in Nova Scotia). There was new growth as well in local commercial agriculture.

After the American War of Independence, Halifax became an important strategic base on the North American continent for the British Royal Navy. The British merchants of Halifax had maritime interests in both the United Kingdom and the British West Indies. The Halifax-based Bank of Nova Scotia was chartered in 1832, and Samuel Cunard of Nova Scotia began his fleet of ocean liners in the 1840s. As in the United Province of Canada, the second resource economy had begun to expand its commercial ties with the rapidly growing northern states of the American Republic.

By the 1850s the beginnings of local manufacturing and of the "new industrialism" had appeared in both the Atlantic provinces and United Canada. The Great Lakes region of old Upper Canada had the advantage of proximity to early industrial growth in the northeastern American Midwest —as well as a rapidly growing population of its own. Both the Massey and Harris families had begun to manufacture agricultural equipment and machinery in the heartland of the first Canadian wheat economy, in what is now central and southwestern Ontario. (Only a half century later, this first Central Canadian wheat economy would move on to become the second wheat economy in Western Canada.)

The buoyant North American boom era of the 1850s brought the beginnings of the railway age to Nova Scotia, New Brunswick, and the United

Province of Canada. In the United Province, early railway development helped link the upstart interior mini-metropolis of Toronto with railway networks in the United States that ultimately flowed into the city of New York.

The railways also linked Toronto more effectively with Montreal and strengthened Montreal's connections to London, England. What's more, elected colonial politicians engaged in a series of contentious discussions on the subject of an Intercolonial Railroad that would directly link the United Province and the British Atlantic provinces.

In a somewhat haphazard way, along with the beginnings of colonial democracy on the British parliamentary model, there was a groping toward a modern economic base — a successor to the ancient unity of the fur trade.

Even in the Northwest, by the late 1850s the United Province of Canada and, independently as it were, the British Empire had dispatched missions of exploration and discovery into the western interior to guard against any overly aggressive impulses on the American frontier and to probe the potential for a wider future. In 1859 two former employees of *The Globe* in Toronto started a newspaper called *The Nor'Wester* in the Red River–Fort Garry area that would later become Winnipeg — among the Indians and the fur traders, Lord Selkirk's early settlers, handfuls of new British, American, and even French and English Canadian arrivals, and a strong contingent of Métis heirs of the vanished North West Company.

The modern Canadian future would prove to be complex, difficult, replete with regional conflicts, cultural and even racial warfare, and many other internal and external tensions. Nonetheless, by the middle of the nineteenth century, backed by the might of what was still the greatest empire since Rome, the country had begun to stake its claims.

4
CREATING THE CONFEDERATION

Within not much more than a decade, the emerging Canadian nation suddenly achieved a modest political shape in the Confederation of the 1860s and 1870s.

In a fundamental sense, Confederation arose in response to its own internal logic. To start with, there was the French and Indian legacy of the sixteenth and seventeenth centuries. Then, among those who subsequently took over the legacy in official imperial circles in the United Kingdom, the prospect of bringing together the British North American colonies that remained after the War of Independence had been broached as early as the late eighteenth century. In both imperial and colonial circles, it was again broached in the 1820s and the late 1830s. Humanity being what it is, once the boundary of British North America was completed with the Treaty of Oregon in 1846, some larger political enterprise was bound to arise within the vast northern territory from the Atlantic Ocean to the Pacific.

Modern Canada, however, has grown up on the sidelines of larger developments elsewhere, especially the United Kingdom and the United States. To no small extent, Confederation was a response to two seminal Anglo-American events of the nineteenth century. The first was a historic shift to "free trade" in the British Empire during the late 1840s. This led to a free trade or "reciprocity" agreement, between the British North American provinces and the United States, in the mid-1850s. The second event was the great nineteenth century North American trauma of the American Civil War in the first half of the 1860s.

Undoubtedly, external pressure prompted Confederation to happen when it did. Arguably, it happened too soon — before the various parts of the new whole had developed to the point where a larger reach made complete practical sense; and before the necessarily complicated structure and diverse purposes of the greater political enterprise could be altogether or even largely understood.

This was in fact claimed by some at the time. Yet a cardinal discipline of modern Canada is that it has seldom enjoyed the luxury of too many choices. In the world watched over by the British Empire and the American Republic, if there was to be any kind of wider Canadian future — *a mari usque ad mare* ("from sea to sea") — it had to begin in the 1860s and 1870s. (That the same era also witnessed the creation of the modern German, Italian, and Japanese national states suggests still larger forces at work.)

From this standpoint, the lasting achievement of the men who most directly created the original Canadian Confederation was not so much that they had created wisely and well, but that they had had enough foresight and hindsight to create something, before it was too late.

External Forces: Free Trade and Reciprocity

The historic shift to British Empire free trade began with the abolition of the Corn Laws in the United Kingdom in 1846 and culminated with the abolition of the ancient Navigation Acts in 1849.

The old, centrally regulated "mercantilist" imperial trading system, with roots as far back as Oliver Cromwell in the seventeenth century, and even reaching back to the defeat of the Spanish Armada in 1588, was abandoned. In its place arose a new, more open-ended and decentralized system. The Empire at last acceded to the laissez-faire economic doctrines that Adam Smith had propounded in *The Wealth of Nations* at the time of the American War of Independence.

The shift to imperial free trade coincided with the final triumph of the British North American provinces in the struggle for colonial democracy. This triumph was not accidental. Since British officials no longer found it necessary to regulate the Empire's trading system so closely, the decisive imperial objection to colonial self-government disappeared.

In the 1860s and 1870s, the same logic would make it possible for the United Kingdom to transform its remaining British North American colonies into what would ultimately become the beginnings of a rival national state. It could be argued that had the imperial shift to free trade taken place in the 1770s, instead of the 1840s, an American "war of independence" might not have been necessary.

On the other hand, imperial free trade also brought economic dislocation to the provinces. Fundamental parts of the provincial economies, and particularly the designs of the Montreal merchants for a second northern resource economy of lumber and wheat, had been organized to take special advantage of the highly regulated old mercantilist trading system. Along with old political restraints, old economic privileges in the home markets of the United Kingdom disappeared.

One obvious solution was to take greater advantage of new American markets that the dramatic growth of the Republic had already begun to open up by the 1840s. Imports of Canadian lumber at the Great Lakes port of Oswego in New York State, for instance, had risen from two million feet in 1840, to 60 million feet in 1850.

Some believed that this pointed toward the annexation of the British North American provinces by the United States — an option briefly encouraged even by a few Montreal merchants in 1849. But more were interested in what the *Montreal Gazette* would call, in 1856, "the hope of founding here, apart from the United States, a Northern nationality for ourselves." In the end, the key instrument for resolving the economic problems created by British Empire free trade was the Reciprocity Treaty of 1854, a free trade agreement between the British North American provinces (which did not, at this point, include still more colonially organized British territory west of the United Province of Canada) and the United States.

In effect, the British Empire pressured a somewhat reluctant American Republic into the agreement, using free American access to British Atlantic fishing territory as enticement. The fishing issue was already the object of an international Anglo-American dispute, and the managers of the Empire had heated it up, by dispatching imperial warships to British Atlantic waters in 1852. The Empire itself had initially acted on North American free trade with a degree of reluctance, giving in to pressure from the British North American provincial governments, especially from the United Province of Canada.

The Treaty of 1854 provided for provincial free trade with the United States in resource products only. Fledgling British North American manufacturing interests remained under the protection of provincial governments. Nova Scotia was not altogether happy about free American access to the British Atlantic fisheries, and British Empire free trade proved to be less of a disincentive for continuing British North American exports to the United Kingdom than had at first been feared. Yet in both the Atlantic provinces and the United Province of Canada, the Reciprocity Treaty with the United States helped make the 1850s the first great boom era in modern Canadian economic history.

More External Forces: Reciprocity and Civil War

Along with pressure from the British Empire, north-south sectional cleavage inside the American Republic had decisively facilitated ratification of the Reciprocity Treaty of 1854 by a fractious U.S. Congress. This cleavage had reached crisis proportions by the 1850s and would finally lead to the bloody Civil War — the first major example of a terrifying new kind of military conflict in the new age of global industrialism — from April 1861 to April 1865.

To many northern U.S. politicians, free trade with the "British provinces" was only an irksome alternative to the best solution for all British North America's problems: annexation to the United States. In 1855 the American journalist Horace Greeley, coiner of the immortal phrase "go west, young man," wrote to the old English Canadian rebel of the 1830s, William Lyon Mackenzie:

> You know that I am an annexationist. The time is coming when those states that persist in deifying slavery will secede from the Union and I am for letting them go peace-fully .... Then I would like to form a union with Canada and have a Great Free Republic, the strongest and truest in the world. You and I will not live to see this, for the Reciprocity bill has postponed its advent but it is the right thing and so certain to come about. You see I too believe in Manifest Destiny.

The understanding that the Reciprocity Treaty of 1854 would "postpone" American annexation of the British North American provinces formed the treaty's crucial attraction for southern U.S. politicians during the decade before the 11 states of the short-lived Southern Confederacy finally did secede, beginning with South Carolina in late December 1860. Unlike northerners of Horace Greeley's ilk, the South did not want the British provinces in the American Union. The underlying, if not decisive issue of the Civil War was indeed the South's "deification" of black slavery. And, like the U.S. northern states, by the 1850s the British North American provinces were resolutely "free."

(There had in fact been handfuls of Afro-American slaves, even in the old French Canada and Acadia. Some 2,000 more had arrived with the American Loyalists in both Nova Scotia and Upper Canada. An additional 3,500 who had won freedom through loyalty to the Empire settled in the Atlantic provinces at the same time. Slavery was "gradually abolished" in Upper Canada in 1793, on the model of several neighbouring northern states. Within the next few decades slavery had become illegal in virtually all the British North American provinces. For greater certainty, slavery was formally abolished by the British Empire in 1834. In the 1840s and particularly the 1850s, the United Province of Canada became a refuge for fugitive slaves from the American Republic — the most northern terminus of the Underground Railway.)

In the same spirit, most of the 4,000 to 40,000 British North Americans estimated to have fought in the American Civil War served on the winning side of the North, thus confirming Greeley's instincts about where mainstream British North American sentiment lay, in at least this respect. And the North was quite clearly the side publicly endorsed by various prominent provincial Reformers, who had only so recently won the struggle for responsible government.

The managers of the British Empire, however, recognized the South as a legitimate belligerent in the war, to enormous Northern irritation. And by the late 1850s, in the United Province of Canada, the historic French and English Reform alliance that LaFontaine and Baldwin pioneered had begun to lose its way. Into the breech stepped a new French and English "Liberal-Conservative" alliance, co-led by George-Etienne Cartier of Montreal and John A. Macdonald from, in a favourite phrase of Macdonald's, the "loyal old town of Kingston." This was, in several respects, a sly revival of the legacy of the earlier Tory oligarchs and Roman Catholic bishops, adapted here to the cause of economic progress and the new colonial democratic age. It had some sympathy for the Southern Confederacy, for reasons quite unrelated to the narrow question of black slavery. George Brown of Toronto, the brightest new light of English Canadian reform in the 1850s (and, like both John A. Macdonald and William Lyon Mackenzie, of Scottish birth), viewed the "Slavocracy" in the American South as in some ways equivalent to what he called the "Priestocracy" in French Catholic Lower Canada. And the Priestocracy Brown despised was, in the partisan jargon of the day, a loyal "Bleu" supporter of Cartier and Macdonald.

All the British provincial governments made genuine efforts to enforce an official stance of strict neutrality once the Civil War had broken out. But the St. Alban's Raid in October 1864 showed without a doubt that British

North America was nonetheless a haven for Southern saboteurs. This only added to an increasingly pronounced hostility toward all things British — including the British North American provinces — in the ultimately victorious northern section of the Union. Even before the end of the Civil War in 1865, this hostility had helped seal the fate of the Reciprocity Treaty of 1854, in a U.S. Congress that contained no representatives from the as yet unreconstructed states of the Southern Confederacy.

Following an option provided for in the original agreement, in March 1865 Congress voted to abrogate (or cancel) the Reciprocity Treaty in 1866. Economic reasons were advanced to support the decision. It was a grievance among northern U.S. politicians, for instance, that the agreement had not provided for free trade in manufactured as well as resource products, but political instincts mobilized by the trauma of the Civil War were paramount. In late January and early February of 1866, delegates from the United Province of Canada, Nova Scotia, and New Brunswick visited Washington to lobby for a renewal of the treaty. Chairman Morrill of the Ways and Means Committee in the House of Representatives told them: "That will have to be postponed until you, gentlemen, assume your seats *here.*"

This response helped mobilize nascent feelings in mid–nineteenth century British North America about a new "Northern nationality ... apart from the United States." Certain pioneer businessmen in the British provinces also viewed a northern Confederation, one that would pick up the transcontinental torch from the vanished North West Company, as utterly essential in any future that did not include a free trade agreement with the United States. Others urged that only a new, confederated British North America would be strong enough to negotiate any eventual renewal of the abrogated treaty.

For the first time since the War of 1812, there were apparently serious prospects of an invasion of British North America — this time by the conquering northern armies of a new, more centralizing and expansionist American Union, reforged in the bloody crucible of more than 200,000 deaths in battle, more than 280,000 through disease, and an additional more than 500,000 wounded in action.

While such prospects finally proved only apparent, not real, at the end of the war there was a raid on the British North American border at Niagara, by demobilized American "Fenian" sympathizers of the Irish nationalist cause in the United Kingdom. The issue of the fundamental defence of British North America had been raised in a serious way. In both colonial and especially in imperial circles, it gave the question of a new and stronger political enterprise in British North America a hard and practical edge.

Internal Forces in the United Province

As it happened, history turned out exactly opposite to the preference Horace Greeley had confessed to William Lyon Mackenzie in 1855. The northern states of the old Union did not form a new union with Canada, while letting a new Southern Confederacy go its own way. The southern states were compelled to remain in the Union by force of arms, and a new northern Canadian Confederation was allowed to set down roots under the protection of the British Empire. (On 29 January 1861, however, three days after Louisiana became the sixth state to join the Southern Confederacy, the reformist *Globe* in Toronto had cited with good-humoured approval a brash piece of Canadian regionalist wit in the conservative Toronto *Leader*: "Should the Northern States seriously ask to be allowed to join Canada," there was "every likelihood" that the request would "receive a fair and candid consideration.")

One of Greeley's mistakes was that he had anticipated neither the steely resolve of Abraham Lincoln, nor the fiercely united American Republic he represented "I have no purpose ... to interfere with slavery," Lincoln had declared in his first inaugural address of 1861, but "no state, on its own mere action, can get out of the Union."

Another of Greeley's mistakes was that he did not appreciate how, despite its comparatively small population, the newly developing society of British North America was fundamentally more diverse than any vision of William Lyon Mackenzie's could accommodate.

This was grasped in a noble spirit by the scholarly Edmund Head, colonial democratic British governor of the United Province of Canada in the late 1850s. In 1857 Governor Head had advised officials across the ocean that

> whatever may be the personal convictions, and whatever may be the religious beliefs of a Canadian politician, if he means to lead his countrymen as a whole, he must school his mind to principles of tolerance and he must learn to respect the feelings and even the prejudices of others who differ widely from himself.

With the Indians increasingly relegated to the sidelines, the greatest source of diversity in the United Province was the French Canadian fact, so tenaciously dedicated to "la survivance". And, after the triumph of colonial democracy in the late 1840s, it was the newly radicalized English Canadian Reform movement's failure to grasp Head's wisdom that opened the door for the more conservative French and English alliance of Cartier and Macdonald.

The unifying bond of the struggle for responsible government had carried with it a principled recognition of French rights, at least wherever French Canadians could command electoral majorities. But once the struggle had been won, the old French and English Reform alliance confronted a stark practical reality.

There were profound social and economic differences, between the "British" variation on the English Protestant culture of the North American frontier that had now set down roots in the Great Lakes region, and the traditional "French" Catholic culture of the seigneur, priest, and habitant, that continued to dominate the St. Lawrence Valley. Once colonial democracy was established, these differences could only be bridged — for as long as a generation, time would eventually tell — by the more conservative instincts in early English Canada that harkened back to the spiritual legacies of the American Loyalists.

In the increasingly Byzantine early democratic politics that shaped the narrow world of the United Province, even the French and English conservative alliance forged by Cartier and Macdonald could not produce stable governments.

The characteristic problem of the Reformers was that while they came to dominate the western, predominantly English section of the province (under the leadership of George Brown from Toronto), their support grew lamentably thin in the eastern, predominantly French section. Here they were led by the "Rouge" Antoine-Aimé Dorion, in some respects a spiritual ancestor of both Wilfrid Laurier and René Lévesque.

At the same time, while the urbane George-Etienne Cartier easily came to dominate French Canada, even the near-alcoholic geniality and high political skill of John A. Macdonald could not command English Canada without the wider English-speaking political base in the British Atlantic provinces and the British Northwest Territories, (support from these areas would only come with the Confederation of the 1860s and 1870s).

The situation was complicated yet again by divisions between Protestants and Catholics, as well as French and English. These unfolded in a setting where the Catholics included Highland Scottish and Irish migrants from the United Kingdom, as well as French Canadians, and where the Protestants included a substantial body of strident new Empire Loyalists from among the Orangemen of Northern Ireland.

Mixed in with the racial and religious conflict was a rising political and economic struggle between the established British merchants of Montreal, who looked first to London, England, and the upstart Canadian merchants of Toronto, who looked first to New York City. It is a gross oversimplification to say that the English Canadian Reformers of mid–nineteenth century Canada West leaned toward the metropolitan ambitions of upstart Toronto, while the English Canadian Tories (or in John A. Macdonald's more subtle European terminology, Liberal-Conservatives) leaned toward the ambitions of established Montreal. But it is also broadly correct.

The issue that, more than any other, repeatedly brought the political system of the United Province to the edge of collapse was what a much later generation would call "cultural." Very broadly, it focused on the requisite fine balance between overtly Catholic majority and Protestant minority confessional schools in what is now Quebec, and nominally "public," but essentially Protestant, and Catholic "separate" schools in what is now Ontario. (And this was, in several intriguing respects, a prefiguration of the debate over "official bilingualism" in the wider Canadian Confederation of the mid- to late twentieth century, after the demise of the British Empire had brought still more fundamental tensions between the French and English languages into the open.)

The first scheme to resolve the problems of racial, religious, political, and economic deadlock in the United Province of Canada, through a wider British North American political enterprise, was drawn up in the late 1850s by Alexander Tilloch Galt, economic friend to the British merchants of Montreal and political ally of George-Etienne Cartier and John A. Macdonald. As the modern historian W.L. Morton relates, Galt's scheme, though quite like "the scheme that was eventually to be adopted," was put forward too much as a "party measure" to win broad support, even inside the United Province itself. From an imperial standpoint, it also lacked the urgent context of the American Civil War.

A legislative committee under the direction of George Brown of Toronto drew up the final, politically viable scheme in the late spring of 1864. By this point, the recurrent rise and fall of ten provincial governments in as many years, the American Civil War, and rumours about American abrogation of the 1854 Reciprocity Treaty had brought the politics of the United Province to a rolling boil.

Brown's scheme provided for the division of United Canada into two provinces (modern Ontario and Quebec), each of which could manage its own local affairs, especially including education; the joining of these two provinces with the British Atlantic provinces and with what would soon become the united colony of British Columbia, in a larger British North American federation; and the annexation by this federation of the remaining Hudson's Bay Company territories of the British Northwest.

The scheme was quickly endorsed by Cartier, Macdonald, and virtually every other United Canada politician with a substantial following, though not by the Rouge A.A. Dorion, or several radical Upper Canadian Reformers. In the late summer of 1864, Cartier, Macdonald, Brown, and five other delegates from the United Province travelled down the St. Lawrence River to Charlottetown, Prince Edward Island, to present their handiwork to delegates from P.E.I., Nova Scotia, and New Brunswick.

Internal Forces on the Atlantic (and Pacific) Coast

In the 1840s and 1850s, and even before, interest in the concept of a British North American federation had not been confined to the United Province of Canada. The first formal debate on the subject in a provincial assembly was actually held in Nova Scotia in February 1854.

Suggesting some degree of mid–nineteenth century confusion about the word "Canada," the Nova Scotian legislator M.I. Wilkins had declared: "The Canadian, the New Brunswicker, the Nova Scotian and the inhabitants of the other Canadas should be so united as to feel, to know, and to be assured, that they are for ever henceforth to be one and the same people."

Yet Wilkinson was not typical of his region. As Innis would later stress, the first resource economy of the international cod fisheries promoted extreme decentralization on the north Atlantic Coast. Even under the French regime, Acadia had been something different from Canada — and Newfoundland was different again. There were four Atlantic provinces in the middle of the nineteenth century, not one province as in Canada. They were also distinct from the United Province, even if outsiders sometimes lumped the Atlantic provinces together with Canada. Especially in Joseph Howe's Nova Scotia, the struggle for responsible government had been won on the back of regional patriotism.

The Atlantic provinces were fundamentally loyal to the British Empire — more loyal, in their own estimation, than the French and English United Province of Canada. This in itself made the concept of a new "Northern nationality ... apart from the United States" less meaningful for the regional patriots of the British Atlantic Coast. To some the concept was even more "pretentious" than the nativist stirrings of the American Republic. (And on the eve of the Civil War the Republic itself was still, as modern American historian S.L. Mayer has explained, "an ex-British colony, with a post-colonial economy, largely dependent on Britain for its industrial products and protected from Europe by the Royal Navy.")

Because of the expulsion of so many Acadians in the 1750s, and because the ancient Acadiens were never so numerous or so entrenched as the ancient Canadiens to the west, the French fact in the Atlantic provinces had grown weak. Such British Atlantic regional patriots as Joseph Howe had profound doubts about the prospects of any French and English "catamaran of a Confederacy," in which the much more tenacious French-speaking people of Canada were bound, through sheer numbers, to play an important role.

A fundamental dilemma for the Atlantic provinces, in any wider scheme of British North American federation, was the marked discrepancy between their populations and economic bases and those of the United Province of Canada. In the early 1870s, Ontario and Quebec would have more than 75% of the population in the Confederation that finally emerged, compared with just over 20% in Nova Scotia, New Brunswick, and P.E.I. Tortuous negotiations on the projected Intercolonial Railroad in the 1850s and early 1860s, which time and time again stumbled over the increasingly congenital Canadian political instability, did nothing to reassure Maritimers about the good intentions of the United Province.

As the various North American storms of the era gathered, eastern attention increasingly focused on the alternative concept of a "Maritime Union" of the three, or perhaps even four, Atlantic provinces — either as a longer-term future in itself or as an essential, strengthening prelude to some form of eventual wider association with the United Province of Canada. When Cartier, Macdonald, Brown, and the other Canadians travelled from the United Province to Charlottetown in the late summer of 1864, they went to a conference that had originally been called to discuss Maritime Union, among Nova Scotia, New Brunswick, and Prince Edward Island alone.

Yet, though Maritime Union reflected pervasive Atlantic regional instincts that would thrive long after the Confederation set down roots, it would finally prove to be fatally flawed as a concept in its own right. For New Brunswick and Prince Edward Island it raised fears of Nova Scotian dominance, comparable to the wider Atlantic fears of Canadian dominance in a British North American federation (to say nothing of the apprehensions of Newfoundland, very much it own region, even among its Atlantic brothers).

Moreover, under Maritime Union each of the Atlantic provinces would in effect disappear — a particular concern for Prince Edward Island. Under the wider Confederation option proposed by the United Province in 1864, all the provinces would at least continue to exist within a transcontinental federal system, like that of the American Republic.

By the mid–1860s the imperial officialdom across the ocean had also concluded that wider confederation was the best option for the future defence of British North America. Maritime Union might have made some sense in the open-ended northern New World of the first half of the nineteenth century when the region was dominated by a notably decentralized United States, still haunted by African slavery, and recurrently preoccupied with arguments about states' rights and its own versions of regional patriotism. But any merely Maritime Union — a new British version of the old French Acadia — would be a frail vessel in the world of the new, conquering, "free", and expansionist America that had emerged from the Civil War.

As the ultimate fate of Newfoundland proved, under responsible government the old parent state in the United Kingdom could not dictate to its new self-governing colonies. Yet, especially in a region so loyal to the Empire, and still so dependent on the Royal Navy, it retained great powers of persuasion.

Similar powers would shape the fate of the still very new colony of British Columbia on the Pacific Coast. Here responsible government remained in the wings, and the great majority of people were still Salish, Nootka, Kwakiutl, Bella Coola, Tsimishian, Haida, and Tlinkit Indians.

By the 1860s, there was a "Canadian party" among the as yet extremely small white population of the British Pacific Northwest. And there was the improbable ex-Nova Scotian "Amor De Cosmos" (a polyglot concoction of Latin, French, and Greek, meaning "lover of the universe": he was born plain William Smith). De Cosmos, a former friend of the Mormons in Utah and photographer in the California goldfields, was now a journalist in Victoria and a colonial politician full of bold enthusiasm for British North American confederation and a new Canadian transcontinental nation. But in British Columbia there were also British Americans and plain Americans from south of the forty-ninth parallel — at least some of whom were profoundly sceptical about both Canada and the British Empire.

The Confederation Decade, 1864– 73

Tradition has it that the birthday of the modern Canadian Confederation is 1 July 1867, just three days before the celebration of the 1776 Declaration of Independence in the American Republic. Yet, though there is some logic to the date, it cannot have the depth of mythic significance that 4 July 1776 has in the United States. In terms more suited to the case in point, the creation of the Canadian Confederation began in 1864 and did not end until 1873.

The year 1864 marks the Charlottetown Conference and then the Quebec Conference, where provincial delegates first put a design for the new political enterprise on paper. The year 1873 marks the entry of what is still the Confederation's smallest and least populous province, Prince Edward Island. It also marks the death of George-Etienne Cartier — in some still too unacknowledged respects, as his modern English Canadian biographer, Alastair Sweeny, has urged, "the first among the Fathers of Confederation."

At Charlottetown in September 1864, representatives from the United Province at last managed to convince Atlantic representatives that there was room for Atlantic voices in a new transcontinental, self-governing political enterprise. The promise of equal regional representation in the upper house of the new Confederation Parliament, ultimately to become the Canadian Senate, played an important role in the discussions.

It also counted for something that — whatever French and English dualism it might reflect, whatever quest for some future northern nationality it might embody, and however committed it was to the continuing evolution of parliamentary democracy — the new Confederation would remain, in form, a constitutional monarchy within the wider political framework of the British Empire. The provincial delegates agreed to repair to Quebec City, ancient capital of the historic French and Indian empire in America, for more detailed discussions, to which even Newfoundland finally agreed to add its voice.

At Quebec City in October 1864, representatives from the United Province of Canada, Nova Scotia, New Brunswick, Newfoundland, and Prince Edward Island debated and revised 72 sometimes highly controversial resolutions, typically introduced by the United Province and frequently by John A. Macdonald. With some subsequent modifications, these became the basis of the imperial British North America Act, 1867 which would mark the bare beginnings of the modern Canadian Constitution. The act was described by the British MP Charles Adderly, who would eventually introduce the legislation in the imperial Parliament, as "a matter of most delicate mutual treaty and compact between the provinces."

The imperial officialdom across the ocean moved quickly to endorse the work of the Quebec Conference. But in British North America itself, 1865 brought winds of disagreement. Even in the United Province of Canada there were some politicians, especially but not exclusively French-speaking, who opposed the Confederation. Others urged with no ultimate success that it ought to be put to a fresh vote of the electorate, not to a mere vote in the current assembly as on the strictly "British" parliamentary convention.

The winds of disagreement blew still stronger in the Atlantic provinces. An election in New Brunswick seemed to return a majority against the work of the Quebec Conference. In the mid–nineteenth century party system, still rather undisciplined by late twentieth century standards, the matter was not altogether clear. It did become quite clear, however, that both Newfoundland and Prince Edward Island still had many concerns about the fate of their regional identities in the larger enterprise.

Nonetheless, by 1866 the uncertain implications of the end of the American Civil War, the final clarification of the attitude of the new American Union toward the 1854 Reciprocity Treaty, and the prestigious voices of imperial officials had turned opinion around again in New Brunswick. Similarly, at least majorities in the current assemblies of Nova Scotia and United Canada continued to support the Confederation project.

In December 1866, representatives of the United Province, Nova Scotia, and New Brunswick met in the imperial metropolis of London. Here they made the final revisions to the work of the Quebec Conference. As at Quebec in 1864, the success of the negotiations leaned on what W.L. Morton has called "a failure to disagree for lack of understanding and clear definition."

*The Charlottetown Conference, September 1864. In a dispatch dated "7th September" the **Halifax Chronicle** reported: "The Conference sits daily now, from ten to three, without interruption or adjournment. Yesterday morning, before the hour of business, they all repaired to the lawn in front of Government House, and were photographed in a group, by an artist named Roberts, from St. John."*

George-Etienne Cartier is standing, just to the left of John A. Macdonald, who is seated on the steps in the centre of the group. Charles Tupper from Nova Scotia is standing, third from the left, in the back row. Samuel Leonard Tilley from New Brunswick is standing on the same step that John A. Macdonald is sitting on, immediately left of the man waving his hat, who is Andrew G. McDonald from Prince Edward Island.

The provincial delegates unanimously elected John A. Macdonald chairman of the 1866 London Conference. This reflected his unique technical mastery of the details of the Quebec resolutions. Earlier on, Macdonald had been only the junior partner to Cartier, in the unstable French and English conservative alliances of the United Province. As the initial consummation of the wider Confederation drew within sight, he had become, as his colleague Hector Langevin, described him, "a sharp fox ... a very well informed man, ingratiating, clever, and very popular ... *the man* of the conference." Cartier was now merely "No. 2."

On the basis of this status among his peers, Lord Monck, first British governor general of the new Confederation of Nova Scotia, New Brunswick, Quebec, and Ontario, appointed John A. Macdonald modern Canada's first prime minister. This took effect on 1 July 1867, the date set for the official birth of the enterprise. Over the summer of 1867, Macdonald and Cartier, supported by such Atlantic luminaries as Charles Tupper of Nova Scotia and Samuel Leonard Tilley of New Brunswick, organized a leisurely first Canadian federal election, which lasted six weeks.

This, as both luck and the more human skills of the sharp fox would have it, confirmed Macdonald's status among the electorate of the new Confederation. The resulting first federal conservative alliance would win a second election in 1872, by only eight seats and 0.8% of the popular vote, and preside over the remainder of the Confederation decade, to Cartier's death in 1873.

There had been some debate about what the new self-governing country of the British Empire should be called. At an evening ball during the 1864 Quebec Conference, Macdonald had told Lord Monck's sister-in-law that "in some speech he had said that to please the Nova Scotians it should be called 'Acadia.'" Around the same time, other wits had proposed "Canadia" — a combination of Canada and Acadia. According to W.L. Morton (born much later, in Manitoba), "a Maritimer" finally proposed the name Canada.

At the London Conference in 1866, Macdonald and other provincial delegates had also wanted to call the new Canada a "Kingdom" or "Viceroyalty." Imperial officials felt that this would be too much of a red flag to the American Republic. The term "Dominion" was finally agreed on. One story has it that this evoked the "Old Dominion" of Virginia, spiritual homeland of some among the more prominent American Loyalists of the 1780s. Another claims that the devout Samuel Tilley from New Brunswick (also, according to Langevin, "a deft trimmer, clever and adroit") pointed to Psalm 72, verse 8, in the Christian Bible: "He shall have dominion also from sea to sea, and from the river unto the ends of the earth."

Only some two months after the first federal election in the new Dominion of Canada, a provincial election in Nova Scotia returned what seemed to be an "anti-confederate" majority. By 1868, Joseph Howe, the conservative Reformer who had earlier led the Nova Scotian struggle for responsible government, had raised the alternative prospects of Maritime Union once again. To stem this tide, the financial terms of the original Confederation bargain were renegotiated. With pressure from imperial officials, urgings from Maritime pro-confederates, and all manner of warm overtures from John A. Macdonald, Joseph Howe was persuaded to take a seat in the new federal Cabinet at Ottawa in January 1869.

The next crisis arose when the new Dominion, as had already been planned, purchased the old Prince Rupert's Land of the British Northwest from the Hudson's Bay Company, in December 1869. This prompted a protest among the Métis and Indian heirs of the vanished North West Company, in the Red River area adjacent to what would officially become known as Winnipeg in 1876. The protest quickly developed into the Red River (or first Northwest) Rebellion, led by the mystical and charismatic Métis prophet Louis Riel. And, right at the birth of the Confederation, this inaugurated the theme of western alienation in modern Canadian history.

The immediate result was the creation of the original "postage stamp" province of Manitoba in 1870 — an unusually small geographic box in the south end of the Manitoba of today. Not long after, to complete the sweep to the Pacific, the Crown Colony of British Columbia became the sixth province of the new Dominion of Canada, in 1871. The officials of the Empire gently managed the arrangements.

A petition for annexation to the United States had been circulated — though not widely signed — in British Columbia in 1869. Although Indians accounted for three-quarters of all the people in British Columbia when it joined Confederation, much of its small white population was still resolutely "British." There were memories, as well as a few commercial survivals of the old Montreal-based transcontinental fur trade. There were such exotic enthusiasts for the new transcontinental nation as the Nova Scotian born Amor De Cosmos. And Anthony Musgrave, the appointed governor of the Crown Colony, had earlier been governor of Newfoundland when it had spurned the Confederation project. On the Pacific Coast, he worked harder to fulfil the pro-Confederation wishes of his masters across the Atlantic Ocean.

Unlike Newfoundland, British Columbia still lacked responsible government, which would only come when it became a province of the new Dominion. This made Musgrave's task easier. By the spring of 1870 he had secured enough agreement among his local colonial advisers to dispatch a delegation of three (R.W. Carrall, J.W. Trutch, and J.S. Helmcken) to Ottawa — via the recently completed Central Union and Pacific railways in the United States.

At this point, Macdonald was recuperating from the earlier crises of the new Dominion at a resort on Prince Edward Island. Cartier, who had also played a leading role in the drama over Manitoba, managed the negotiations. He impressed the delegates from the Pacific Coast with his personal warmth, and his buoyant faith in the destiny of the Confederation. A key British Columbian demand was a railway from Central Canada to the Pacific — a western analogue to the eastern Intercolonial Railroad. The new Domin-

ion agreed: as Musgrave later reported, "the Railway ... is *guaranteed* .... Sir George Cartier says they will do that or 'burst.'"

In the spring of 1873 Prince Edward Island at last set aside its earlier reservations and became the seventh province of the first self-governing dominion of the British Empire. There would be no similar change of heart in Newfoundland. It would remain aloof until 1949 — a rugged symbol of the extreme tenacity of regional attachments on the Atlantic Coast.

Soon afterwards, on 20 May 1873, George-Etienne Cartier died while on a trip to London, England. His daughter Josephine reported: "Almost his last words were to say how happy he was that the union with Prince Edward Island had been completed."

John A. Macdonald, *"the man"* of the 1866 London Conference, had become the first prime minister of the new Canada, with its new English-speaking majority. Yet George-Etienne Cartier spoke for the first people to call themselves Canadians. "Nations," he had declared in 1865,

> now are formed by the joining together of various people
> having similar interests and sympathies ... we shall form a
> political nationality independent of the national origin and
> religion of individuals .... The idea of a fusion of all races is
> Utopian ... diversity is the order of the physical, moral, and
> political world.

Part Two

THE OLD DOMINION

5
THE MUTED VOICE OF REGION

Even in the late twentieth century, one side of English Canada still believes that if the country is to have a real "Northern nationality ... apart from the United States," it must have its own miniaturized versions of all the patriotic trappings in the mythology of the American Republic. Thus, John A. Macdonald is sometimes misleadingly assigned the part of "Canada's George Washington."

One partial antidote to this tendency is to stress Macdonald's crucial partnership with George-Etienne Cartier, without which Confederation would have been impossible. Yet even this response, obscures something fundamental about what Canada would become. To no small extent, Cartier and Macdonald shared a particular constitutional vision. Its hallmark was a profound belief in the essential primacy of the federal government at Ottawa in the life of the Confederation.

It would be naive to imagine that this belief flowed from any inability to grasp the significance of the abiding regionalism of the new "dominion also from sea to sea." Macdonald and Cartier received their immediate political education in the congenitally unstable United Province of Canada, which was finally immobilized by relentless regional bickering between predominantly French Canada East and predominantly English Canada West. They also lived in a North America where regional conflict between North and South in the American Republic had led to a traumatic Civil War, in which the total number of dead and wounded would be greater than the total population of all the British Atlantic provinces combined. They felt that because the new Confederation had so many "natural" tendencies toward decentralization, its constitution must promote strong institutional tendencies in the opposite direction.

In one respect, the vision in its purest sense, most narrowly identified with John A. Macdonald alone, had already been cut off at its knees by the time of Macdonald's death in 1891. In its final form the British North America Act, 1867, did seem to suggest that the new "confederation" had some notable biases toward centralization. The provincial governments, in the view of Macdonald and those who shared his most rigorously pro-Ottawa reading of the act, were to be no more than "glorified County councils." In the 1870s and 1880s, however, the new provincial governments of Quebec and, especially, Ontario, with support from such places as Nova Scotia and Manitoba, took a series of constitutional issues to the Judicial Committee of the Privy Council in the United Kingdom — the final court of appeal for Canadian constitutional disputes until 1949. The upshot was a series of legal interpretations that dramatically increased the effective powers of the provincial governments in the Confederation and thwarted federal powers to reserve and disallow provincial legislation.

In another respect, however, the vision of the English-speaking "sharp fox" and his urbane French-speaking partner lived on, down to the present. The new federal Parliament at Ottawa was divided into two houses. The House of Commons was composed of members elected from geographic constituencies fundamentally based on population, from the Atlantic to the Pacific. The Senate was composed of members appointed to represent the major geographic regions or "sections" of the Confederation.

At the 1864 Quebec Conference, arrangements for the Senate had been debated for six days, more thoroughly and over a longer time than any other feature of the new political enterprise. For many provincial delegates, especially from outside the United Province, the Senate was meant to ensure that each major region, regardless of disparities in population and "natural" economic power, would have its own equal and effective voice in the decisions of the federal government at Ottawa.

Yet the original Canadian Senate was constructed in such a way that it could not hope to fulfil this purpose practically. As the modern political scientist F.A. Kunz would explain much later, in the mid–1960s, the real Senate of Canada became merely "a rhetorical device, a psychological rather than a political remedy" for the abiding regionalism of the Confederation.

Old Tory Heirlooms

To start with, the Senate would be burdened with additional purposes. As its name suggests, it was partly modelled on the Senate in the federal system of the United States. (So would be, to a much greater extent, the Senate created by the new Commonwealth of Australia, which became the second self-governing dominion of the British Empire in 1901.) Like the U.S. Senate, the Canadian Senate was a response to the nation-building need for territorial representation, as a counterweight to representation by population, in a geographically large, transcontinental country.

Yet the Canadian Senate was also modelled, as was, to some extent, the U.S. Senate itself, on practices of British colonial government that reflected the mother country's historic institution known as the House of Lords. And in the self-governing Canada that remained a part of the British Empire, this particular institutional legacy would carry unusual weight.

Under the typical British colonial constitution — in the old Thirteen Colonies, as well as in British North America after the War of Independence — the governor appointed by imperial officialdom was advised by two local bodies: an elected assembly and an appointed council. In the two Canadas created by the Constitutional Act, 1791, three such bodies were established: an elected Legislative Assembly, an appointed Legislative Council, and an appointed Executive Council. In terms of the Canadian Constitution today, at the federal level, the colonial Legislative Assembly is the ancestor of the modern House of Commons; the colonial Executive Council, the ancestor of the modern Cabinet; and the colonial Legislative Council, the ancestor of the modern Senate.

The Maritime provinces began with only an elected assembly and an appointed council, as in the old Thirteen Colonies. New Brunswick, however, adopted separate Executive and Legislative Councils in 1834, as in the two Canadas, and Nova Scotia and Prince Edward Island followed suit in 1837.

In all of British North America after the War of Independence the appointed Legislative Councils tended to become bastions of the Tory oligarchs — just as the elected Legislative Assemblies became the institutional arenas that spawned the provincial Reform movements. The provisions of the Constitutional Act, 1791 that established the province of Upper Canada had even envisioned the creation of a hereditary aristocracy, whose political position would be bolstered by representation on the Legislative Council. Even in Canada under the British flag, this jarred far too much with the democratic realities of North American agrarian frontier culture to ever receive any enduring breath of life. It nonetheless reflected Old World conservative instincts that would play a part in the creation of the Canadian federal Senate in the 1860s.

Reformers made significant and even, as the examples of Brown and later Howe show, crucial contributions to the new Dominion of Canada. But in all the British provinces the Confederation movement, as it gathered momentum, increasingly tended to be led by such more conservative politicians as Cartier, Macdonald, Tupper, and Tilley. The most radical Reformers tended to be staunch regionalists, who in many cases had at least initially opposed the Confederation project. (Before his death in 1861, William Lyon Mackenzie's last failed cause was a campaign for the dissolution of the old United Province of Canada.)

It is, as well, sometimes stressed that the Dominion of Canada established in the 1860s and 1870s was not a democracy, but a constitutional monarchy. In a related sense, the United States of America established in the 1770s and 1780s was not a democracy either, but a republic. In fact, the complete rhetoric and practice of modern liberal democracy was not fully accepted in Canada until the late nineteenth and early twentieth centuries. Though its effective practice was in advance of the mother country, Canada tended to follow the political rhetoric of the constitutional monarchy in the United Kingdom, rather than that of the republic to the south. The United States can be said to have become "a democracy" somewhat before either the United Kingdom or Canada, as reflected in the title of de Tocqueville's monumental book of the 1830s, *Democracy in America*.

Thus, along with its functions of regional representation, the Canadian Senate was also assigned functions that reflected modern variations on the ancient purposes of the British House of Lords. In Macdonald and Cartier's Liberal-Conservative revival of the earlier ethos of the Tory oligarchs, the old claims of aspiring colonial aristocrats had given way to the new claims of established colonial businessmen. And as Macdonald put the point on the second day of the Quebec Conference in 1864, there would be a large property qualification for membership in the Senate, "which is then the representative of property." Or, as he put it more bluntly on another occasion, the "rights of the minority must be protected, and the rich are always fewer in number than the poor."

Cartier, coming from a milieu where the never altogether convincing claims of the ancient French Canadian seigneurs had only begun to fade, put a sharper political focus on the issue: "The weak point in democratic institutions is the leaving of all power in the hands of the popular element .... In order that institutions may be stable and work harmoniously there must be a power of resistance to oppose the democratic element."

Here, lie the origins of the modern Canadian Senate which has sometimes resembled a gentlemen's club for retired luminaries of the Canadian business establishment — an institution that the political scientist Colin Campbell attacked in the 1970s as *A Lobby from Within*, and that Winnipeg-born Toronto wit Larry Zolf satirized in the 1980s, in a book of Canadian political humour called *The Survival of the Fattest*.

The Debate over Regional Representation

Another problem with the original Canadian Senate was that its regional representation functions were, in effect, shared with another body. In the 1920s R.A. MacKay, eminent contributor to the slender historical literature on the subject, noted that "the Fathers of the federation did not expect that the Senate would be the chief line of defence for the protection of provincial or sectional rights. The first great check on the central government would be in the federal nature of the Cabinet; the upper house would be only a last means of defence."

To no small extent, this reflected a grafting of the historic practices of the old United Province of Canada onto the new Confederation. In the United Province virtually every Cabinet position had been divided regionally. There had been, for instance, an attorney general east, representing modern Quebec, and an attorney general west, representing modern Ontario.

The new Dominion's Cabinet would not go to such extremes. But it did become and remain an unwritten convention that each major region, or even province of the Confederation, customarily receives some representation in the federal Cabinet.

This was not provided for in the British North America Act or any other document. It was merely a necessary informal practice that a shrewd observer could deduce from the ultimate formal arrangements. In one of the few genuine intellectual achievements of the Confederation debates of the 1860s, the inevitably "federal nature" of the future Cabinet at Ottawa was clarified by Christopher Dunkin — "an acid independent from Lower Canada" (in W.L. Morton's characterization). Dunkin, intending his clarification as a criticism of the design for the Senate complained: "It is admitted that the Provinces are not really represented to federal intent in the Legislative Council. The Cabinet here must discharge that kind of function which in the United States is performed in the federal sense by the Senate."

It is far from clear that the generality of provincial delegates at the Charlottetown, Quebec, and London conferences (as opposed to such leading "Fathers of the federation" as Macdonald, Cartier, and their particular colleagues) altogether grasped the full significance of Dunkin's clarification. If provincial delegates underrated the importance of regional representation in the Senate to the extent that Dunkin did, albeit correctly enough, it is hard to explain why the Quebec Conference spent six of its 14 days arguing about the details of the Senate's composition. It is equally hard to explain why the smallest province, Prince Edward Island, pressed so doggedly for provincial

Christopher Dunkin, who shrewdly complained in the 1860s that "the Provinces are not really represented to federal intent" in what would become the Senate of Canada, appears in this illustration of the members and staff of a special court or commission, established in 1855 to at last wind down the ancient quasi-aristocratic seigneurial system of land tenure in Lower Canada or Canada East.

Dunkin is the gentleman with a goatee in the foreground, just to the right of the centre of the picture. (Immediately above him, in the background, is Louis Hippolyte LaFontaine, co-leader with Robert Baldwin of the French and English Reform alliance that had at last brought colonial democracy to the United Province of Canada, in the late 1840s.)

The special court had been mandated under an "Act for the Abolition of Feudal Rights and Duties in Lower Canada." Yet, as Dunkin bemoaned, in several senses the social and political ethos underlying the abolished rights and duties — a French analogue for the somewhat parallel aristocratic pretensions of the English Tory oligarchs and at least some among the American Loyalists — would live on in the structure of the federal Senate in the new Dominion of Canada.

66

rather than merely regional or sectional representation — and then remained aloof from the Confederation for half a dozen years when its demand was spurned.

As in the federal nature of the Cabinet, the decision to represent regions or sections rather than provinces in the original Canadian Senate can be traced to the earlier experience of the United Province and the complexities created by its French and English dualism. Though the United Province Assembly had been popularly elected, Canada East and Canada West had each been assigned equal numbers of seats. In the new federal House of Commons there would be strict representation by population, giving the now more populous Ontario more seats than Quebec.

Thus, the leading Canada West Reformer, George Brown, who was also the leading proponent of "representation by population" in the federal successor to the elected assembly, saw the logic of the federal Senate as implicitly tied to the French and English character of the new Dominion: "Our Lower Canadian friends have agreed to give us representation by population in the Lower House, on the express condition that they could have equality in the Upper House. On no other condition could we have advanced a step."

From this old Canadian, or new Central Canadian, standpoint, representation in the Senate by sections or regions rather than provinces was meant to protect the position of the French Canadian heartland in what was at once the old province of Lower Canada, the old section or region of Canada East, and the new province of Quebec — on the banks of the lower St. Lawrence River. Equal representation for each province in the Senate would have reduced the claims of the French fact in the Confederation to no more than the claims of the province of Prince Edward Island, an extremely small geographic territory with only 2.5% of the new Dominion's total population.

This was the background to John A. Macdonald's initial proposal at Quebec (based on an earlier proposal by George Brown) that the federal Senate, (still described as a Legislative Council or upper house at this stage) be composed of 24 members from the region or section of the new province of Quebec, 24 members from the region or section of the new province of Ontario, and 24 members from the region or section of the Maritime provinces.

In theory, this followed the logic of Maritime Union as a prelude to Confederation, gave what Harold Innis would much later describe as at least "a substantial number of senators" to the Maritime provinces as "a guarantee of maritime rights," and yet still acknowledged the particular importance of Quebec as the heartland of French Canada. A specific geographic allocation of Quebec's 24 Senate seats was also designed to represent the English and Protestant minorities in the province.

Only Prince Edward Island consistently opposed Macdonald's proposal, favouring instead equal representation for each province. Its arguments won intermittent support from other Maritimers but even Tilley from New Brunswick proposed that the Maritime section have 32 not 24 senators. The allocation of Maritime senators among the Maritime provinces proved an inflammatory issue as well — especially when Newfoundland, which had not been represented at Charlottetown, joined the delegates at Quebec.

More broadly, virtually all Atlantic delegates at the Quebec Conference initially resisted the principle of merely equal sectional representation with each of the new provinces of Ontario and Quebec. On this issue, as Morton has phrased the point, "the conference nearly broke up."

CANADIAN REGIONAL DEMOGRAPHICS IN THE EARLY 1870s

Province/Region	Population 1871 (000s)	% Total Confederation
Nova Scotia	388	10.5
New Brunswick	286	7.8
Prince Edward Island	94	2.5
Maritimes (Total)	768	20.8
Quebec (old Canada East)	1,191	32.3
Ontario (old Canada West)	1,621	43.9
Manitoba	25	0.7
Northwest Territories	48	1.3
British Columbia	36	1.0
West (Total)	109	3.0
ALL CANADA	3,689	100.0

Atlantic complaints in turn, however, raised even more inflammatory fears among the partisans of the French fact. The P.E.I. delegate Edward Whelan reported: "The French Canadians seem to apprehend that they will be swamped in the Upper House, and desire a larger representation than the Maritime Provinces ask for, so that they may not be overpowered by the British element."

In the end, a majority at the Quebec Conference finally agreed on John A. Macdonald's original proposal for three 24-member sections. Newfoundland was treated as separate from the Maritime section, and assigned four senators in its own right — a principle that would in fact give the four Atlantic provinces combined a slightly larger number of senators than either Ontario or Quebec.

Neither Prince Edward Island nor Newfoundland was happy with this arrangement. By the London Conference of 1866, however, they had dropped out. It was agreed that if and when P.E.I. joined the Confederation, it would have four senators, and Nova Scotia and New Brunswick 10 each. Meanwhile, Nova Scotia and New Brunswick would have 12 each. If and when Newfoundland should join, it would have four senators in its own right, as agreed at Quebec.

To bring the subject swiftly down to the present, when Manitoba became a province in 1870, it was allocated two senators. British Columbia was given three when it joined the Confederation in 1871. The prescribed adjustments among the three Maritime provinces took place when P.E.I. joined in 1873. When the new provinces of Alberta and Saskatchewan were created in 1905, they were assigned four senators each. Then in 1915 the four western provinces of Manitoba, Saskatchewan, Alberta, and British Columbia were established as a new 24-member Senate section, with six members each. In the same year it was provided that if and when Newfoundland joined, it could also have six senators, an outcome realized at last in 1949. Finally, in 1975 the Yukon and Northwest Territories were assigned one senator each.

The Election vs. Appointment Issue

Perhaps the most striking point about the 1860s debates over regional and provincial representation in the second chamber of the new federal Parliament is how much insignificant sound and fury they amount to in retrospect — given the lame and ineffectual, or even, to its most acidic critics, vaguely ridiculous, institution the Canadian Senate eventually became. Yet it is arguable that, even with the compromise of representation by regions instead of provinces, the Senate might have done more to integrate the abiding regionalism of the new Confederation into the workings of the federal government, had it not also been for what Macdonald called the "mode of appointment to the Upper House."

Macdonald himself framed this issue when he introduced his Senate proposals on the second day of the Quebec Conference: "Many are in favour of election and many are in favour of appointment by the crown."

Even in the model of the American Republic, direct popular election of senators would not arrive until 1913. Before this, U.S. senators were chosen by the state legislatures. (It is also intriguing that, even with direct election, the American Senate, like its Canadian counterpart, has frequently been characterized as "a millionaire's club.")

In the 1860s, however, there were some British North American precedents for popular election of the upper house. On cues from one strain in the pre-Confederation Reform movement, the Legislative Council in the United Province of Canada had in fact been turned into an elected body in the later 1850s, with allowances for the gradual retirement of earlier members who had been appointed for life. Even after it finally joined Confederation, Prince Edward Island would have an elected provincial Legislative Council, first created in 1862, until 1893.

As Macdonald's framing of the issue itself implies, some delegates at the 1864 Quebec Conference advocated an elected Senate. Two prominent Canada West Reformers are noted in the traditional literature. The first is William McDougall, one of the original Clear Grits who radicalized the English Canadian Reform movement after the triumph of responsible government. (McDougall had also been the owner of a Toronto newspaper called *The North American*, subsequently absorbed by George Brown's *Globe*.) The second is Oliver Mowat, who would later serve for 24 uninterrupted years as the Liberal premier of Ontario (1872–1896) and lead the largely successful struggle for provincial rights at the Judicial Committee of the Privy Council in the United Kingdom.

One reservation about an elected Senate, on the part of a more conservative majority at the Quebec Conference, centred on the complications it appeared to raise for the evolving British North American traditions of parliamentary democracy — as opposed to the separation-of-powers constitutional system in the United States. Under "British institutions," democracy would come to mean that the will of the elected House of Commons was the paramount political expression of the sovereign power in the national state. What would happen if the will of an elected Senate were to clash with the will of an elected House of Commons? This was a conflict, Macdonald implied, that the elected Legislative Council had already threatened to raise in the United Province.

In fact, such an essentially technical problem was not an altogether decisive objection to an elected upper house. This would be demonstrated by the Commonwealth of Australia, another parliamentary democracy on the British model, when it created an elected Senate in 1901. Furthermore, even with an appointed Senate in Canada, the United Kingdom was concerned about a potential deadlock between the Canadian Senate and House of Commons. The Earl of Carnarvon and the Colonial Office in the United Kingdom successfully urged that the confederating partners adopt an emergency provision, subsequently never used, for the creation of extra senators, to resolve such a conflict.

Another reservation about electing senators sprang from the majority of the provincial delegates' genuine conservative concern for some "power of resistance to oppose the democratic element," as voiced by Cartier. In expressing his preference for selection of senators through "appointment by the crown," Macdonald himself frankly appealed to elitist instincts, in the old Tory tradition. It would be, he argued, in "the interest of each section to be represented by its very best men, and the members of the Administration who belong to each section will see that such men are chosen." To further promote Cartier's desire for harmony and stability, they would be chosen for life, as in the original Legislative Councils.

Macdonald's language here also reveals, or perhaps obscures, a crucial final point about the mode of senatorial appointment in the new Confederation. This point may or may not have been clear to the majority of provincial delegates at Quebec. On 19 October 1864, Jonathan McCully of Nova Scotia

William McDougall: radical "Clear Grit" in the Canada West of the mid-nineteenth century, founder of the short-lived Toronto newspaper known as **The North American,** *and proponent of an elected Senate for the new Confederation at the Quebec Conference of 1864.*

had moved

> that the members of the first Legislative Council in the
> Federal Legislature shall be appointed by the Crown at the
> recommendation of the Federal Executive Government upon
> the nomination of the respective Local Governments. And
> that in such nomination due regard be had to the claims of
> the members of the Legislative Council of the Opposition in
> each Province, so as that all political parties be as nearly as
> possible fairly represented.

This particular phraseology — which, in some respects, anticipates the 1987 Meech Lake Accord by almost 123 years — was apparently agreed to by all the delegates at Quebec, but it did not find its way into the final British North America Act, 1867. All the act would say was that the "Governor General shall from Time to Time, in the Queen's name, by Instrument under the Great Seal of Canada, summon qualified Persons to the Senate."

As the sharp fox John A. Macdonald no doubt appreciated, in practice all this really meant was that members of the Senate would be selected by the federal prime minister. The Senate of Canada would become a body *chosen by the head of the central government* to represent, among other things, the interests of the major regions or sections of the Confederation.

Powers of the Senate and Its Ultimate Role

The triumph of equal sectional rather than equal provincial representation in the original Canadian Senate, and of "appointment by the crown" rather than popular election, could be viewed as evidence for what historian Carl Berger has called an "interpretation of Canadian history as simply the imperialist expansion of central Canada." Thus, the specific principle of regional representation finally adopted can be formulated as follows: the two most populous, central provinces — Ontario and Quebec — are sections in their own right; all the other, less populous, "hinterland" provinces are merely parts of other sections.

At the same time, Macdonald, Cartier, and other like-minded, leading "Fathers of the federation" did assign the Senate extensive formal authority. With only two qualifications, it would have the same broad powers as the House of Commons. Much more recently, limitations have been placed on the Senate's powers in connection with amendments to the Constitution. But it remains true in Canada today that no ordinary federal legislation can become law until it has been passed by majorities in both the Senate and the House of Commons.

Within this framework, the first original qualification to the Senate's authority was narrowly legal, and was specified in the British North America Act, 1867. So-called money bills — or, in the the language of the act, "Bills for appropriating any Part of the Public Revenue, or for imposing any Tax or Impost" — had to "originate" in the House of Commons. Even so, the Senate had the power to prevent any such bill from becoming law, if it chose. This qualification stands to the present day.

The second original qualification was merely conventional. Many provincial delegates at the Charlottetown, Quebec, and London conferences seem to have agreed that in practice the Senate would tend to be a legislature that specialized in review and revision, a chamber of "sober second thought" in Macdonald's legendary formulation. Macdonald stressed the Senate's value as "a regulating body, calmly considering the legislation initiated by the popular branch, and preventing any hasty or ill-considered legislation which may come from that body." Despite this perception, however, the upper house retained the power to initiate whatever legislation it so desired, apart from money bills. And Macdonald's own federal Cabinets of the late nineteenth century would typically introduce as much as 20% of their legislation in the Senate.

By the early twentieth century, the triumph of the democratic ethos in the United Kingdom and Canada, as well as the United States, would put a very blunt edge on the broad, formal powers of the Canadian Senate. In the more explicitly democratic country that would rise from the ashes of Cartier, Macdonald, Tupper, and Tilley, and involve a much larger role for provincial governments than anything Macdonald in particular had imagined, a legislature merely appointed by the federal prime minister could not aspire to any vigorous exercise of practical political power.

The kinds of members actually appointed to the Senate, once the new Dominion of Canada was established, only further eroded what public credibility it otherwise enjoyed. John A. Macdonald, for instance, was a man with at least sentimental attachments to old British Tory traditions. Or, from a more cosmopolitan angle, he was a mid–nineteenth century European "liberal conservative," somewhat in the manner of Count Camille de Cavour, who presided over the modern unification of Italy. Yet he was also a shrewd, tough manager of a late nineteenth century North American democratic political party machine.

For Macdonald, as for virtually all his successors as prime minister, in the robust real world of democratic party politics the typical types of "very best men" to serve in the Senate, were those with the most obvious qualifications. They were politicians and businessmen, or later even journalists and academics, who had laboured long and hard in the interests of the federal governing party — or who had done well representing the party in their regions, rather than the other way around.

In the language of mid–twentieth century political science, the most "functional" role that the Senate would finally play in the Canadian political system was to serve as the apex of federal political party patronage. And if this is not the altogether salacious mission it is sometimes made out to be, it is still considerably less than what most of the provincial delegates who argued for six days at the Quebec Conference of 1864 seem to have had in mind.

During the late nineteenth century, the Canadian Senate did play a slightly more elevated part in the life of the federal government than it would in the twentieth century. Macdonald and Cartier's first federal Cabinet had drawn five of its 13 members from the Senate rather than the House of Commons. After the Reformers, or Liberals, of the new Dominion tried unsuccessfully to forge a durable federal governing party, following Cartier's death in 1873, John A. Macdonald's Conservatives, still officially labelled Liberal-Conservatives, returned to power at Ottawa in 1878. There they remained, even without Macdonald, until 1896. John Joseph Abbott and Mackenzie Bowell even served as prime ministers from seats in the Senate, for a total of some two years and eight and a half months after Macdonald's death in 1891.

Even in the twentieth century, most federal Cabinets have included some representation from the Senate, though typically only one or two members. In the quite recent past, both federal Conservative and Liberal governments have drawn important Cabinet ministers from the Senate when they lacked elected members in the House of Commons from, respectively, Quebec and Western Canada.

In spite of such qualifications, the original Canadian Senate would largely become what Harold Innis called it in the late 1940s — "that unique institution" that "has lent itself to political manipulation" and "supported the growth of a strong party organization." In the twentieth century the most elevated issue it would recurrently encounter would be its own abolition or reform.

6
WEST IS WEST ...

In some respects, the Canada created by Confederation was a late nineteenth century example of a "new nation." This is a political and economic phenomenon that the world has watched more recently, in the post-colonial wave of new nations created in the mid–twentieth century.

As seems common enough in such cases, the new Dominion had its share of difficulty at the beginning. In the standard multi-volume history of the country, the volume that describes the 1874–96 era is aptly entitled *Arduous Destiny*.

Briefly, in the mid–1870s the new Dominion of Canada entered a prolonged economic slump. Despite a short-lived recovery in the early 1880s, it did not completely emerge from its troubles until the late 1890s. The early part of the slump had North American and even international origins, in the financial Panic of 1873. The later part has been explained in various ways by various authorities: broadly, it reflected the Dominion's particular troubles in adjusting to the birth pangs of a new phase in the development of the modern world economy.

By the early 1890s, the slump had grown gloomy enough to prompt Goldwin Smith, the expatriate intellectual from Toronto, to write the sceptical early classic of modern English Canadian political literature, *Canada and the Canadian Question*. Smith wondered

> whether the four blocks of territory constituting the Dominion can for ever be kept by political agencies united among themselves and separate from their Continent, of which geographically, economically, and with the exception of Quebec ethnologically, they are parts.

With virtually all his direct experience of the situation having taken place during the difficult era of "arduous destiny," his answer was probably not.

Yet, oddly enough, Smith himself pointed to that aspect of Canada's future that would finally make his scepticism look merely weak-hearted. As he reviewed the lay of the land in the early 1890s, he could not help enthusing about at least one part of the British Dominion of Canada:

> It is a sensation not to be forgotten ... as, standing upon the platform of the railway car ... you shoot out upon that oceanic expanse of prairie, purple with evening, while an electric light perhaps shines on the horizon like a star of advancing civilization. What is the extent of the fertile land in the North-West, and how great are the capabilities of the

region are hardly yet known, but it is known that they are vast.

Less than a decade later, the long slump was over. The ancient British Northwest was at last being transformed into the modern Western Canada. The new region — with only 3% of the Dominion's total population in the early 1870s — boomed dramatically in the early twentieth century. And its boom set the scepticism of Goldwin Smith's Canadian question aside.

By this time the old Tory, "Sir John Macdonald," was dead. But the Liberals, modern heirs of the colonial Reformers, had at last managed to create a reformed version of Sir John's model federal governing party, under the French Canadian Wilfrid Laurier. "Sir Wilfrid" would remain prime minister of Canada from 1896 to 1911. After another 10-year Conservative regime under Robert Borden from Nova Scotia, Laurier would be succeeded as Liberal leader by his admiring English Canadian follower, William Lyon Mackenzie King, who, with only two interruptions, would remain prime minister of Canada until 1948.

Eventually, Western Canada would become the region most concerned to do something sensible with the old Tory heirloom of the Canadian Senate. Though the ultimate germination of its concern would only arrive in the late 1970s, various vague hints appeared in the first half of the twentieth century. In the end, the unique variety of modern Canadian regionalism that evolved in the former Crown Colony of British Columbia, and in the old Hudson's Bay Company territories purchased by the new Dominion would have crucial implications for the long journey to Senate reform.

The Complicated Legend of Louis Riel

The story starts with two romantic and still controversial events in Canada's history. Historian George F.G. Stanley's pioneering book of the 1930s, *The Birth of Western Canada.*, was appropriately subtitled *A History of the Riel Rebellions.*

The first rebellion led by the Métis prophet Louis Riel had taken place in the Red River area. It stimulated the establishment of the province of Manitoba, in 1870. The second (known as the Northwest Rebellion) took place in 1885. It climaxed with a confused victory of red-coated Canadian militia over Métis insurgents at Batoche, in what would later become the province of Saskatchewan. After the first rebellion, Louis Riel, like William Lyon Mackenzie and Louis Joseph Papineau just over a generation before, went into exile in the American Republic. After the second rebellion, Riel was tried by a court of the Dominion of Canada, and hanged for treason.

There have been several interpretations of these events. Following strict linear logic, the interpretations conflict with each other, but from a more multicultural perspective, they add up to Western Canada's unique variation on the modern national diversity.

To start with, in the 1930s Stanley interpreted both Riel rebellions as

> the manifestation in Western Canada of the problem of the
> frontier .... In all parts of the world, in South Africa, New
> Zealand and North America, the penetration of white settle-
> ment into territories inhabited by native peoples has led to
> friction and wars; Canadian expansion into the North-West
> led to a similar result.

In taking this view, Stanley was reacting against earlier writers who had read "the prejudices of Old Canada" into the Riel rebellions, and "regarded the valleys of the Red and Saskatchewan Rivers as the western battleground of the traditional hostilities of French Catholic Quebec and English Protestant Ontario." In the late 1960s and 1970s, however, Pierre Trudeau revived ancient constitutional issues, in the Canada that blossomed in the wake of the Second World War and the demise of the British Empire. These issues drew some fresh attention to the earlier views, and eventually (despite Trudeau's initial thoughts on the matter) also shed new light on the heritage of the Indians and the Métis themselves.

George-Etienne Cartier, for instance, had in fact used the first Riel rebellion of 1869–70 to bolster the case for French Catholic as well as English Protestant institutions in the modern political framework of the old British Northwest. These institutions amounted to an elaboration of the Catholic separate schools in Ontario, which had taken root during the old French and English dualism of the United Province. They were meant to ensure that the new Canadian West would be a place for French-speaking as well as English-speaking Canadians. In the new province of Manitoba created by the federal government in 1870 — unlike in Ontario — French and English had even been given equal status before the provincial courts and legislature.

Yet, as a practical matter, the defeat of the second Riel rebellion in 1885 also amounted to a defeat for any vigorous growth of French Catholic institutions in the West, as well as a not quite final defeat for the ancient cultures of the Indians of Canada. This would be confirmed by the pro–English Protestant compromises that Wilfrid Laurier, modern Canada's first French Canadian prime minister, felt compelled to make over the Manitoba School Question in the late 1890s. As well, at the start of the decade the Manitoba Legislative Assembly, now dominated by English-speaking elected repre-sentatives, had repealed the earlier recognition of French in the provincial courts and legislature. Despite the historic legacies of La Vérendrye and the French and Indian fur trade, in the twentieth century most of Western Canada would become an even more predominantly English-speaking re-gion than either Ontario or most of the old Acadia on the Atlantic Coast.

In 1979 the Supreme Court of Canada at long last declared the province of Manitoba's 1890 repeal of the status of French in its courts and legislature *ultra vires*. And in 1984, Trudeau's last year in power, the provincial govern-ment of Manitoba agreed to reinstate the original provisions of 1870. But in the 1970s and 1980s, new popular interpretations of the Riel rebellions brought an ironic twist to the legend of Louis Riel, shaped by the most recent expressions of western regionalism. Riel's latest incarnation in spite of his French, Catholic, Métis, and Indian connections, is as the first inspired regional patriot of modern Western Canada — which overwhelmingly speaks English.

"Beardy's Warriors," Duck Lake, N.W.T. (now part of Saskatchewan).

Riel's 1885 rebellion began late in March with a clash at the small Duck Lake settlement to the west of Batoche. On one side was a detachment of North West Mounted Police, augmented by local militia. On the other was a force of Métis and Indians, led by Riel's military commander Gabriel Dumont. The Métis and Indians won the battle, sending panic all the way to Ottawa. By 10 April, militia reinforcements from Nova Scotia, Quebec, and especially Ontario had reached what is now Qu'Appelle, Saskatchewan, on the newly completed Canadian Pacific Railway.

According to an early twentieth century military history, Dumont was "a brave and resourceful leader, skilled in all the arts of Indian warfare. The result was that while the rebels of 1870 fled ignominiously ... those of 1885 gave a very good account of themselves."

In the end, more than 5,000 troops would help put down the 1885 rebellion, some 1,700 of whom came from the West itself. Unlike Riel, Dumont escaped to the United States when the fighting was over, and eventually returned to Canada under the terms of a general amnesty.

Riel's supporters in 1885 did in fact include not just Indians and French and English-speaking Métis, but even some among the handfuls of early English-speaking white settlers, who had begun to open up the new Canadian Northwest Territories for the culture of the Anglo-American frontier. Early in 1884, the *Bulletin* in the still extremely raw frontier town of Edmonton bemoaned:

> If it was not by — not threatening, but actual — rebellion and appeals to the British government for justice that the people of Ontario gained the rights they enjoy today and freed themselves from a condition precisely similar to that in which the North-West is being rapidly forced, how was it?

At the time, Manitoba was still a "postage stamp" province, involved in a boundary dispute with the much larger Ontario to its east, and yet still siding with the provincial government of Ontario in protests against "the centralizing proclivities of the Macdonald clique" at Ottawa. British Columbia, in splendid isolation to the west of the Mountain Barrier, had waited almost 14 years for the transcontinental railway that Cartier had promised in 1871. It would reach the Pacific Ocean in 1885, but only arrive in Vancouver in 1887.

In the early 1880s, the handfuls of early white, English-speaking agricultural settlers in the new Canadian Northwest Territories — between Manitoba and British Columbia— still accounted for not much more than 1% of the Confederation's total population. They were unusually dependent on decisions by often disorganized federal bureaucrats in distant Ottawa for the claims to their land, and they had absolutely no representation in the federal House of Commons. (As a direct result of the 1885 rebellion, they would be granted one seat.)

WESTERN CANADA AND THE NORTHWEST, 1871–1891

Province/Region	% of Total Canadian Population		
	1871	1881	1891
Manitoba	0.7	1.4	3.2
Northwest Territories	1.3	1.3	2.0
British Columbia	1.0	1.2	2.0
Western Canada	**3.0**	**3.9**	**7.2**
Total Canadian Population (000s)	3,689	4,325	4,833

Above all else, to many new English-speaking people who came to live in the Northwest, it seemed that Ottawa viewed the region chiefly as a field for the ambitions of the merchants of Montreal and Toronto: inheritors of the mantle of the old North West Company and the transcontinental fur trade. White settlers from the town of Prince Albert helped pay for Louis Riel's journey to Batoche. In at least a subtle sense, in the Northwest rebellion of 1885, Toronto's earlier resistance to the domination of Montreal in Central Canada, was echoed by Western Canada's new resistance to the combined domination of Montreal and Toronto in the wider Confederation.

There were also some complicated symbolic connections between the rebellion of 1885 and the fabled "last spike" on the Canadian Pacific Railway, which was driven in the same year. British Columbia had demanded the CPR. Along with its successors, the railway would become the backbone of early Western Canadian economic development. Some white settlers who sympathized with Riel's rebellion were actually angry that the new railroad was located so far south of their own homesteads.

Yet the CPR was the technologically up-to-date successor both to the ancient Indian canoe and portage waterways that had taken Alexander Mackenzie to the Pacific Ocean in 1793, and to the Great Lakes–St. Lawrence canals of the first half of the nineteenth century. Headquartered in Montreal, with a western outpost in Winnipeg, it was under the new imperial command of the English-speaking merchants of Ontario and Quebec. Like many railroads in the United States, it would become the bane of the western farmer and, among western businessmen, the despised channel for the domination of wide-open western commerce by the effete elitist traditions of eastern high finance.

At Last, the Last Best West

Since the romantic and fractious age of Louis Riel, a key feature of development in Western Canada has been unusually pronounced cycles of slow growth followed by heady bursts of rapid expansion and change, or vice-versa. Frustration over slow western development during the difficult arduous-destiny era for the wider Dominion of Canada in the late nineteenth century had even played some part in stimulating the second Riel rebellion.

Part of the wider difficulty flowed from the earliest signs of decline in the British Empire, to which Canada was still politically and, even with imperial free trade, economically attached. Another related aspect flowed from the U.S. government's continuing refusal to renew the abrogated Reciprocity Treaty of 1854, with any Canadian Confederation that insisted on remaining politically aloof from the American Republic.

By the late 1890s, however, the British Empire had begun the early brilliant phases of its long twentieth century sunset. It gave off a last great burst of energy prompting a new wave of industrialization in an expanding world economy. Gold was discovered in the most northwestern part of Canada, leading to the establishment of the modern Yukon Territory in 1898.

Population growth in Western Canada suddenly jumped from a mere 174,000 people between 1881 and 1891 and 265,000 between 1891 and 1901, to more than 1.1 million between 1901 and 1911.

This almost intoxicating burst of western progress in the first decade of the twentieth century grew out of a long-awaited but nonetheless dramatic expansion in the second Canadian resource economy of lumber and wheat, and then mining and pulp and paper as well. Lumbering found a new frontier in the forests of British Columbia; both lumbering and the new technology of hydroelectricity brought a pulp and paper industry to the Canadian Shield. Major mining industries became established on the Shield and in parts of the B.C. Mountain Barrier.

The southern (or, more particularly, southwestern) regions of Quebec and especially Ontario had become sites for at least locally notable industrial manufacturing in the late nineteenth century. In 1911, a Canadian branch of the new North American automobile industry was setting down roots in Cenrtal Canada. By the early twentieth century the wheat economy of Central Canada (which had peaked in the 1880s) had, figuratively, picked itself up and moved onto the vast, flat horizons of the Western Canadian prairies, in a northern variation on east-west development patterns in the United States. Western Canada alone accounted for some 208 million of the 230 million bushels of wheat produced in all of the Dominion. And the western wheat economy had become a strategic engine of both regional and national development.

WESTERN CANADA IN CONFEDERATION, 1901–1921

Province/ Region	% Total Canadian Population		
	1901	1911	1921
Manitoba	4.7	6.4	6.9
Saskatchewan	1.7	6.8	8.6
Alberta	1.4	5.2	6.7
British Columbia	3.3	5.5	6.0
Western Canada	**11.1**	**23.9**	**28.2**
Total Canadian Population (000s)	5,371	7,207	8,788

To no small extent, the new wheat economy's growth was stage-managed by the Canadian federal government at Ottawa. As provided for in what is now the Constitution Act, 1867 (and as in the earlier case of Manitoba), the federal government created the provinces of Saskatchewan and Alberta in 1905. In 1912 the boundaries of the original postage stamp province of Manitoba, already expanded somewhat in the 1880s, were extended to their present limits (as were the boundaries of Ontario and Quebec). In 1915, two years after the Seventeenth Amendment, which provided for the election of senators in the United States, Western Canada was constituted as a distinct 24-member section of the Canadian Senate, with six members from each of the four Western provinces.

Yet, despite repeated protests, the management of natural resources in the three post-Confederation provinces of Manitoba, Saskatchewan, and Alberta remained in the hands of the federal government at Ottawa until 1930. All the other provinces which had not been created by the government at Ottawa but had themselves been partners in establishing the federal regime, managed their own natural resources. The theory for the three prairie provinces was that, at least in the initial phases of their growth, only the federal government could mobilize all the resources necessary for effective regional development. Even some westerners agreed that the theory was not altogether wrong.

The enduring contribution of Macdonald's federal Conservatives had been to preside over and financially assist the building of the Canadian Pacific Railway, during which the Midwest American railroad builder, William Van Horne, transformed himself into a Montreal-based merchant of Central Canada. For reasons largely beyond their control, in the late nineteenth century Macdonald's Conservatives had not been able to push the enterprise further.

Starting less than a decade after Macdonald's death, the large-scale mass settlement of the "Last Best West" on the North American frontier in the lexicon of a buoyant new Canadian boosterism would be aggressively promoted by Wilfrid Laurier's federal Liberals. Especially prominent in the work of promotion was Laurier's minister of the interior, Clifford Sifton. Moving from Ontario to Manitoba in 1875, Sifton had begun his political career in Manitoba provincial politics. To many he became a symbol of the domination by the eastern establishment of western development. He died a multimillionaire in New York City, some half a dozen months before the stock market crash of 1929.

To some extent, Western Canada was settled by migrants from Ontario, Atlantic Canada, and to a very limited degree, Quebec. Like Clifford Sifton, Walter Scott, first premier of Saskatchewan, most populous of the new provinces, had been born in Ontario. As if to show that his compromises over the Manitoba School Question in the 1890s did not imply the complete surrender of French culture in the west, Wilfrid Laurier appointed Amédée-Emmanuel Forget as Saskatchewan's first lieutenant-governor. Under pressures from Quebec and even the Vatican in Rome, Laurier put enough about potential Catholic schools in the legislation creating both Saskatchewan and Alberta to prompt Sifton's resignation from the federal Cabinet. Yet, as in the case of the earlier mass European settlement of Atlantic and Central Canada, immigration from other places would be the vital engine of Western Canadian population growth. For virtually all practical public purposes, English would be the language that immigrants to the West were expected to speak.

Some of the immigration to Canada came from the traditionally favoured source of the United Kingdom. Unlike the rural British migrants of the nineteenth century, those of the twentieth tended to be urbanites, many of whom found the rising cities of Ontario more congenial. (The one place in

Celebrating the inauguration of the Province of Alberta, Edmonton, 1 September 1905 — only 20 years after the 1885 Northwest Rebellion.

The sign behind the assembled young ladies reads "Our Fair Dominion ... Alberta Our Home." The name of the province, derived from one of the four provisional districts of the old Northwest Territories, and honoured Princess Louise Caroline Alberta, fourth daughter of Queen Victoria and wife of the governor general, the Marquis of Lorne. Originally, the southern part of the territory was home to the Blackfoot nation, while the Plains Cree and other woodland tribes dominated the north.

the West that did have special attractions for this group was the growing urban-centred wilderness resource economy in British Columbia.)

More enthusiastic prairie agricultural settlers came from the United States, where the closing of the American West in the 1890s had prompted the beginnings of Frederick Jackson Turner's seminal meditations on the role of the frontier in American history. On the trail blazed by the neutral Yankees of Nova Scotia in the mid-eighteenth century, and by the "late Loyalists" of Ontario in the early nineteenth century, the nostalgic last pioneers of the Anglo-American frontier drove the last covered wagons into the Last Best West of Canada, in the early twentieth century.

Clifford Sifton's federal immigration policy also systematically reached out to the peasants who grew wheat on the vast plains of Eastern Europe. This had the ultimate effect of giving Western Canada a more cosmopolitan demographic profile in the first half of the twentieth century than any other part of the country. Still, recurrent conflicts over early Asian immigration to British Columbia, along with the problems of the increasingly beleaguered native Indians and Métis, showed the specific limits of the cosmopolitanism involved. One branch of the fiercely sectarian Russian Doukhobors would provide newspaper headlines for two generations, by parading naked to protest what they regarded as harshly conformist public pressures, even on the free and democratic frontier of the New World.

After the First World War, the Western Canadian economy, and especially the western wheat economy, stumbled somewhat, like regional and national economies in many other places. The great burst of more than a million new people in the first decade of the twentieth century had already fallen to 760,000 between 1911 and 1921, and would fall again to 568,000 between 1921 and 1931. But by the mid-1920s the earlier buoyancy seemed to have returned.

The 208 million bushels of Western Canadian wheat in 1911 had become more than 544 million bushels in 1928. In 1931 Western Canada, home to less than 4% of all Dominion residents a half century before, had more than three million people, and accounted for more than 29% of the total Canadian population. Saskatchewan alone had some 922,000 people, making it the third most populous of the now nine provinces of the Confederation, after Ontario and Quebec.

The Northern Grapes of Wrath

It is juvenille to imagine that a convincing Canadian political nation must have its own miniature variations of all the elements in the national mythology of the American Republic. The twentieth century history of Canada illustrates how social and economic trends almost identical to those in the United States produce somewhat different results when handled by somewhat different human institutions that flow from a somewhat different past.

The dismal North American economic depression and ecological drought of the 1930s brought the same havoc to the wheat economy of Western

Canada that it brought to John Steinbeck's grief-struck agrarian wanderers of the era in the southwestern United States. In the uniquely Western Canadian regional tradition, a generation of heady expansion was quickly succeeded by a generation of hardship and contracting horizons, even worse than in the earlier slow growth of the late nineteenth century. Men and women who had travelled long distances and worked long hours to build new futures for their children saw dreams collapse overnight. Hopes that had risen very high were suddenly dashed very low.

It would be wrong to exaggerate the northern grapes of wrath on the western prairie of the 1930s. In the fall of 1932 W.L. MacTavish, editor of the *Winnipeg Tribune*, owned by the Toronto-based Southam chain, told the Canadian Club of Canada's second-largest city: "I believe you in Eastern Canada are taking and have taken somewhat too gloomy a view of Western conditions." He had slyly prefaced his remarks with: "We, in the hinterlands, of course, regard Toronto as the cultural capital of the Dominion." He reminded the cultural capital's more eminent residents that "more than sixty-two per cent of the farmers in Western Canada are free of mortgage debt." He then offered the opinion, based on extensive recent travels in the region, that not "a farm could be found," in any of the three prairie provinces, "in which there is not sufficient livestock at least to provide for most of the wants of the family."

On the other hand, population statistics alone suggest a story of notable grief for quite large numbers of people. The Saskatchewan that would so briefly reign as Canada's third most populous province was the hardest hit. (As even editor MacTavish had acknowledged in 1932, "There is a small area in Southern Saskatchewan which has had crop failures for four years in succession.") The population of Saskatchewan at large declined absolutely by some 26,000 people between 1931 and 1941, and would decline again by another 64,000 between 1941 and 1951. Not until the early 1960s would it return to its early 1930s high of more than 920,000 people.

Even after its recovery in the 1950s, the wheat economy of the West would never again exude quite the same energy and high aspiration that had marked its meteoric rise in the first two decades of the twentieth century. Manitoba, with some industrial and service diversific ation, and especially Alberta where cattle ranching complemented wheat growing and where there was also some coal to be found, did not fare quite as badly as Saskatchewan. Neither lost population absolutely, but both declined in relative importance in the Confederation at large.

Even before the 1930s, there were clear signs of limits to growth in the Western Canada that was driven by wheat. The great boom in the first decade of the century had stimulated two new Canadian transcontinental railway projects to compete with the CPR. Both benefited from British capital, hungry for any fresh opportunities. The Grand Trunk Pacific was essentially a second Montreal-headquartered operation — an extension of the British St. Lawrence merchants' mid-nineteenth century railroad into Southern Ontario. The Canadian Northern reflected a bid by the merchants of Toronto (who tended to look first to New York City, not London, England) for their own western railway, out from under the domination of Montreal.

WESTERN CANADA IN CONFEDERATION, 1931–1941

Region/Province	% Total Canadian Population	
	1931	1941
Manitoba	6.7	6.4
Saskatchewan	8.9	7.8
Alberta	7.1	6.9
British Columbia	6.7	7.1
Western Canada	**29.4**	**28.2**
Total Canadian Population (000s)	10,377	11,507

By the early 1920s both enterprises, in deep financial trouble for almost a decade, had been taken over by the Canadian federal government (which had already heavily subsidized the Canadian Northern and had actually built part of the transcontinental network operated by the Grand Trunk Pacific). They were merged with the old Intercolonial Railroad to Atlantic Canada, an essentially government enterprise from the very beginning, to form the modern, publicly owned Canadian National Railways.

The "northern grapes of wrath" in Western Canada also stimulated regional and national innovations in the Canadian political party system that have endured to the present. In 1932 W.L. MacTavish confessed to his eminent Central Canadian audience that

> we have our troubles in respect to political farmers and other earnest agitators in the West. We have a large number of gentlemen much disturbed about this and that. We have more than our share of the sons of the wild jackass. Fortunately perhaps for the West and for Canada as a whole they are far from unanimous as to the causes of their displeasure.

As the leading Canadian radical historian of the era, Frank Underhill, pointed out, such sentiments could easily have come from the lips of an early nineteenth century Tory oligarch in Upper Canada. Less eminent persons, even in Toronto, took a different view of the matter.

In the end, the West of the 1930s was the birthplace of the right-wing populist Social Credit Party, which would recurrently govern Alberta and, after the Second World War, British Columbia, and play some role in national politics down to the 1960s. It was, as well, the more consistently honoured birthplace of the left-wing populist Co-operative Commonwealth Federation or CCF—ancestor of the modern New Democratic Party or NDP, North America's only enduring "social democratic" political party.

Starting in the mid-1940s, the CCF/NDP would recurrently govern Saskatchewan and then Manitoba, and rule much more briefly in the British Columbia of the mid-1970s. In the mid-1980s New Democrats would form a brief accord with Liberals to help govern Ontario. They continue to win substantial numbers of seats in Canadian federal elections down to the present, and they have almost replaced the Liberals as the major left-wing party in both the provincial and federal politics of Western Canada today.

The North Pacific Slope and New Ontario

For all practical purposes, the deepest gloom of the Depression in Canada as in the United States, stopped at the Rocky Mountains. One Western Canadian province — British Columbia — actually increased its share of the national population in the 1930s.

In some important ways, British Columbia today has become merely the most western part of the West. It identifies with the wider region whose first inspired modern patriot is Louis Riel, and shares many of its understandings about the still wider Canadian Confederation. In other ways, British Columbia began as and has remained almost a region unto itself. Isolated by the Mountain Barrier, it has basked in the benign geography of the North Pacific Slope. Just as the exotic tribes of the Pacific Coast had been unique among the ancient Indians of Canada, British Columbia would be unique among the modern provinces of Canada in the twentieth century.

Lumbering and mining, not wheat, formed the backbone of B.C.'s participation in the dramatic economic expansion that marked the century's first decades. British Columbia had joined Confederation in 1871 as at least a British Crown colony, if not quite a self-governing "province". Unlike the three prairie provinces of the old British Northwest, it had not been created by the government at Ottawa.

As in Ontario, British immigration would play an especially important role in B.C.'s early twentieth century development. And, unlike most other parts of Canada, but like its American regional cousins on the Pacific Coast, early twentieth century British Columbia struggled with its conscience over the rights of early Asian immigrants to the new European-oriented civilization of the New World. "The most lively thing" about Victoria in the early 1890s, according to Goldwin Smith, was its "Chinese Colony, where we come into contact with the advance guard of that countless host which ... can hardly be arrested in its march, and may some day possess the coast of the Pacific."

British Columbia did not grow as suddenly between 1901 and 1911 as Saskatchewan and Alberta, though it did advance somewhat more quickly than Manitoba. On the other hand, if its rise was not as meteoric as that of the two provinces due east, it would prove to be more steady and ultimately more profound. Unlike the three prairie provinces, B.C.'s share of the Canadian population regularly increased. The opening of the Panama Canal in 1914 stimulated Vancouver's growth as a versatile Pacific seaport. By 1931 Vancouver replaced Winnipeg as Canada's third largest city — a status it has retained down to the present. In 1951 British Columbia replaced Saskatchewan as the third most populous province in Canada.

If British Columbia was a part of Western Canada that was in some ways separate from it, there was another booming Canadian place of the early twentieth century that, though separate from Western Canada, was also in some ways, a part of it. The place is now called Northern Ontario, but "New Ontario" was the more common term for the generation that also coined the "Last Best West."

In the 1880s Oliver Mowat of Ontario had fought boundary disputes with both Manitoba and, much more critically, John A. Macdonald's federal government. Mowat finally took the question of the northwestern extent of Canada's most populous province to the Judicial Committee of the Privy Council in the United Kingdom. The result was an Ontario that extended much farther north, and west, than Macdonald had originally envisioned (and would be extended still further with the final boundary settlement of 1912). In the early twentieth century, aggressive provincial efforts to promote a second Ontario agricultural frontier on the northern "Clay Belts" of the Canadian Shield never remotely lived up to initial expectations. But the place did prove to be a virtual treasure-trove for the crucial resource industries of forestry and mining. In this respect, as in a few others, it was somewhat like British Columbia.

The population of Northern Ontario did not grow at all as fast, or become at all as large, as any of the western provinces. The place had just over 75,000 people in 1891, and some 385,000 in 1931, compared with 98,000 in 1891 and 694,000 in 1931, in slow-but-steady British Columbia. Similarly, unlike Western Canada, the more easterly parts of the region became a notable destination for French-speaking migrants from Quebec. Thus, Sudbury in modern Northern Ontario — or Nouvelle Ontario to at least some Ontario French Canadians — is an officially bilingual city.

At the same time, like Western Canada, Northern Ontario became a resource hinterland for the new urban, industrial areas in the southern parts of Ontario and Quebec. Winnipeg became the effective metropolis for the more western parts of Northern Ontario, and much of the region came to share many Western Canadian attitudes toward the wider Confederation.

Finally, in the wider development of Canadian regionalism, mining on the Northern Ontario Shield became a golden opportunity for the merchants of Toronto. Though the great mass of endless rock north of the Great Lakes defeated large-scale human settlement, it proved a repository for virtually every known economic mineral, except coal and tin. More than any other single factor, mining in Northern Ontario would put a fledgling Toronto financial sector on its feet and carry it through the 1930s Depression relatively unscathed. By the end of the decade Toronto had the third largest stock exchange in North America.

The great boom in Western Canada did play some role in the growth of Toronto. But it was even more important in the growth of Montreal. And, fundamentally, it was Northern Ontario in the first half of the twentieth century that gave Toronto the critical momentum to replace Montreal as Canada's largest city, in the second half of the twentieth century.

7
... AND EAST IS EAST

It is only a slight exaggeration to say that the Confederation of the 1860s and 1870s made modern Western Canada. The region had links with the golden age of the Montreal fur trade. And even though the southern part of British Columbia and the area around Winnipeg, had enjoyed more autonomous origins, in all places, the Canadian Pacific Railway that the new Dominion pushed through the rugged wilderness in the late nineteenth century was an agent of transformation. If the West grew up in a perpetual quarrel with Confederation, it was nonetheless a family quarrel with the broader being that begat Western Canada itself.

In what became Atlantic Canada, on the stroke of midnight 1 July 1867, the relationship that would evolve down to the end of the Second World War was different. Even under the French regime, Acadiens had been distinct from Canadiens. After this, in Innis's formulation, "staple products coming down the St. Lawrence system made for a centralization of exports, whereas fishing from numerous ports of an extended coast line made for decentralization."

After the American War of Independence, the Maritime provinces enjoyed their own brief golden age as a principal Atlantic outpost of the British Empire in the Western Hemisphere. But this began to wane with imperial free trade. As new forces of progress gathered in the North American interior, Maritime involvement with a wider Canadian Confederation acquired a fresh regional logic. To many who lived in the region, however, the logic was never altogether compelling.

Newfoundland's long aloofness, down to 1949, was an extreme symbol of the continuing impulses toward decentralization in the three Atlantic provinces that did join Canada. In the late nineteenth century, Newfoundland almost joined too — in the midst of its own arduous northern destiny. There was another near miss in the First World War era, when the Dominion of Canada had an Atlantic prime minister. But then Newfoundland gradually evolved into a British dominion in its own right. This extreme local response to Atlantic decentralizing impulses finally proved unworkable, for reasons that include yet another striking difference between the modern histories of Western and Atlantic Canada.

The characteristic problem of the West would be the volatility of its economic development, its exaggerated cycles of boom and bust. Yet, fundamentally, Western Canada was a positive creation of what Innis called the shift from "commercialism" to "capitalism." It was a flower of the brave new industrial world that took hold after the American Civil War, not just in North America, but in the Europe of German and Italian unification and in the Japan of the "Meji Restoration" as well. The Canadian West became the newest and, in several senses, the most progressive part of the Confederation, even though the most obvious industrialization, in the narrowest meaning of the term, took place in Central Canada.

In Atlantic Canada, on the other hand, what economic history textbooks called the "new industrialism" was more a force of destruction than creation. As Innis wrote, "the impact of machine industry has been a major calamity to the fishing regions." The share of the total Canadian population in the new Atlantic Canada of the late nineteenth century — Nova Scotia, New Brunswick, and Prince Edward Island — would progressively decline in the twentieth century. By 1940 Innis had pronounced that, in the ancient realm of the cod fisheries, the "transition from dependence on a maritime economy to dependence on a continental economy has been slow, painful, and disastrous."

The region's situation was complicated by its fervent cultural and commercial connections to the British Empire. There was, however a more positive political and cultural side to Atlantic Canada's first three-quarters of a century in the Confederation. Even materially, the place remained well enough off in a global context. Yet all this was like an austerely beautiful flower that struggled to blossom in a hard and rocky soil. What immediately struck everyone's eye was the hard and rocky soil.

The Uninspiring Demographics

The most objective picture of the historic troubles of Atlantic Canada is the region's pattern of population growth, from the late nineteenth to the middle of the twentieth century.

ATLANTIC CANADA IN CONFEDERATION, 1871–1901

Province/Region	% of Total Canadian Population			
	1871	1881	1891	1901
Nova Scotia	10.5	10.2	9.3	8.6
New Brunswick	7.8	7.4	6.6	6.2
Prince Edward Island	2.5	2.5	2.3	1.9
Atlantic Canada	**20.8**	**20.1**	**18.2**	**16.7**
Total Canadian Population (000s)	3,689	4,325	4,833	5,371

Two of the three Maritime provinces — Prince Edward Island and Nova Scotia — actually sustained bouts of absolute population loss. P.E.I. fell from 109,000 people in 1891 to 103,000 in 1901, 94,000 in 1911, 89,000 in 1921, and

88,000 in 1931. Nova Scotia's loss was confined to the era of what was elsewhere known as the Roaring Twenties. Its population fell from 524,000 in 1921 to 513,000 in 1931.

New Brunswick, more securely attached to the continent and thus less disastrously affected by the shift from a maritime to a continental economy, fared marginally better. Its population never declined absolutely. Yet, as in other parts of the Confederation, it stalled profoundly in the 1880s, at the height of the collective economic troubles.

Compared to the rest of Canada, population growth in the new Atlantic Canada was not utterly dismal. The region still had just under 17% of all people living in Canada in 1901. Though under its more than 20% of 1871, it still amounted to more demographic weight than had so far developed in the new Canadian West.

The situation changed suddenly, however, in the first decade of the twentieth century. While Western Canada boomed like there was no tomorrow, Nova Scotia and New Brunswick enjoyed only very modest growth and Prince Edward Island lost some 9,000 people. By 1911 Western Canada had more than 23% of the total Canadian population, and Atlantic Canada only 13%. From here until 1931, the Maritimes' share of the people of the Dominion continued to decline.

ATLANTIC CANADA IN CONFEDERATION, 1911–1941

Province/Region	% of Total Canadian Population			
	1911	1921	1931	1941
Nova Scotia	6.8	6.0	5.0	5.0
New Brunswick	4.9	4.4	3.9	4.0
Prince Edward Island	1.3	1.0	0.8	0.8
Atlantic Canada	**13.0**	**11.4**	**9.7**	**9.8**
Total Canadian Population (000s)	7,207	8,788	10,377	11,507

There were precedents for such statistics elsewhere on the North American continent. In 1750 the Atlantic regions of Massachusetts and Virginia, the two largest of the old Thirteen Colonies, had together accounted for more than 35% of the total population of what subsequently became the United States. But by 1900 their collective share of the American population had shrunk to only 6%. Virginia actually lost population absolutely in the 1830s, as did Maine and New Hampshire in the 1860s and Mississippi in the decade between 1910 and 1920.

In Canada, Ontario accounted for only 33% of all Canadians in 1941, down from 44% in 1871. Even Quebec, famous for the French Canadian "revenge of the cradle," had fallen somewhat, from more than 31% in 1871 to 29% in 1941. Yet, when the West finally boomed, none of the other original three Senate sections of the Confederation fared at all as badly as Atlantic Canada. By 1931 neither Ontario nor Quebec had seen its share of the Dominion's population decline by anything like more than half.

As if to highlight the Atlantic region's somewhat perverse unique identity, the only bright spot in its early demographic history came during the Great Depression of the 1930s. With the forces of progress and the new industrial civilization at bay everywhere, some old Maritimers in other places went home, while others decided not to leave. Prince Edward Island actually gained population for the first time since the 1880s. Nova Scotia recovered its population loss of the 1920s and went on to grow at a faster rate than it had known since the 1870s. New Brunswick actually managed to increase its share of the Dominion's total population by one-tenth of 1%.

The Grievance

Given these uninspiring demographics, and given the comparative reluctance with which Nova Scotia, New Brunswick, and Prince Edward Island had originally joined the enterprise, it is understandable enough that many in the region attributed its "lagging growth" to the Canadian Confederation itself.

In 1886, in the midst of the collective economic grief, the Liberal W.S. Fielding won a Nova Scotia provincial election on a campaign that explicitly raised the prospect of repealing Confederation in the province. This was offset in a federal election of February 1887, when John A. Macdonald and Charles Tupper convincingly took 14 of Nova Scotia's 21 seats for the nation-building Conservatives. Fielding himself would become a powerful minister of finance in Wilfrid Laurier's reformed federal governing party of the late nineteenth and early twentieth centuries. Yet in the early 1890s Goldwin Smith, the Toronto-based English inventor of the Canadian question, exaggerated only slightly when he declared: "No inhabitant of Nova Scotia or New Brunswick calls himself a Canadian."

By the dawn of the twentieth century, in Atlantic Canada, as in the West, there was fertile ground for the argument that the Dominion of Canada was fundamentally tilted in favour of the two most populous provinces, the only two that were also Senate sections in their own right, Ontario and Quebec.

English-speaking Montreal, with 415,000 people in 1901, not Halifax, with only 51,000, became a regional metropolis for the Canadian Atlantic Coast. Merchants in Montreal and, to a lesser extent, Toronto (with 303,000 people in 1901) became distribution agents for merchants in the Maritimes.

In 1901 the Merchants' Bank of Halifax, founded in 1869, moved its headquarters to Montreal and changed its name to the Royal Bank of Canada. It would become Canada's largest chartered bank, but by the

William Stevens Fielding, premier of Nova Scotia, 1884–96, minister of finance for the Dominion of Canada, 1896–1911, 1921–25.

Though Fielding almost took Nova Scotia out of Confederation in the 1880s, he went on to become a crucial figure in both Wilfrid Laurier's federal regime at Ottawa and the early federal regime of William Lyon Mackenzie King.

middle of the twentieth century few would remember that it had its origins in the Maritimes. At about the same time, the Bank of Nova Scotia, founded in 1832, erected a Toronto office building with more space than the bank's official headquarters. These remained in Halifax but were increasingly eclipsed as a business and decision-making centre by the bank's Toronto-based operations.

A popular Atlantic tradition of resentment against John A. Macdonald's historic high-tariff National Policy (launched in 1879 to help cope with the late nineteenth century economic troubles) developed as well. In this respect, as in some others, there was a parallel with Western Canada (about which more must be said later). Even after the Second World War, the Nova Scotia wit Will R. Bird could report a conversation with an irate New Brunswicker on the subject: "Nova Scotia and we were seduced into Confederation at a time when we were getting along all right. Then they put on tariffs to protect Upper and Lower Canada, and they've been protecting them ever since and paralysing the Maritimes."

In fact, tariffs had equally protected early efforts to establish a Maritime manufacturing sector. The Manufacturers Association of Nova Scotia had been a proponent of Macdonald's National Policy in the 1870s. The domestic Canadian market, however, was not remotely large enough to support significant manufacturing in both Atlantic and Central Canada. And Central Canada had the advantage of being the largest part of the market.

The National Policy included tariffs on coal, presumably designed to protect the Canadian market for the coal of Nova Scotia. Yet even with these tariffs, it was usually cheaper for the manufacturers of Central Canada to buy their coal in Pennsylvania. To Will Bird's irate New Brunswicker, this could only imply that a protected Canadian market for textiles or automobiles made for sound national policy, when that suited the interests of Ontario and Quebec; but when Central Canadians could profit more from a continental market for coal, that was also in the national interest.

Miriam Chapin, an unusually insightful American who published three intriguing books about Canada in the middle of the twentieth century, would try to explain the result. In Atlantic Canada Confederation had become, above all else, a "grievance." Down deep, or often enough even quite close to the surface, most Maritimers felt that, during the Dominion of Canada's first 75 years, the "Federal Government wronged them, and the wound persists."

"A Neglected Part of the British Empire"

Will Bird's New Brunswicker had at least a rhetorical solution to the difficulties of Atlantic Canada: "Then they put tariffs on to protect Upper and Lower Canada and they've been protecting them ever since and paralysing the Maritimes. We ought to leave them and join New England."

At the bottom of this impulse was Goldwin Smith's home truth that each of the four east-west "blocks of territory constituting the Dominion" also enjoyed important north-south connections with analogous regions of the United States. For their part, Maritimers often felt that they had more in common with their neighbours in the "Boston States" than with Central or Western Canada. In the 1860s, between the Quebec and London conferences, there had been a faction in New Brunswick bold (or vain) enough to imagine that it might be able to strike its own renewal of the 1854 Reciprocity Treaty with the United States, separate from the rest of British North America.

As Smith's point made clear, there were residents in all parts of the Dominion with similar feelings. Still, in Atlantic Canada, as elsewhere, the prospect of actually joining New England — or, more accurately, the United States — remained a domestic debating point, not a practical proposal. After he had made the point, Bird's irate New Brunswicker quickly felt obliged to add, even to a fellow Maritimer, "I'm sorry .... I really get hot under the collar and say more than I mean."

There was an obvious practical question, formulated later by Miriam Chapin as: "Would the Atlantic Provinces be any better off if they had joined New England and not Canada? New England has fallen behind in the competition with the rest of the United States for some of the same reasons that they have lagged behind in Canada."

Perhaps even more important were questions of sentiment. Among a people still so reluctant to call themselves Canadians, these questions finally focused not on the Dominion of Canada, but on its continuing membership in the noble, cosmopolitan, and well-managed global civilization of the British Empire. Had there been a strong and highly developed native "Canadian" patriotism in the rest of English-speaking Canada, this might have isolated the Maritimes from the larger Dominion even more. But there was not. In the early 1890s the patriarchal premier of Ontario, Oliver Mowat, explained the situation. The provinces that made up the Confederation "are not yet sufficiently welded together to form Canada into an independent nation ... the strongest tie which up to this moment binds the provinces together is their common British connection."

As Mowat himself understood, more generously than most English Canadians of his era, this was not at all true of the French-speaking majority in Quebec. Here what emerging patriotism toward the larger Dominion there was, flowed from a native "Canadien" sense of nationality. And by the 1920s, 1930s, and 1940s it had also become somewhat less true of Ontario and Western Canada, where various gentle forms of nativist Canadian attachment were setting down new roots. But Mowat's late nineteenth century insights on the "common British connection" had a particular relevance for Atlantic Canada, well into the middle of the twentieth century.

Despite Toronto's pretensions as a cultural capital, English-speaking Atlantic Canada saw itself — and was frequently seen by the rest of English-speaking Canada — as the Dominion's purest, most committed, and most able exponent of the global English language culture of the British Empire. With the possible exception of Eastern Ontario, on the banks of the upper St. Lawrence River, Atlantic Canada was the one part of the Confederation where the old Loyalist heritage could convincingly be said to have real cultural and social depth.

All this brought practical as well as spiritual opportunities to at least some who began life as Atlantic Canadians. Loyal Maritime academics, teachers, and clergymen would help lead a not altogether vain quest to civilize the philistine pioneers of gritty old Ontario and the new and feisty Canadian West.

A classic case is "Sir Robert Falconer," born in Charlottetown, educated in the United Kingdom and Germany, a lecturer in "New Testament Exegesis" at the Presbyterian College in Halifax, and finally venerated president of the University of Toronto from 1907 to 1932. His career illustrates another dimension of Atlantic Canada's special relationship with the British Empire. Though born on Prince Edward Island, he spent much of his youth, with his parents, in "Trinidad, B.W.I." This reflected an old link in the chain of imperial commerce, between the British Maritimes and the islands of the Caribbean Sea. As Innis would explain in 1940:

> The tradition of Nova Scotia's assertiveness prior to Confederation contributed to the conspicuous advance in extraterritorial sovereignty after Confederation. Agreements with the West Indies ... in 1915 provided improved communications and preferential arrangements by which fish excluded from the United States could be sold more advantageously in the West Indies.

Even these original creations of Maritime assertiveness ultimately devolved to the advantage of a larger Central Canadian establishment, headquartered in Montreal and Toronto. The Canadian chartered banks would develop branches in the Caribbean, as well as in the Channel Islands of the United Kingdom — another link between Atlantic Canada and the old fishing economy of the Empire. Even when much later migration from the West Indies became an important element in Canadian population growth, it would focus on Central not Atlantic Canada, despite the presence of a historic African American community in Nova Scotia.

Another side of Atlantic Canada's special imperial relationship was equally a two-edged sword. For a brief period in the 1920s Bonar Law from New Brunswick became not a mere prime minister of Canada, like Nova Scotians Robert Borden, John Thompson, and Charles Tupper, but a prime minister of the United Kingdom — top political job in all of the Empire. And Max Aitken from New Brunswick spent some time in Montreal, but ultimately became Lord Beaverbrook, leading press baron in the global metropolis of London, England.

For the time being, all this made it possible for Maritimers to worry somewhat less about their increasingly small population weight in the Dominion. The real prize was not Canada: it was all of the Empire, on which the sun never set. By the 1930s it was clear enough that the sunset was

Sir Robert Falconer, a son of Atlantic Canada who served as president of the University of Toronto for a quarter of a century. According to an admiring contemporary, he shouldered his responsibilities as an academic administrator "with the coolness and method of a railway magnate, and the studied impartiality of a Chief Justice."

growing dimmer. Even more than in the Dominion at large, the British Empire could not continue to be part of the solution to Atlantic Canada's problem. At bottom, it was a symbol, even a part of the problem itself.

The Royal Commission on Maritime Claims

Even in the wider world the Atlantic region was notable for its problems. They were reflected in the subtitle of an intriguing travel book, published in 1931 by George Nestler Tricoche: *Rambles Through the Maritime Provinces of Canada: A Neglected Part of the British Empire*. Tricoche was a Prince Edward Island Acadian, who published books in French, in Paris, France, as well as books in English, in London, England. It was a sign of how much the symbiotic problems of slow growth and low income obsessed Atlantic Canada, however, that even in his 1931 English travel book, he felt obliged to include a discussion of regional economic problems. His views were somewhat different from those of Will Bird's New Brunswicker. Tricoche urged that when

> one looks deeper into the causes of economic depression ... it becomes clear that, roughly speaking, they arise from three sources: the eccentric situation of the Maritimes, as compared with the rest of the Dominion; the failure of the Federal Government to make up for this geographical inferiority by granting them at least the same facilities as those given to the western provinces, instead of following the present policy of according almost all its attention to the latter; and, lastly, the lack of enterprise of the Maritime population itself.

The careers of Max Aitken, Robert Borden, Robert Falconer, Bonar Law, and the men who built the Merchants' Bank of Halifax suggest, however, that Atlantic Canada did create some highly enterprising people. The problem was that they so frequently left for greener pastures elsewhere.

Yet there was a more profound, or at least influential insight, behind the other elements in Tricoche's particular version of the Maritime dilemma in Confederation. The root of the trouble was not really federal tariffs, (though he had earlier revealed some harsh views on tariffs, as well as the more diffuse imperialism of Central Canada.) It was Atlantic Canada's "eccentric situation" and "geographical inferiority." And at least part of the solution would have been the same kind of federal development policy apparently at work in Western Canada.

Western Canadians might have found this odd. And Tricoche was writing before the full impact of the depression had set in on the Canadian prairies. At bottom, however, it was only a variation on a popular enough Western argument: the only problem with John A. Macdonald's National Policy was that it was the wrong national policy. It worked for Central

Canada, but not for the rest of the country. What was needed was a national policy that worked for everyone.

Evidence for Tricoche's particular argument could be seen in the pre-Confederation history of railroad building in Atlantic Canada. In the old United Province, or the states of the more perfect Union to the south, one form or another of government subsidization had played an important role in early railway development, but railroads were nonetheless largely built and operated by private enterprise and private capital. On the other hand, as the regional historian J.S. Martell would explain in the late 1930s, in the old British North America before Confederation, "the railways in Nova Scotia were owned and run by the government."

There is a similar contrast between the Intercolonial Railroad that linked Atlantic and Central Canada, and the Canadian Pacific Railway from Montreal to the Pacific Coast. Though the CPR enjoyed much subsidization and other federal encouragement, it was ultimately owned and operated by a private business organization. The Montreal-headquartered Canadian Pacific Ltd. would go on to become one of Canada's five largest industrial corporations, even in the late 1980s. On the other hand, from the moment it was finally completed, in fact only about a decade before the CPR, the Intercolonial would be owned and operated by the government at Ottawa. It is the earliest ancestor of the publicly owned transcontinental Canadian National Railway, which stumbled into full-blown existence in the 1920s.

Almost as an act of God, it could be argued, because of its underlying geography Atlantic Canada was simply not the kind of region that could generate enough surplus capital, to have such things as railroads built and operated by its regional private sector. For the same reason, outside private investors were not much attracted to the place either, on any strict free market logic. (The logic of the late eighteenth and early nineteenth century British imperial position in the region had been strategic, in the context of the old mercantilist system, before imperial free trade.) Nor, for that matter, were immigrants from outside North America, most of whom — like many Atlantic Canadians themselves — went to Central or Western Canada, or the United States.

From all this, it was only a short step to the argument that Atlantic Canada could only develop effectively through extra-large doses of government intervention in its regional economy. And that was, or ought to be, one of the purposes of the larger Confederation, just as it was, as Tricoche had observed, in the West. By the 1920s views of this sort had helped create an amorphous Maritime Rights political protest movement, led by such regional luminaries as H.S. Congdon from Nova Scotia, A.M. Belding from New Brunswick, and A.E. MacLean from Prince Edward Island.

This kind of thinking had not impressed Wilfrid Laurier. As early as 1887, he told an audience in his native province of Quebec: "You cannot legislate against geography." Nonetheless, it was part of Laurier's revised Liberal strategy for actually governing the fractious Confederation to appoint W.S. Fielding, former premier of Nova Scotia, as the federal minister of finance.

Robert Borden, the Nova Scotia Conservative who defeated Laurier in 1911, favoured many forms of government intervention, in theory. But he also had many more pressing concerns — and, he sometimes seemed to plead, not yet enough resources to work with. The First World War, however, did allow his government at Ottawa to inaugurate the modern federal income tax.

Finally, in the midst of the Maritime Rights movement of the 1920s, the Mackenzie King Liberal regime that succeeded Borden's Conservatives found itself in need of ways to shore up its electoral support in Atlantic Canada. Despite the accident of being born in southwestern Ontario, King understood that one of Canada's fundamental problems was "too much geography." In 1926 he appointed The Royal Commission on Maritime Claims.

The commissioners did their work well enough. At a Dominion-Provincial Conference in 1927, it was agreed that, in view of Atlantic Canada's unique situation in the wider Confederation, the share of federal grants destined for its three provinces would be increased. In the same year, taking a leaf that was already in the Western Canadian book, Dominion railway freight rates were tilted somewhat in favour of Atlantic Canadian locations.

The Regional Renaissance of the 1930s

It would be saying far too much to link new freight rates, and the modest increase in federal grants to the Maritime provinces in the late 1920s, with the political and cultural blossoming the region enjoyed in the 1930s. But there was nonetheless such a blossoming. Harold Innis suggested what it involved in his 1940 conclusion to *The Cod Fisheries:*

> The postwar period has been marked in part by a return movement of "Maritimers" and immigration of Canadians from other parts of Canada. A renaissance has been apparent in the cooperative movement sponsored by St. Francis Xavier University, in the activities of Maritime universities, in the rejuvenation of the interest in cultural growth, in the development of museums, in the preservation of archives, and in a revival of pride in a notable past.

The numbers behind the renaissance were the population statistics that at last showed a modest surge in Atlantic Canadian demographic strength in the 1930s. There was a rough justice to the bright flowers that the Great Depression strew across the region's hard and rocky soil. When Canada's version of the new industrialism and the shift from commercialism to capitalism had boomed, Atlantic Canada had suffered. Now that the new industrialism and all that went with it had busted, it was only fair that the modern Maritime provinces should, in at least some ways, blossom and thrive.

In 1933 public bankruptcy in Newfoundland and loss of the old colonial democracy also cast a slightly brighter light on the fate of the three Atlantic provinces that had finally decided, however reluctantly, to become part of the Canadian Confederation in the nineteenth century. By the 1930s it was possible for Maritimers to take some pride in the contribution their region had made to the wider history of Canada, even if most still did not warm to the idea of actually calling themselves "Canadians."

Charles Tupper, Samuel Tilley, and even Joseph Howe had been crucial figures in the initial creation of the new Dominion of Canada's federal government at Ottawa. Amor De Cosmos, from Windsor, Nova Scotia, had helped bring British Columbia into the Confederation in 1871, and then served as B.C.'s second premier, from 1872 to 1874.

"The Rev. George M. Grant of Halifax, N.S." had written one of the first classics of a new Canadian national literature, *Ocean to Ocean: Sanford Fleming's Expedition through Canada in 1872.* "Travel a thousand miles up the St. Lawrence," the book began,

> another thousand on great lakes and a wilderness of lakelets and streams; a thousand miles across prairies and up the valley of the Saskatchewan; and nearly a thousand through woods and over great ranges of mountains, and you have travelled from Ocean to Ocean through Canada. All this country is a single Colony of the British Empire; and this Colony is dreaming magnificent dreams of a future when it shall be the Greater Britain, and the highway across which the fabrics and products of Asia shall be carried, to the Eastern as well as to the Western sides of the Atlantic.

Subsequently, Grant would become the venerated Principal Grant of Queen's University in Kingston, Ontario. As already noted, two of the four short-lived Conservative prime ministers of Canada who had held John A. Macdonald's old regime together between his death in 1891 and Laurier's victory in 1896 — John Thompson and Charles Tupper — were from Nova Scotia. So was Robert Borden, the Conservative who defeated Laurier in 1911, formed a "Unionist" government that attracted some maverick Liberals during the First World War, and remained prime minister until the summer of 1920.

The Royal Commission on Maritime Claims in the later 1920s would be a precedent for the Canada-wide "Rowell-Sirois" Royal Commission on Dominion-Provincial Relations in the late 1930s. The Atlantic co-operative movement that reached out from St. Francis Xavier University in Nova Scotia during the 1930s and 1940s was a variation on themes that the Great Depression had brought to Western Canada and many other parts of the world. It was not accompanied by the kind of political blossoming that brought forth the Co-operative Commonwealth Federation that distinguished the West, but it did suggest an approach to the future that would find some echoes, for instance, in Manitoba and Saskatchewan.

In the characteristically sweeping and rather oracular concluding sentences of *The Cod Fisheries*, Harold Innis hinted at more particular Atlantic variations on these themes:

> The tremendous initiative which characterized commercialism based on the fishing industry could be measured in ... the history of Newfoundland and New England, the defeat of France and the breakdown of the colonial system, the disappearance of the Navigation Acts, and even the rise of responsible government and the establishment of Confederation. This is an initiative which cannot be suddenly replaced. The effects of the tragedy of the replacement of commercialism by capitalism call for a long period of expensive readjustment and restoration, and this cannot take place without policies which foster the revival of initiative under responsible governments.

With the Empire that had long ago begun the tremendous initiative about to conduct its final finest hour, here at last were some beginnings to a new national future for the people of Canada's Atlantic Coast. The old sense of regional grievance would persist, in many different ways, even down to the present. But, whatever they might have been in the waning Empire, the Maritime provinces of Canada would at least not be a neglected part of the new Canadian Confederation, that would arise in the wake of the Second World War.

8
"THE UNREFORMED SENATE OF CANADA"

In their different ways, both Western and Atlantic Canada developed lists of regional grievances during the first half century of the modern Canadian Confederation. In theory the Senate was supposed to be an important means by which such grievances were brought to bear on the national agenda. At bottom, things did not work this way because of what the Senate became in practice — "a bribery fund in the hands of the Government" at Ottawa, according to Goldwin Smith. It is logical enough to ask, however: then why didn't Western and Atlantic Canada mount some early twentieth century crusade for Senate reform?

Part of the answer is that there were, in fact, some impulses for change in the Senate, especially during the second and third decades of the century. Western Canada was a frequent supporter of the impulses. Prime Minister Robert Borden from Nova Scotia made serious but ultimately aborted plans for change, and at least introduced the legislation that gave Western Canada its own 24-member Senate section in 1915.

These early reforming impulses did promote the beginnings of a slender national literature on the Canadian Parliament's second chamber, including *The Senate of Canada*, published in 1914 by George Ross, a former premier of Ontario, and R.A. MacKay's more durable *The Unreformed Senate of Canada*, first published in 1926. Yet they did not lead to the kind of major structural debate about Senate reform that would arise in the 1970s. One underlying reason points to some striking differences in the structure of Canadian regional politics before and after the Second World War.

Today the most popular stereotype pictures "metropolitan" Central Canada, and especially Ontario, allied with the federal government against the regionalist pressures of the eight "hinterland" provinces — four in Atlantic Canada and four in the West. But in the late nineteenth and early twentieth centuries, Central Canada was itself the great pioneer of regional power in the Confederation.

To start with, the provincial government of predominantly French-speaking Quebec became, logically enough, the principal spokesman for the historic French Canadian fact in a predominantly English-speaking dominion of the British Empire. This gave the democratically elected government of Quebec, if not the business elite of English-speaking Montreal, frequent occasions to resist the authority of a federal government at Ottawa that spoke for the will of the national majority, *a mari usque ad mare*.

At the same time, Montreal, in Quebec, would remain the unchallenged economic capital of the Dominion until after the Second World War. Toronto, in Ontario, was only a junior partner in the national dream, at best the

English-speaking cultural capital. (In 1920 Harold Innis explained to his fiancée from Illinois that Toronto was "the literary centre of Canada if not the industrial centre ... the second largest city.") This gave the provincial government of Ontario reasons to resist a federal government often thought to speak most clearly for the merchants of Montreal. As strange as it may seem today, late nineteenth century Ontario, under its regional "Cromwell," Oliver Mowat, was the founder of the modern tradition of "province building" in English-speaking Canada.

The underlying geographic regionalism of Canada made it easy enough for Ontario and Quebec to bring other provinces on board, in periodic protests against the "centralizing proclivities" of the federal government at Ottawa. Yet in a more fundamental sense, the deepest dilemma for Atlantic and at least one side of Western Canada was not so much to find some means of strengthening the expression of regional power in the Confederation, but to find some shield against the too formidable regional power of Ontario and Quebec.

The Great Depression of the 1930s finally cast all this in bold relief. In keeping with the spirit of the age, the countervailing idea whose time ultimately came was a more genuinely national federal government, from ocean to ocean, strong enough to resist the regionalism of Central Canada. Senate reform did not seem much or even at all related to this kind of hinterland agenda, even if we of the late twentieth century, with the easy wisdom of hindsight, can construct arguments about the demographic dominance of Ontario and Quebec in the House of Commons to show that the structure and role of the Senate was, logically at least, extremely important.

The Earliest Impulses toward Senate Reform

Part of the difficulty was that, by the early twentieth century, the regional representation function of the Senate bequeathed by Cartier, Macdonald, Tupper, and Tilley had been significantly obscured by its qualities as an old Tory heirloom.

This was not how events had initially begun to unfold. The first actual debate on Senate reform in the federal Parliament took place in 1874, not long after the first and only electoral defeat of John A. Macdonald's (and George-Etienne Cartier's) founding federal regime. The debate was instigated by the Liberal-Reformer David Mills, who would much later succeed the aged Oliver Mowat in his brief and largely honorary tenure as Wilfrid Laurier's first minister of justice. Mills urged that

> the present mode of constituting the Senate is inconsistent with the Federal principle in our system ... and our Constitution ought to be so amended as to confer upon each Province the power of selecting its own Senators, and to defining the mode of election.

This focus on the issue flowed from the same fundamental concern for the Senate's role as an instrument of regional representation that would arise in the late twentieth century. It also flowed, however, strictly from a point of principle, which, in the late nineteenth century, lacked the support of an organized and articulate political constituency. David Mills raised his point of principle again in 1875, and then he and everyone else forgot about it under the pressure of more immediate concerns, especially after Macdonald's return to power in 1878.

A generation later, the question of Senate reform arose again in the federal Parliament — and this time as a more practical issue. But the focus was no longer on regional representation and "the Federal principle in our system." By this point it had become clear that Canada was developing into a country of unusually long-lived governing parties. The Senate's most immediately controversial feature had become its tendency to artificially extend the influence of the former federal governing party, most recently defeated by the voters at the polls.

Macdonald's Conservative regime, for instance, held office continuously from 1878 to 1896, with Abbott, Thompson, Mackenzie Bowell, and Tupper tacked on at the end. It appointed Conservative senators. Thus, when Laurier came to power in 1896, his Liberal majority in the House of Commons faced a Conservative majority in the Senate. Then Laurier's Liberal regime held office continuously from 1896 to 1911. It appointed Liberal senators. When the Conservative Robert Borden came to power in 1911, he faced a Liberal majority in the Senate. Then Borden's Conservative (and then Unionist) regime held office continuously from 1911 to 1921, with Arthur Meighen tacked on at the end. And when the Liberal Mackenzie King came to power in 1921, he faced a Senate with a Conservative majority.

Under these circumstances, the most practical motivation for talk about Senate reform typically involved legislation being first passed by a House of Commons elected majority and then defeated by a rejected governing party that nonetheless still held a majority in the appointed Senate. In 1906 — a year when the Senate's handling of an emotional federal Sunday Observance Bill had prompted some heated parliamentary debate — Gilbert McIntyre, member of Parliament for Perth, Ontario, moved in the House of Commons that "the Constitution of the Senate should be brought into greater accord with the spirit of representative and popular government, and the genius of the Canadian people."

Three years later, in the Senate of Canada itself, Richard Scott argued that "the time has arrived for so amending the Constitution of this branch of Parliament as to bring the modes of selection of Senators more into harmony with public opinion." Similar concerns would ultimately animate both Robert Borden's aborted approach to actual Senate reform in the First World War era and, in more subtle, Machiavellian ways, Mackenzie King's more or less decisive barking on the subject in the 1920s.

This framing of the issue reflected the extent to which the shift from John A. Macdonald in the late nineteenth century to Wilfrid Laurier in the early

David Mills from southwestern Ontario was Alexander Mackenzie's minister of the interior when he complained in the 1870s that Canada's appointed Senate was "inconsistent with the Federal principle in our system." By the time he served as Wilfrid Laurier's justice minister in the 1890s, he had himself accepted a Senate appointment.

twentieth century had signalled the final triumph of an essentially democratic constitutionalism in Canada. Laurier's immediate successor, "Sir Robert Borden," who retired in 1920, was the last Canadian prime minister to bear a British knighthood in office. By the end of the First World War, even the highly abridged late nineteenth century version of the old Tory elitism failed to move people and events as it had in the 1860s and 1870s.

At the same time, recurrent bouts of righteous indignation at the essentially undemocratic interventions of an appointed Senate, in an increasingly democratic national political system, drew attention away from any positive role the Senate might have played as a defender of regional interests in Atlantic and Western Canada, or even, as George Brown had stressed in the mid-1860s, in Quebec.

Lord Bryce's Mistake

One reflection of just how much the Senate's regional representation functions had become obscured by the end of the First World War is a description of the institution in a short book of the early 1920s, entitled *Canada: An Actual Democracy*. It was the work of "The Right Honourable Viscount Bryce, O.M., P.C., D.C.L., F.R.S.," easily the era's most eminent British authority on the government and politics of the Western world. Lord Bryce was also the author of *The American Commonwealth*, the classic study of American politics after the Civil War and a worthy successor to de Tocqueville's account of the 1830s, and of the comparative survey *Modern Democracies*. His short study of the Canadian scene is both convincing and compelling, but he was only human, and, like all eminent authorities in all times and places, he sometimes made mistakes.

One of them concerned the selection of Canadian senators. In Canada, Lord Bryce reported, the "Senate consists of 96 persons nominated for life by the Governor-General, i.e. by the Ministry for the time being, as vacancies occur by death or resignation. A number of senators proportionate to population is assigned to each Province."

The mistake was in the phrase "proportionate to population." In fact, 24 senators were assigned to the three provinces of Atlantic Canada, 24 to the province of Quebec, 24 to the province of Ontario, and, by Lord Bryce's time, 24 to the four provinces of Western Canada — to offset, in at least some degree, inequities in the geographic distribution of population.

What seems most striking, is that so eminent and well-informed an authority should have missed this point. His error implied, a domestic critic might have argued, that, for all the apparent good it did anyone, the equal sectional representation in the Canadian Senate might just as well be representation by population, as in the House of Commons.

Nonetheless, that Western Canada had been given its own 24-member Senate section, not too long before Lord Bryce made his mistake, showed how the Senate's regional representation function had not been completely forgotten inside the Dominion of Canada itself. This was officially the work of Borden's Conservative regime at Ottawa, though Laurier, now Liberal opposition leader, played a part as well. The story is something of a notable stopover on the long journey to Senate reform in Canada.

Laurier, Borden, and the New Western Section

Borden first bumped into the subject when he was opposition leader, casting about for some winning new policies. In 1906, the year of the emotional federal Sunday Observance Bill and McIntyre's Senate reform motion in the House of Commons, Rodmond Roblin, the Conservative premier of Manitoba, urged Borden to adopt an "advanced" federal party program that included a popularly elected Senate.

At this point, Borden himself felt that "if any change should be made in the Senate I would rather prefer the United States system of an election by State legislatures." And, still a loyal follower of Macdonald in at least this respect, he ultimately believed "the present system would be better than any that has been suggested" if only party politics could be removed from the appointment process.

His mind began to change after he came to power in 1911. At the opening of the 1911–12 parliamentary session, there were 62 Liberals in the Senate and only 19 Conservatives. In the wake of an emotional 1911 election on free trade with the United States, a contest Borden's Conservatives had won with only 50.9% of the popular vote, the Liberal majority in the Senate systematically tried to block government legislation.

Particularly irksome to Borden was the Senate's rejection of bills for a new tariff commission, federal grants for provincial highways, and an "emergency contribution" to the Imperial Navy, based in the United Kingdom. In the last case, adroitly covering the question of its own lack of democratic legitimacy, the Senate had returned Borden's legislation to the Commons with the curt message: "This House is not justified in giving its assent to the Bill until it is submitted to the judgement of the country."

As all this was unfolding in Canada, a serious move for Senate reform was afoot in the United States, as part of the early twentieth century "progressive impulse" that would also leave some marks on Borden. A campaign for a constitutional amendment requiring direct popular election of American senators had begun in 1903. Its progress was slow at first. To move the cause along, a number of states established primary elections, in which voters expressed Senate preferences that state legislatures then found it impolitic to ignore. Finally, in 1913, the Seventeenth Amendment to the U.S. Constitution provided for direct popular election of all senators throughout the Republic.

By this time, a bipartisan committee in the Canadian House of Commons, of the sort frequently struck to make recommendations on the redistribution of Commons seats, had also recommended some changes in the distribution of Senate seats — to catch up with the rapid growth of the Dominion in the first decade of the twentieth century. Then, as Borden's memoirs for the parliamentary year of 1914 put the matter, the question of Senate representation "had been under discussion several times during the session. ... Sir Wilfrid Laurier ... had suggested a fourth division, comprising the Western Provinces, which should be represented by twenty-four members and I concurred in that view."

Expanding the Senate to make room for the full representation of the now four provinces of Western Canada was a modest bow to the rising assertiveness of the Confederation's newest section. (Late in 1913, the Prairie premiers had written to Borden, raising the thorny issue of responsibility for natural resources in the three provinces created by the federal government.) It also offered to give Borden an opportunity to appoint some new Conservative senators, thus evening up the odds in the Liberal-dominated Senate that was thwarting his legislative program.

Accordingly, on 11 June 1914 Borden introduced legislation for the new Western Senate section, and for some related housekeeping changes. (These included an appeal to the Imperial Parliament in the United Kingdom, for an amendment to the British North America Act, 1867, with respect to British Columbia's Senate seats. Representation for the three Prairie provinces created by the federal government was within the constitutional competence of the Canadian Parliament alone.)

Borden's legislation received unanimous approval in the elected Commons. The Liberal-dominated Senate, however, kept up its tricks. It returned the legislation with an amendment providing that "this Act shall not take effect until the termination of the now-existing Canadian Parliament" — that is, until after the next federal election. The issue here was who would appoint the new Western Canadian senators. Without the amendment, it would be Borden and the Conservatives. With the amendment, there was at least a chance that it would be the Liberals.

The prime minister from Nova Scotia was at last full of fury. Advisers urged him to call an election, which it was thought the Conservatives could win, before the economic difficulties that had appeared in 1913 grew worse. To start off, a resolution was drawn up for a national plebiscite on the question: "Are you in favour of abolishing the Senate of Canada as at present constituted and of substituting therefor a Senate elected by the people?"

The preamble to the question noted: "Since 1867 the evolution and development of Federal systems both within the British Empire and in foreign countries has strongly tended in the direction of election of members of the Upper House instead of appointment thereto by the Executive." (The reference to the Empire covered, directly, the creation of an elected Senate in Australia in 1901 and, indirectly, a historic reduction in the ancient powers of the British House of Lords in 1911, as part of a political crisis surrounding early welfare-state legislation in the United Kingdom.)

Then, suddenly, a poor Conservative showing in a Manitoba provincial election, rumours of the imminent death of the Ontario Conservative premier James Pliny Whitney, and the outbreak of the First World War in Europe prompted the prime minister to decide not to call an election. And, as his initial fury subsided, Borden became convinced that, as his modern biographer

Robert Craig Brown has put the point, "Senate reform was a perpetual topic of debate among politicians, a perpetual bore to the electorate."

Even so, on 25 March 1915, Robert Borden reintroduced his legislation for a new Senate section for Western Canada in the House of Commons. Again the House unanimously approved, and the bill went to the Senate. Again it came back with an amendment stipulating that it could not take effect until after the next election. Borden's deepest instincts were genuinely above such sordid hi-jinks. This time, he tells us in his memoirs, "as it seemed impossible to pass this desirable and necessary legislation without the Senate's unnecessary and obstructive amendment, I felt disposed to accept the Senate's proposal."

The Confederation would not get an elected Senate, but the West would at least get something. Now each of Atlantic Canada, Quebec, Ontario, and Western Canada would be equally represented in the unreformed Senate of Canada. (On the other hand, meteoric western population growth quickly blunted this particular edge of change. By 1921 the only section that could really be said to enjoy potential benefit from equal Senate representation was Atlantic Canada. Each of Quebec, Ontario, and Western Canada actually had a greater share of the national population than of Senate seats. Even if the regional representation functions of the Senate had been important, this particular arrangement would not in fact have brought much extra national influence to Western Canada.)

Mackenzie King's Incredible Canadianism

As it happened, Borden won the next election — postponed until 1917, owing to the emergency circumstances of the First World War. He appointed the new Western senators, as well as new senators in other sections. The balance of power in the chamber of sober second thought shifted toward the Conservatives.

They had their vengeance for the partisan insults of 1912–15, after William Lyon Mackenzie King defeated Borden's successor, Arthur Meighen, and a new Canadian Progressive Party in the federal election of December 1921. This time a Conservative-dominated Senate, with equal sectional representation from ocean to ocean, could harass an elected Liberal government.

The harassment came to a head in 1924 when the Senate defeated a series of government bills for railway branch lines in various parts of the Dominion, bills that Mackenzie King regarded as particularly important to his larger purposes. Shortly after this, the prime minister who would be called *The Incredible Canadian* (by his popular biographer Bruce Hutchison, from British Columbia) announced in Parliament that he would soon be introducing measures of Senate reform. In the meantime, he would exact from any new senators he appointed a pledge to support "whatever reform the Government proposes."

The kind of reform Mackenzie King had in mind was not the popularly elected Senate that Borden had mulled over in 1914. As the scholarly biographer of his middle period, H. Blair Neatby, has explained, King believed that "he and his colleagues" in the federal Cabinet "were more effective spokesmen for racial and religious minorities and for provincial rights" than any kind of Senate could possibly be — in a country where (as King himself once put it) "the difficulty of maintaining unity ... is very great indeed." What's more, according to King's view of how Canada worked best, it was "helpful to be able to reward loyal party members by appointing them to the Senate."

William Lyon Mackenzie King was in fact the great wizard of Canadian political development in the difficult but important era of the 1920s, 1930s, and 1940s. Along a path so subtle and devious that it would sometimes seem to fool even him, he would finally lead Canada to its first steps out of the British Empire and into its own modern, post-colonial future. More than any other prime minister before or since, he grasped the deepest meaning of Christopher Dunkin's old criticism that, under the arrangements bequeathed by the 1860s and 1870s, the "Cabinet here must discharge that kind of function which in the United States is performed in the federal sense by the Senate."

Above all else, according to this view, in a highly diverse, still not quite independent country, prone to racial, religious, and geographic discord, it was the primary responsibility of the federal executive to manage the regionalism of the country. The appropriate means were deft compromises, cunning stratagems, shrewd and often cynical appointments, exasperating tactics of delay, sensitivity to the disparate voices of the people, caution, the indispensable Ernest Lapointe as French Canadian lieutenant, John W. Dafoe of the *Winnipeg Free Press* as a frequently valued counsellor, and even, on rare occasions, the advice of spiritualists, mediums, psychics, and the prime minister's dead mother — venerated daughter of William Lyon Mackenzie, leader of the Upper Canadian Rebellion of 1837.

In this struggle, the Senate was merely meant to be a loyal ally of the prime minister and Cabinet. Or as R.A. MacKay's pioneering and, as it turned out, increasingly authoritative book of 1926 would explain, in the eyes of the fathers of the federation "it was not anticipated that the Senate would be a first line of defence" for "peculiar sectional and (in the case especially of Quebec) ... peculiar provincial, interests ... it would be in effect a reserve line after the House of Commons and the Cabinet."

The agenda for Senate reform that flowed from such conceptions was simply to remove the old Tory fangs that Cartier, Macdonald, Tupper, and Tilley had foolishly given to the chamber of sober second thought in the first place. If the Senate could contribute something useful to the resolution of Canada's regional problems, or anything else, well and good. If not, it should at least stay out of the way of the man who could or, as the grandson of the Upper Canadian rebel leader of 1837 liked to put it, of the elected "Parliament," which represented the people. Thus, Mackenzie King's plan was merely to reduce the powers of the Senate — much as the powers of the British House of Lords had only recently been reduced, in 1911, clearing the way for a new age of democracy, even in the bosom of the ancient Canadian parent state.

It appears that King first hoped to do this merely by talking and threatening, and exacting pledges of support for whatever reforms he proposed from his own new senatorial appointees. However, the Senate's defeat of early federal government legislation for modest old age pensions in 1926 finally prompted somewhat stronger action. In the end, Mackenzie King did not formally change anything. Yet, in a characteristically roundabout way, he did gently remove the Senate of Canada's remaining fangs.

The Birth of Federal-Provincial Diplomacy

The arena in which the final acts of Mackenzie King's subtle quest for Senate reform in the 1920s took place suggested an alternative institution for addressing the political problems of Canadian regionalism — not one invented by the men who created the Confederation in the 1860s and 1870s, but one that gradually evolved out of Canada's subsequent hard experience.

Like Borden before him, King concluded that Senate reform was not the kind of issue to be fought altogether on the electoral battlefield. In the 1925 federal election, he told voters, in Neatby's words, "that the government had found itself hampered during the past years ... by a hostile Senate. The Senate must be made more responsive to the popular will, and a Dominion-Provincial conference would be called to discuss reform."

In the 1926 election that soon followed (as a result of the "King-Byng Crisis" or "King-Byng-Wing-Ding," over the alleged unconstitutional interference of the British governor general in Canadian affairs), Mackenzie King also made something of the Senate's particular rejection of his old age pension bill. Then, having won the 1926 election with a decisive enough majority, the prime minister convened his Dominion-Provincial Conference in early November 1927.

This was only the third of what would much later be generically labelled "First Ministers' Conferences" in the history of the Confederation. But the very earliest precedent for such gatherings went back as far as the Interprovincial Conference of 1887. This had been hosted by Honoré Mercier of Quebec, chaired by Oliver Mowat of Ontario, and attended by Nova Scotia, New Brunswick, and Manitoba. (Prince Edward Island, British Columbia, and Macdonald's federal government of the day declined invitations.) John A. Macdonald had derided the event as an impotent partisan gathering of Liberal malcontents from the provinces. But when Mowat and W.S. Fielding of Nova Scotia joined Laurier's reformed federal governing party in 1896, the precedent began to take on a more positive significance.

At the request of the provinces, and after a second, strictly interprovincial gathering in 1902, Laurier himself convened the first "Conference of the Representatives of the Government of Canada and the Various Provinces" in early October 1906, the same year that Robert Borden had canvassed his opposition Conservatives for their views on Rodmond Roblin's elected Senate proposal. A second conference in November 1918 was called by Borden.

Following the third conference in 1927, five conferences would be held in the 1930s, three in the 1940s, seven in the 1950s, 15 in the 1960s, and 16 in the 1970s. Much more than the Senate, and even more than the federal Cabinet (at least after the wizardry of Mackenzie King), these conferences would ultimately evolve into a primary mechanism for addressing the political problems of Canadian regionalism — giving rise to what the political scientist Richard Simeon would finally christen *Federal-Provincial Diplomacy*, in a seminal book of the early 1970s.

The Dominion-Provincial Conference of 1927 was not in fact particularly notable for its discussion of Senate reform, though this was the lead item on the agenda. The substantive federal-provincial diplomacy that took place turned around Western and Central Canadian support for increased federal subsidies to Atlantic Canada, as recommended by the Royal Commission on Maritime Claims, in return for Atlantic and Central Canadian support for at last giving all Western provinces control over natural resources, and in

The provincial premiers and their colleagues, assembled in Ottawa for the first federal-provincial conference in October 1906. Seated in the centre of the front row is Lomer Gouin, premier of Quebec, the province that had hosted the first conference of premiers alone, in 1887. In 1918 Gouin would give a celebrated speech in the Quebec Legislative Assembly against "the Francoeur motion," introduced in the wake of the 1917 Canadian crisis over conscription for wartime service.

The motion had declared that "the Province of Quebec would be disposed to agree to breaking the Federation pact of 1867 if the other Provinces consider that Quebec is an obstacle to the unity, progress and development of Canada." Gouin urged that, despite the just complaints of French Canadians, the best hope for the French fact in North America lay with "the development and maintenance of the Canadian Confederation."

return for Western and Atlantic Canadian support for giving Ontario and Quebec provincial control over hydro power on navigable streams. The highest longer-term constitutional significance of the conference was that it marked the beginning of some 54 years of federal-provincial discussion on how to "patriate" the power to amend the British North America Act from the United Kingdom — a process that would reach fruition in 1981.

Mackenzie King's victory in the 1926 election gave him the upper hand over the Senate that he wanted. He signalled the new status of the upper house by refusing to appoint any of its members to his Cabinet. This, together with promises of support exacted from new appointees, prompted the senators to approve the prime minister's federal old age pension bill that they had earlier blocked.

The Western premiers were interested in more substantive changes in the Senate, and the subject was duly debated at the 1927 conference. Ernest Lapointe, the prime minister's French Canadian lieutenant and minister of justice, proposed adopting an age limit for senators, together with either "the British practice which enabled the lower House to overcome the opposition of the upper House by passing a measure in three successive sessions" or "the American system of a joint sitting of the two Houses, with a large majority in the lower House able to over-ride the opposition of reluctant Senators."

While the premiers from Western Canada continued to express concern that something be done, they were not certain that this was the solution. The premiers of Central and Atlantic Canada concluded that it was best to leave things as they were for the time being, and Premier Taschereau of Quebec was particularly concerned that any strong action would only "open the door to further amendments" of the delicate arrangements that held the highly diverse Confederation together. The final conference report simply indicated that everyone present had expressed "frank and candid views."

As far as Mackenzie King was concerned, the Senate reform that desperately needed to take place had in fact happened. The formally unreformed Senate of Canada retained its vast theoretical powers, equal in almost all respects to those of the House of Commons. But it had finally come to understand that if it continued to try to use these powers in any serious and consistent manner, by one means or another they would be taken away.

9
THE ROWELL-SIROIS SOLUTION

Mackenzie King's approach to Senate reform in the 1920s could be character-ized in language he himself would later use in Quebec during the Second World War, describing his federal government's position on conscription for overseas military service: Senate reform if necessary, but not necessarily Senate reform.

This approach did broadly resolve the one urgent practical difficulty created by the Canadian Senate in the early twentieth century. It effectively neutralized the theoretical power of the appointed upper house to thwart the will of the democratically elected House of Commons. But it did nothing for the underlying problems of Canadian regionalism that the Senate was meant to help manage. Ultimately, the Great Depression of the 1930s brought these problems to a point where they had to be confronted, even systematically, in some other way.

Strictly from Mackenzie King's standpoint of practical politics, there were two key sources of pressure. The first was simply that the Depression affected some parts of the Dominion more than others. While a prolonged economic slump coincided with a cultural renaissance in Atlantic Canada, on the prairies of Western Canada it coincided with a prolonged period of recurrent drought that did not affect either Atlantic or Central Canada, or even, for that matter, British Columbia.

A second source of pressure was the demand for government action on Depression issues that arose in many parts of the world. In Canada, this was complicated by the federal-provincial division of powers set down in the British North America Act, 1867.

To Macdonald, Cartier, Tupper, and Tilley, the local needs of the people were not among the important responsibilities of government. Insofar as government did have such responsibilities, they were assigned to the prov-inces — which is where the earliest beginnings of the modern welfare state in Canada first appeared, during the late nineteenth and early twentieth centu-ries.

Since it had not been anticipated at the time of Confederation that provincial governments would devote many resources to their merely local responsibilities, the lion's share of public revenues had been assigned to the federal government at Ottawa. Even apart from the eventual welfare respon-sibilities of provincial governments, difficulties with this arrangement were raised by the late nineteenth century decisions of the Judicial Committee of the Privy Council in the United Kingdom, which strengthened provincial powers in the Confederation in a way unanticipated by Macdonald and Cartier.

The result was that conflict between strong federal revenues on the one hand and strong provincial responsibilities on the other had appeared as a practical political issue of Canadian federalism well before the Great Depression. It had been a key concern at the first federal-provincial conference of 1906 — which had led to a general round of increased federal financial grants to provincial governments. Yet this did not at all exhaust the problem in principle. In the end, severe economic troubles in the 1930s only brought federal-provincial tensions that had been bubbling for a generation to a boil.

The Complicated Legend of the National Policy

One step removed from practical politics, in both Atlantic and especially Western Canada these tensions were filtered through some popular regionalist traditions, which focused on the legacies of John A. Macdonald's founding federal regime at Ottawa.

By the 1930s these traditions had been evolving for some half a century. Their point of departure was the late 1870s, when it became unmistakably clear that the post–Civil War federal government at Washington would not renew the American-abrogated Reciprocity Treaty of 1854 for any British Dominion of Canada. In response, Macdonald's Conservative returned to power at Ottawa in 1878 on a platform that stressed growth and development inside Canada's own borders.

Part of the resulting federal development strategy rejuvenated ongoing work on the Canadian Pacific Railway, which would finally reach the Pacific Ocean in 1885. In frank imitation of national policies pursued by the model republic to the south, however, the distinguishing feature of the new National Policy Macdonald's government introduced in 1879 was high tariffs on imported manufactured goods, designed to protect the Canadian market for a fledgling industrial manufacturing sector that was setting down its deepest roots in southwestern Quebec and central and southwestern Ontario.

In the late nineteenth century, Laurier's Liberals opposed this particular Canadian trade design in favour of a new reciprocity agreement with the United States. Yet in the continuing absence of a new treaty, they too finally succumbed to the logic of Macdonald's scheme of 1879. They even supplemented the concept with one of the Macdonald regime's unimplemented aspirations — an "Imperial Preference" for British goods in the Canadian market, intended to prompt special treatment for Canadian resource and manufactured goods in the markets of the free trading British Empire.

When it seemed that Washington might at last have changed its mind about its trade future with Canada, Laurier's Liberals did negotiate a new Canada-U.S. Reciprocity Treaty in 1911. Yet others claimed that the Americans had only become more devious and that both the aspiring nation and the historic link with the Empire were threatened. Laurier's agreement was (rather narrowly) defeated in a Canadian federal election, dominated by the votes of Canada's most populous and industrializing province, Ontario, and by the financial resources of a Central Canadian business establishment — newly invigorated by the early twentieth century economic boom, which the West had played so prominent a part in creating.

Mackenzie King would himself lay the groundwork for a more open Canada-U.S. trade relationship in the 1930s, and Canadian tariff barriers against all countries would decline dramatically after the Second World War under the international General Agreement on Tariffs and Trade. But from the election of 1911 to the election of 1988, all Canadian federal governments would continue to pay some degree of homage to the principles of John A. Macdonald's National Policy.

To many in Western Canada the evolution of the National Policy confirmed the late nineteenth century grievance that Ottawa viewed the West chiefly as a preserve for the ambitions of the Central Canadian merchants. Western producers paid high prices for protected manufactured goods from Central Canada (often enough made by branch plants of American multinational corporations), and then faced high American tariffs when they tried to sell their resource products into adjacent protected American markets.

Western Canada, it seemed, was paying for the industrialization of Central Canada and gaining virtually no compensating advantage in return. The so-called National Policy was no more than a Central Canadian regional policy, designed to make and keep the West a resource colony of newly industrializing Ontario and Quebec.

This popular western critique of the National Policy had its equally popular counterpart in Atlantic Canada — despite otherwise fundamental differences between the Western and Atlantic regional economies. It was seldom as convincing in Central Canada, however, and not always for reasons of naked self-interest. To start with, even to thoughtful Central Canadians who liked to think of themselves as fair-minded, it was obvious that the part of the Canadian market in Ontario and Quebec was simply that much larger than the parts in Western or Atlantic Canada — even at the height of the West's relative population base in the early 1930s.

Still more to the point, the entire east-west domestic market from the Atlantic to the Pacific was never large enough, in itself, to stimulate a vigorous manufacturing sector in any part of the country. The two strongest Ontario manufacturing industries in the 1920s — agricultural machinery and automobiles — depended a great deal on markets outside North America altogether, especially in the British Empire.

For its part, much of French Canada in Quebec benefited only marginally from the prosperity of the Montreal that would reign until the end of the Second World War as the undisputed economic capital of Canada. It would also often enough be argued, even in Ontario, that the National Policy created only a hothouse industrialism, congenitally small-scale, inefficient, and overdependent on branch plants of American corporations, that did Central Canada little long-term good.

Even from a more "natural" (or continental free market) perspective on economic geography, the concentration of Canadian manufacturing in Central Canada was in many respects only a northern variation on the concentration of American manufacturing in the Northeast and Midwest. Ontario's own early twentieth century forward momentum depended at least as much on forestry and mining in Northern Ontario, as on the stimulus to its "forced" industrialization brought about by the growth of the West.

On the other hand, there was much intellectual sustenance for regionalists interested in ridiculing Macdonald's National Policy in Goldwin Smith's influential, late nineteeth century, highbrow jounalism. And, as the premier of Prince Edward Island would observe in the late twentieth century, the "reality of Canada is that the perspective changes depending on where you are."

For those who were in Western Canada, the chain of Montreal and Toronto banks and Eaton's department stores that stretched across the prairies to the Pacific Ocean by the middle of the twentieth century, was evidence enough of Central Canadian domination in western development. Just as the Merchants' Bank of Halifax's transformation into the Royal Bank of Canada in Montreal had suggested the fate of old eastern financial institutions, the fate of new western financial institutions was suggested when Toronto's Canadian Bank of Commerce absorbed the Bank of British Columbia in 1901. Similarly, Macdonald's National Policy did little more for coal in Alberta than for coal in Nova Scotia. In both cases coal in Pennsylvania was much closer to the Central Canadian manufacturing heartland.

In 1897 the Crow's Nest Pass Agreement, between Laurier's government at Ottawa and the CPR, had established the principle of federally subsidized railway freight rates for wheat and flour moving from Western to Eastern Canada, in response to early complaints from prairie farmers. This itself could be viewed as evidence that even the managers of the federal strategy at Ottawa had to admit its underlying lack of genuine national justice.

When the subsidized rates were lifted in response to the special circumstances of the First World War, western interests fought for their reinstatement in the 1920s. The final result was an agreement that established subsidized rates for grain and unprocessed grain products in 1927, the same year as the report of the Royal Commission on Maritime Claims and Mackenzie King's first Dominion-Provincial Conference.

By itself, the protective tariff of the National Policy may not have been exactly the crux of either Western or Atlantic development problems. But for many people in both regions, it became an easily grasped and compelling symbol of many good reasons for regional discontent in the Dominion of Canada.

New Voices from the West

In Atlantic Canada the perceived inequities of the National Policy amounted to just one more argument for putting the British Empire ahead of the Dominion of Canada as a focus for regional identity. The stereotypical

Atlantic Canadian revenge against Central Canada was to refuse to take the whole idea of Canada seriously, to refuse to be bothered about even being "Canadian."

If some material advantage could be wrung from the federal government at Ottawa, that was worth doing. And some Atlantic Canadians migrated to other parts of the country or made careers for themselves in Ottawa. But for many of those who stayed in the region, the best defence against what the Dominion at large seemed to be doing to them was indifference to the Dominion at large.

In Western Canada circumstances were different. Here there was more incentive to fight back, on behalf of new definitions of what it meant to be Canadian. Despite its capacity to generate deep feelings against the world back east, western alienation from John A. Macdonald's particular National Policy did not imply western alienation from the general concept of a national development policy in any shape or form.

It was a prejudice in parts of Ontario that western recalcitrance in such matters actually reflected a lack of national patriotism, attributable to the newness of mass settlement in the region and, some would add (taking cues from old Upper Canadian Loyalist themes), to the prominence of American frontier migrants in the West's early development. Yet this view made little sense to many Ontario residents who journeyed westward and found so much of themselves in an emerging Western Canadian regional patriotism. In a 1940s novel by Morley Callaghan from Toronto, one of the characters, a migrant from New Zealand, had reflected on how "in other Ontario towns and in the West they jeered at Toronto. But he had soon learned that ... the Toronto spirit was a skeleton hidden in their own closets."

In the 1911 federal election, Alberta and Saskatchewan did give more support to Laurier's new Reciprocity Treaty with the United States than any other part of Canada. Manitoba, however, was notably less enthusiastic and British Columbia gave Laurier less support than any other part of Canada — including the Ontario that had embarked on a new urban and industrial future.

Moreover, while Canada-U.S. free trade contradicted Macdonald's particular National Policy, it was not necessarily incompatible with the more general concept of a Canadian national development strategy. And, in any case, support for free trade with the United States was far from confined to Western Canada. The Central Canadian province of Quebec was also a warm Laurier supporter in 1911. The farming majority of the Liberal Oliver Mowat's late nineteenth century Ontario had equally shown strong convictions about the benefits of reciprocity with the United States.

From yet another angle, there were quite exact parallels between Western Canadian agrarian complaints about high tariffs to support industrial interests in Canada, and western American agrarian complaints about high tariffs to support industrial interests in the United States. In both cases the agrarian democracy of the first half of the twentieth century could look back on its predecessors in the nineteenth century. In the late 1920s the Ontario-born radical historian Frank Underhill, in a discussion of Central Canada before Confederation, noted that

> one is constantly being struck in reading the papers of those days by the many points of similarity between the Clear Grit movement amongst the farmers of Upper Canada and the Progressive movement among the prairie farmers today. Both are protests against much the same factors in Canadian life.

Even before the 1930s, there were western leaders and western interests with some sense of how national development policy formulated in Ottawa, however ineptly and prejudicially, had played an important role in the striking growth and prosperity of Western Canada during the first three decades of the century. As early as 1918 the Canadian Council of Agriculture, a forerunner of the Canadian Progressive movement, had proposed a "New National Policy" that included both free trade with the United States and the nationalization of Canadian railways by the Canadian federal government. As W.L. Morton has explained, one stream of the Canadian Progressive Party that arose after the First World War would argue for a new national development strategy, built around the concept of "the metropolitan area assuming, as part of the whole country, the costs of increased benefits to the hinterland areas."

As the 1930s Depression took hold, a related stream, stronger in the West than in any other part of the country, argued for a still broader and more aggressive new national development strategy for all parts of the Confederation. The clearest expression of the theme was the 1933 Regina Manifesto that gave birth to the Co-operative Commonwealth Federation in Saskatchewan. But in the late 1930s and early 1940s, even the right-wing populist Social Credit premier of Alberta, "Bible Bill" Aberhart, was urging Mitch Hepburn, the right-wing (or perhaps left-wing) populist Liberal premier of Ontario, to help organize a new "All-Canada" federal political party that would "get the country moving again."

From these western perspectives, the problem with John A. Macdonald's old National Policy was not that the federal government should avoid any kind of exercise in national development strategy. It was only that the old National Policy was the wrong national policy. The right one would work for all regions, not just for Central Canada.

Up to the 1920s, much of this could be dismissed as not too much more than the radical rhetoric of people who would never be happy about anything — "sons of the wild jackass," according to W.L. MacTavish in an address to the Canadian Club of Toronto in 1932. The crash of the New York stock market in 1929, however, set the stage for a world in which new claims would have to be reckoned with.

There would be as well latent support for these claims even among those whose roots were on the more studiously indifferent shores of the Atlantic

Coast. As early as 1917, Robert Falconer, Maritime-born president of the University of Toronto, had argued:

> Already the west has begun to influence the policy of the east. Things have been done there which of ourselves we might have pronounced premature, if not impossible. In prohibition and woman suffrage they have led the way, and it is not improbable that they will be fertile in political, social and religious experiment and will compel the reluctant east to follow in their steps.

The 1930s Depression and the Rowell-Sirois Report

Back in the real world of practical politics, Mackenzie King's federal regime sustained its one major electoral defeat at the start of the 1930s. For four years the problems of an increasingly grief-struck, regionally fractious Confederation were in the lap of the Conservative R.B. Bennett, an apostle of the Canadian establishment gospel among the unbelievers of Calgary, Alberta.

To cope with the rising tension, Bennett reached out not to the recently emasculated appointed Senate, but to the evolving new institution of the Dominion-Provincial Conference. Four conferences were held during his one term in office — one more than in the entire history of the Dominion up to this point. The first of these dealt with the 1931 imperial Statute of Westminster, which confirmed the Dominion's new status as a completely autonomous member of a new British Commonwealth of Nations. But the other three all focused on the regional and federal-provincial problems of the Depression.

Mackenzie King called another Dominion-Provincial Conference when he returned to power in 1935. After this, it appears he believed that his vaunted political skills would allow the federal executive to resume the management of regional tensions, as a matter of routine business. By 1937, however, Manitoba and Saskatchewan were about to go bankrupt and had appealed to Ottawa for special aid. This convinced King that some longer-term solution was required. He appointed a Royal Commission on Dominion-Provincial Relations, subsequently known as the Rowell-Sirois Commission, after its leading English- and French-speaking members.

(King also quickly bent to pressure for representation on the Commission from all sections of Canada. Rowell was from Ontario, and Sirois from Quebec. But the prime minister who had originally included J.W. Dafoe of the *Winnipeg Free Press* as well, responded to complaints from the Atlantic and Pacific coasts by adding H.F. Angus from the University of British Columbia and R.A. MacKay, (the Ontario-born author of the 1926 book on the unreformed Senate), from Dalhousie University in Halifax.)

The Rowell-Sirois Commission did not finish its work until 1940. It was a magnet for Canada's early local variation on the "new class" of academics, bureaucrats, and media intellectuals that the new industrialism seemed to be spawning everywhere. It commissioned vast amounts of research, reviewed the history of the Confederation since the 1860s, and became a model for several subsequent Ottawa-inspired exercises in addressing major Canadian problems. Its final report, as a commentator of the day put it, filled "32 large red volumes."

Donald Creighton, author of the relevant volume in the standard late twentieth century multi-volume Canadian history, has summarized the thrust of the Rowell-Sirois recommendations:

> The federal government should be granted the exclusive right to personal income, corporation and inheritance taxes, in return for which it was to assume all existing provincial debt, take over certain costly social responsibilities such as unemployment insurance and unemployment relief, and to pay needy provinces a so-called National Adjustment Grant which would enable them to maintain their provincial services at the average Canadian level.

The immediate problem with all this was confirmed at a Dominion-Provincial Conference on the subject called by Mackenzie King in January 1941. The Conference, in Creighton's words, was held at "the Commons Chamber in Ottawa with bitter sub-zero temperatures outside." Even before it began, four provinces had made known their unbending opposition to the Rowell-Sirois philosophy: Quebec, Ontario, Alberta, and British Columbia.

In fact, by January 1941 Maurice Duplessis, the most ardent Quebec opponent, had been temporarily replaced as provincial premier by the less intransigent Joseph-Adélard Godbout. But the mercurial premier of Ontario, Mitch Hepburn, in a kind of neurotic final blaze of the province-building tradition founded by Oliver Mowat, rang the bell for the intransigence of Central Canada — and of the most western parts of Western Canada.

Hepburn remained convinced that the Rowell-Sirois report, the work of "three professors and a Winnipeg newspaperman," was a licence for the federal government at Ottawa to rob the central provinces and then distribute the stolen goods to a hinterland that foolishly wished to live beyond its means. Aberhart in Alberta and Thomas Dufferin Pattullo in British Columbia perhaps sensed that, along with Central Canada, their provinces had the long-term "natural" advantage in the Confederation. Whatever the case, after two days T.B. McQuestern, Hepburn's minister of municipal affairs, rose to announce that Ontario's "association with this so-called conference is over." Moments later the Dominion-Provincial Conference of 1941 came to an abrupt end.

Nonetheless, in 1942 Mackenzie King's federal regime did assume full responsibility for a new national unemployment insurance program. Furthermore, the emergency circumstances of the Second World War prompted King's government, with much provincial co-operation, to play an aggressive, centralizing role in federal-provincial taxation that would not be altogether abandoned when the war ended. By the late 1950s the Rowell-Sirois principle of National Adjustment Grants had become the inspiration for the modern Canadian system of federal-provincial "equalization payments." And by the 1960s another Rowell-Sirois principle — regular federal-provincial conferences — had become a practical reality.

The Commission's recommendations would never be implemented in any systematic way. But they became vital intellectual capital for the generation of federal politicians and bureaucrats who would inherit the mantle of William Lyon Mackenzie King after the Second World War.

The Dominion-Provincial Conference of 1941, House of Commons Chamber, Ottawa — site of the formal rejection of the Rowell-Sirois Commission's work, which would nonetheless echo profoundly over the next three decades.

Mackenzie King is standing, with his back to the camera. Seated around the table, from his left, are Joseph-Adélard Godbout, Quebec; J.B. McNair, New Brunswick; T.D. Pattullo, British Columbia; W.J. Patterson, Saskatchewan; William Aberhart, Alberta; Thane Campbell, Prince Edward Island; John Bracken, Manitoba; A.S. MacMillan, Nova Scotia; and Mitchell Hepburn, Ontario.

The Principle of Abolishing the Senate

Despite its ultimate stress on strengthening the role of the federal govern-ment in the Confederation, the analysis that underpinned the recommenda-tions in the Rowell-Sirois report reflected essentially regionalist, or even radically regionalist conceptions. A contemporary critique by two inde-pendent commentators, S.A. Saunders and Eleanor Back, declared that the

> entire historical discussion found in the Commission's Report rests on a number of assumptions, which, if true, would almost certainly spell the ultimate dissolution of the Cana-dian federation ... It draws its inspiration from the elo-quence and rhetoric of Goldwin Smith, and the ghost of Goldwin Smith still haunts many a Canadian academic cloister.

At its most logical extreme, this thinking presumed that, fundamentally, there was no"natural"reason for the regions of Canada to remain together. Like Smith, and many among the most ideological Western and Atlantic regionalists, the Rowell-Sirois report saw the transcontinental economy of the British Dominion of Canada as an enterprise largely constructed around the artificial device of John A. Macdonald's National Policy, with its protec-tive tariff and expensive east-west transportation system. The trouble with this arrangement was that it benefited the central provinces but not the hin-terland. National Adjustment Grants, distributed by a strong federal gov-ernment at Ottawa, were meant to restore the balance and give the hinter-land regions a real stake in the country.

As the Rowell-Sirois report itself explained, without Macdonald's kind of national development strategy, each of "the separate regions" of Canada

> would have established its principal commercial relations with the external world rather than with the other regions. Traffic, excepting bulky exports for overseas, would have moved north and south. The tariff was designed to direct the demands into Canadian channels so as to provide east-west traffic to help support the vast overhead of the trans-continental railways and to furnish a stimulus to expansion in the older provinces.

On assumptions of this sort, there was no need for a Senate to bring the interests of the regions to bear on national institutions. By definition, the regions had no interests in national institutions that required clarification through political discussion and debate. Canada was no more than an artificial political construct that benefited the metropolitan area of Central Canada but not the hinterlands of Western and Atlantic Canada. All that could be done to keep it together was to forge a new national policy that extended new artificial benefits to the hinterlands.

Harold Innis's rather different conception of Canada's economic geography also brought insights to bear on the relation between the centre and the periphery in the Canadian national economy. His conception of the much more ancient geographic logic of "east-west traffic" in Canada implied more subtle policy prescriptions. (After all, there were also tensions between centres and peripheries in the supposedly more "natural" United States.) In the early 1940s, not long after the failure of the 1941 Dominion-Provincial Conference, Innis observed:

> The complex problems of regionalization in the recent de-
> velopment of Canada render the political structure obsolete
> and necessitate concentration on the problem of machinery
> by which interests can become more vocal and their de-
> mands be met more efficiently .... The danger that bureauc-
> racies, including Royal Commissions, will suggest legisla-
> tion rather than devices by which the demands of interests
> can be reflected and discussed previous to the enactment of
> legislation has been evident ... the political scientist can es-
> cape from the hocus-pocus of the economist and concen-
> trate on the extremely difficult problems of his own field.
> He can best make a contribution to economic development
> by suggested modifications to political machinery.

Had the Canadian academic cloisters that dominated the thinking behind the Rowell-Sirois report been as impressed by Harold Innis as by Goldwin Smith, the Commission might have paid more attention to the potential role of the Canadian Senate in resolving the political and economic problems of Canadian regionalism. But in the 1940s Innis's thinking was still too subtle and too new (as it still sometimes seems to be today). Even his fervent younger admirer Donald Creighton, who had helped out with the voluminous background research to the Royal Commission's deliberations, was more impressed by the final Rowell-Sirois recommendations than a completely profound grasp of the master's thinking would have implied.

Thus, the ultimate logic of the Commission's broader assumptions was that the Senate should probably be abolished, something Goldwin Smith himself had suggested in the late nineteenth century. This was equally a torch that had been taken up by the Canadian Progressive Party of the 1920s and 1930s, and would subsequently be carried by the CCF and its New Democratic successors. For the generation that immediately followed the Second World War, it might even be said, the most progressive view in virtually all partisan political camps increasingly came to be that at some point Canada should come to its senses and simply get rid of its archaic appointed federal Senate.

The Alberta Feminists and the First Person

For his part, the wizard Mackenzie King had no intention of abolishing the Senate. Even without the objections of Ontario, Quebec, Alberta, and British Columbia, he would not have seen the Rowell-Sirois report as any cosmic blueprint for the future. King did not believe in blueprints for the future. As he once explained to a Cabinet colleague, "it was the academic mind which saw only its theory and objective, and the logic, but left the human factor out of consideration which occasioned so much failure in public affairs."

What's more, earlier on, before the troubles that led to the Rowell-Sirois Commission had surfaced in earnest, King had played a part in another sequence of events. In the real world of practical politics, these events were almost entirely symbolic. But they did suggest that the Senate of Canada was an object of interest for instincts that found their most hospitable home in the same Western Canada that did so much to create the Canadian Progressive Party, the CCF, and the NDP.

The short version of the story is that in 1919 Emily Murphy, pioneering magistrate of an innovative Women's Court in Edmonton, began a campaign to have a woman appointed to the Canadian Senate. The objection among certain elements in the national community was that women were not "qualified Persons," as required for such appointments under Section 24 of the British North America Act, 1867. By the late 1920s, Emily Murphy and four other Alberta feminists had managed to have the question put to the Supreme Court of Canada, where they were represented, intriguingly enough, by the same Newton Rowell from Ontario who would later preside over the Rowell-Sirois Commission.

For judicial reasons reaching back to the Constitutional Act, 1791, on 24 April 1928 the Supreme Court actually decided that women were not "Persons," according to the terms of what passed for a Canadian Constitution. On the same day, however, Ernest Lapointe indicated that the federal government would see to it that women could in fact be appointed to the Canadian Senate.

The vehicle ultimately chosen was a federally sponsored appeal to the Judicial Committee of the Privy Council in the United Kingdom. On 18 October 1929 the Privy Council reversed the Supreme Court of Canada's decision, and pronounced the women of Canada persons qualified to serve in the upper house of their country's Parliament.

Picking up the momentum of events on 15 February 1930 Mackenzie King appointed Canada's first woman senator. The woman he appointed was not Emily Murphy of Alberta, as might have been expected, given her long and staunch exertions on the issue. It was Cairine Wilson, a hard-working and politically sensitive matron from the drawing rooms of Montreal and Ottawa, and the prime minister's personal friend. King informed his diary of the reasons for his choice:

Cairine Wilson, Canada's first woman senator, is escorted to her place in the "red chamber" by Raoul Dandurand, leader of the government in the Senate (left), and George Graham, former Liberal cabinet minister (right), 20 February 1930.

> Mrs. Norman Wilson ... has taken a leading part among the women — speaks English & French & is in a position to help the party & will. Was a close friend of Lady Laurier's, is a lady & there will be less jealousy of her than of any other person.

Emily Murphy and the feminists of Alberta were no doubt entitled to feel that, even on a matter so remote from the real levers of national power as this, the Central Canadian establishment was still not prepared to do justice by its Western Canadian brothers and sisters. On the other hand, the appointment also demonstrated that in both Western Canada and the national capital at Ottawa there were those who believed that the Canadian Senate did have a future — of one sort or another. The youthful regional political culture of Alberta had shown that the new world of the Canadian West did have a voice in what this future would involve.

10
LA REVOLUTION TRANQUILLE

In 1947 Harold Innis began a talk to the Royal Society of Canada with a quotation from the philosopher Hegel: "Minerva's owl begins its flight only in the gathering dusk." The point was that it is only possible to understand an era of the past when the era itself has come to an end. On the same principle, we have only begun to understand the generation in Canadian history that started at the end of the Second World War and finished in the 1970s.

As recently as the early 1960s, it was still possible for English-speaking Canadians to believe that the fundamental significance of modern Canada's political identity revolved around the British Commonwealth of Nations, a still noble development of the old British Empire, updated for the second half of the twentieth century. By the early 1980s even the most unreconstructed patriot of the old Dominion knew that this could no longer be true. An official signal had been sent as early as 1971, when the name of the Canadian federal government's central statistical agency was changed from the Dominion Bureau of Statistics to Statistics Canada.

By the late 1980s it was beginning to be possible to see how, during the 1950s, 1960s, and 1970s, the old Dominion of Canada had been transformed into a new Canadian Confederation, in some respects similar to such other new countries of the late twentieth century as India, Ghana, Nigeria, Kenya, Malaysia, Sri Lanka, or Zimbabwe.

Like all these places, Canada remains a member of a still more recently updated Commonwealth of Nations, with the "British" prefix now removed. In at least one sense, the new Confederation also retains, like Australia and New Zealand, the symbolic form of a constitutional monarchy. According to the current doctrine, however, it is technically an accident that the Queen of Canada happens to be the same person as the Queen of the United Kingdom.

By the 1980s Canada had also become part of a new international organization known as la Francophonie. But the crux of Canadian political identity in the late twentieth century is centred on something quite different from historic ties to any part of the Old World. At bottom, as Pierre Trudeau explained in the early 1960s, "the foundation of the nation is will."

Given the deepest roots of Canada's diverse destiny, it is no surprise that this transformation was begun by the first people who called themselves Canadians, in the predominantly French-speaking province on the banks of the lower St. Lawrence River. It is equally no surprise that it ended with fresh claims by the first peoples who occupied the ancient territory of the Confederation, and with new demands from the people who now occupy those regions not included in the original United Province of Canada.

The Wizard's Last Testament

One key connection between the old Dominion and the new Confederation is the career of William Lyon Mackenzie King. He retired as prime minister on 15 November 1948, and then passed into what he believed would be another version of the world on earth on 22 July 1950. Yet with his customary wizardry, he had grasped something of what lay ahead for Canada after the Second World War. Though he did not believe in blueprints for the future, in his last years in power he did what he could to erect a suitably flexible framework for change.

During his final election campaign in 1945, King promised that Canada would have its own distinctive national flag. After the election it became clear that the highly diverse Confederation was still very divided on this subject. The promise would not be redeemed by Mackenzie King's Liberal successors until 1965. Here as elsewhere, however, he had made a start.

In 1947 the Parliament of Canada passed the Canadian Citizenship Act. This was, in the words of the 1988 edition of the *Canada Year Book*, "the first independent naturalization law to be enacted in the Commonwealth." For the first time in Canadian history, it "created the status of a Canadian citizen as distinct from that of a British subject," or, for that matter, as distinct from the status of a subject of the King of France.

In 1948 Mackenzie King decided against proceeding with negotiations for a new Canadian-American free trade agreement. His reason could not have been that he opposed the principle of Canada-U.S. free trade. He had supported Laurier's failed Reciprocity Treaty of 1911 and had negotiated his own tariff-reduction agreements with Washington in the later 1930s. In some Canadian circles, he was reviled for his commitments to the North American continental economy.

In one of the flashes of intuition he valued so highly, however, Mackenzie King may have grasped that the period after the Second World War was the wrong time to begin new economic arrangements with the colossus to the south. As the new Confederation at last began to draw away from its old mother country in the United Kingdom, it did not want to fall into the lap of a new mother country in the United States, which had itself suddenly become the strongest international power of the postwar world.

King also managed to exert decisive influence over the choice of his successor as leader of the Liberal Party and prime minister of Canada. He pointed to Louis St. Laurent, who had filled in as French Canadian lieutenant after the death of Ernest Lapointe in 1941. A Liberal Party convention in 1948 confirmed the choice, and the Canadian electorate seconded the motion at a federal election in 1949. Whatever weaknesses the new St. Laurent regime would prove to have, it was wise, as King understood, for a French Canadian to lead Canada into the second half of the twentieth century.

Before he retired, Mackenzie King himself began the negotiations that would at long last bring Newfoundland into the Confederation in 1949. In the same year, the Supreme Court of Canada became the final Canadian court of appeal. The era of ultimate supervision by the Judicial Committee of the Privy Council in the United Kingdom had come to an end.

Now Canada was constitutionally dependent on the United Kingdom only for amendments to the British North America Act, 1867, which did not deal strictly with the operations of the federal government. This was only because Canadian federal and provincial governments could still not agree on how to amend what had become the principal "written" part of Canada's Constitution — a question first raised at Mackenzie King's Dominion-Provincial Conference of 1927. Louis St. Laurent's government held two federal-provincial conferences on constitutional amendment in 1950. But it would be another generation before the issue was finally resolved, under another French Canadian prime minister, and even then without the assent of the province of Quebec.

In 1951 St. Laurent's government gave the federal Indian Act its first major revision since the early Confederation era of the late nineteenth century — partly in response to early stirrings among the first peoples of the Confederation that would reach a new high point a generation later, in the early 1980s.

In 1952 Louis St. Laurent appointed Vincent Massey the first Canadian-born governor general of Canada. As confirmed by the Statute of Westminster in 1931, Canadian prime ministers had acquired decisive control over the appointment of the governor general by the late 1920s. Yet even Canadian prime ministers had continued to choose British aristocrats to fill the office. With Massey's appointment, Field Marshal The Viscount Alexander of Tunis, chosen by King in 1946, became the last of the breed. From then on, the governors general of Canada would not merely be appointed by Canadians. They would be Canadians themselves.

Prelude to the Quiet Revolution in Quebec

Since the middle of the nineteenth century there had been nativist strains in Ontario that were no doubt encouraged by Mackenzie King's promise of a distinctive Canadian national flag in 1945. By the early twentieth century, similar elements had set down their own regional roots in Western Canada. As the middle of the twentieth century drew within sight, even a few among the people of the ancient cod fisheries on the Atlantic Coast found the concept of a national flag attractive.

King's 1945 flag proposal, however, had been particularly addressed to the first people who had called themselves Canadians, in the predominantly French-speaking province of Quebec. Ever since Confederation, there had been a side to Quebec that looked on the British Dominion of Canada with profound scepticism. It believed that the final destiny of the French-speaking people in the St. Lawrence Valley was to create a French national state in North America.

Modern Canada's long apprenticeship as little more than an elevated colony of the British Empire had dampened Quebec's extreme nationalist aspiration — which was also the extreme expression of Canadian regional-

The funeral procession of Ernest Lapointe, Quebec City, 29 November 1941.

Lapointe had personified the French Canadian side of Mackenzie King's federal regime. And King's mystical depths were profoundly stirred by the numbers who turned out in Quebec City to watch this particular procession. There had never been, he later told his diary, "at any funeral in Canada heretofore, not excepting Sir Wilfrid's or Sir John Macdonald's ... a larger number of people gathered .... I felt as we walked along how much one owes it to be true to the people ... in the march, I turned to Crerar who was just behind me and said: 'Truly Canada has become a nation.'"

ism inside the Confederation. The ideological marriage of convenience between the Roman Catholic Church in Quebec and the British Empire in Canada, dating back to the Quebec Act, 1774, had intensified the effect.

When Canada began its drift away from the Empire, even in the 1920s, 1930s, and 1940s, the dampening effect began to lift. In Quebec itself, a parallel drift away from the Roman Catholic Church began, and this would reach a point of crisis in the 1960s. In 1950 Pierre Trudeau's colleague Gérard Pelletier tells us, "the Quebec clergy was still all powerful; by 1960 it would be in full flight."

The waning of both the Empire and the Church had begun during the new industrialism after the American Civil War, or what Innis had called the shift from commercialism to capitalism. In one way or another, these trends affected all parts of the old Dominion of Canada. Yet, when set beside the particular political and cultural circumstances of the French Catholic majority in the St. Lawrence Valley, they brought unique consequences to the regional politics of Quebec. These consequences led to what journalists would christen "la révolution tranquille", signalled by the election of the Liberal Jean Lesage as premier of Quebec in 1960. The Quiet Revolution, however, had a long prelude, and it would ultimately point in more noisy directions. The prelude had begun with the election of Maurice Duplessis as premier of Quebec in 1936.

Duplessis was the leader of the Union Nationale, the most successful of several Quebec political movements that arose in the generation between 1920 and 1950. His approach to the new social and economic forces of the century was two-sided. On the one hand, he supported those who could bring economic development to his province: the old British Canadian merchants of Montreal, even the upstart English-speaking merchants of Toronto, and the new American merchants of multinational capitalism. On the other, he intransigently stood up for the traditional French Catholic society of Quebec, dominated by a Roman Catholic clerical hierarchy, a petit-bourgeois professional class, and the ancient ethos of the habitant agricultural community.

"Le Chef," as he would subsequently be nicknamed, cooled his heels in opposition during the early 1940s, while the Liberal Joseph-Adélard Godbout served as premier — or "prime minister," as the head of the provincial government was known, in French in Quebec and, frequently, in English in Ontario as well.

Like his crony, Mitch Hepburn, premier of Ontario in the late 1930s and early 1940s, Maurice Duplessis was an apostle of provincial autonomy. (There are some provocative, awkward 1930s photographs still extant of Duplessis and Hepburn together at a birthday party for the Ontario premier on the Hepburn 1200-acre family farm in southwestern Ontario.) Unlike Hepburn, Duplessis opposed Canadian involvement in the Second World War. Thus, Mackenzie King's federal Liberals had worked hard to help Godbout become premier for the difficult era of wartime centralization. But le Chef returned to power in 1944. There he would remain, without interruption, until his death in 1959.

Duplessis stood for what the contemporary historian Michael D. Behiels has called an "ideology of conservative, clerical nationalism." An expanding struggle against this ideology, led by Quebec's variation on the same new class that had elsewhere been drawn to the Rowell-Sirois Commission, tilled the soil that nourished the Quiet Revolution that would blossom in the 1960s.

Yet Duplessis's sheer capacity to win elections and remain in power until his death testifies to his continuing popularity among large sections of the Quebec population — even allowing for the robust patronage and routine corruption with which critics in both French and English have traditionally branded his regime. In 1948 he introduced a Quebec national flag: a white cross on a light blue background, surrounded by the lilies of old France. This would serve as a banner for the neo-nationalist regional independence movement that would crystallize radical new demands about Quebec's place in Canada during the 1970s.

From the Quiet Revolution to the Parti Québécois

Inside Quebec, the legendary first campaign in the struggle against Duplessis took place during a five-month strike in the small mining town of Asbestos, beginning in February 1949. This brought together, the journalist Gérard Pelletier, the labour organizer Jean Marchand, and the independently wealthy lawyer and intellectual gadfly Pierre Trudeau.

The new mass communications technology of television played an important role in what followed. Radio-Canada, the French-speaking arm of the publicly owned Canadian Broadcasting Corporation (established by the Conservative R.B. Bennett's government in the the first half of the 1930s) began television broadcasts in 1952. As Pelletier tells the story, for the only French-speaking television network in North America "televised debates ... soon became very popular," especially since "this kind of programming was inexpensive."

Following French and English population distributions in the country at large, Radio-Canada's stations were overwhelmingly concentrated in Quebec. René Lévesque, the subsequent inventor of "sovereignty-association," and the ultimate leader of mainstream Quebec separatism, won his first popular following as a television journalist and rising star of such programs as "Conférence de presse" and "Point de mire."

In 1960 Lévesque became minister of natural resources in Jean Lesage's new provincial Cabinet. At this point he was still seeking outside advice from Pelletier, Marchand, and Trudeau. The goal of Lesage's quiet revolutionaries was to preside over Quebec's transformation from a traditional "sacralized" to a more modern secular society that would respect the pluralism and democracy Duplessis had denied.

One part of the initial agenda was to take the traditional educational and social welfare functions of a rigorously conservative Catholic hierarchy and place them in the hands of a new, progressive provincial government. Another part was to use the provincial government to further economic ends, in ways already familiar in other Canadian provinces.

Lévesque's key achievement as minister of natural resources was to bring Quebec's hydroelectric system under public ownership. As he explained to Pelletier, Marchand, and Trudeau in a Montreal restaurant, "If Ontario could nationalize in 1907 or 1912, whenever it was, Quebec can surely do it in 1962 or '63." (In fact, a Conservative provincial government had created Ontario's publicly owned Hydro-Electric Power Commission in 1906.)

As it happened, however, this was only the beginning of events that would finally resound throughout the wider Confederation. From their place in an emerging new social structure, the quiet revolutionaries of Quebec in the 1960s did have much in common with the creators of the Rowell-Sirois report in the Canada of the late 1930s. Even though the report would never be implemented in any systematic way, it remained the decisive intellectual capital for Canadian federal-provincial relations after the Second World War. Yet, despite the formal bow to Sirois, as the Quiet Revolution developed, it became painfully clear that the Rowell-Sirois approach to the problems of Canadian regionalism could not appeal to the transforming French Canadian society of Quebec.

The Rowell-Sirois principle of a more genuinely national federal government, from ocean to ocean, strong enough to resist the regionalism of Central Canada, had already raised the ire of Duplessis in the late 1930s and early 1940s. It was an encroachment on the traditional provincial autonomy of Quebec — something that the quiet revolutionaries were equally concerned to defend.

In the 1950s even Trudeau had supported Duplessis's opposition to federal grants to universities, on the grounds that they interfered with the provinces' constitutional authority over education. As one version or another of the Rowell-Sirois principles increasingly came to figure in the federal-provincial financial negotiations of the 1950s and 1960s, Ottawa and Quebec City increasingly found themselves in conflict.

The quiet revolutionaries had two particular concerns, shared by no other province to any remotely comparable degree of intensity, (though New Brunswick, most successful modern refuge of the ancient Acadians, did have some parallel interests). The first was the promotion of the French language, which trends after the Second World War were placing under stress, not just in Canada or North America, but in the world at large. The second was a gradually emerging, more diffuse quest to make the French Canadians of Quebec "maîtres chez nous." The ultimate meaning of the phrase was French Canadian control of the Quebec regional economy, dominated since the late eighteenth century by the British Canadian merchants of Montreal.

For these purposes, Quebec needed a provincial government quite different from the kind of provincial governments assumed by the Rowell-Sirois report. One wing of the Quiet Revolution continued to believe that this could still be achieved within the existing wider framework of Canadian federalism. Another wing, for which René Lévesque would finally become the leading spokesman, grew increasingly convinced that the historic structure of the Confederation could never truly accommodate the aspirations of the new Quebec.

By 1968 Lévesque had left the Quebec Liberal Party to form the Parti Québécois (PQ) around the demand for sovereignty-association — a radical and even separatist definition of Quebec's relationship with the rest of Canada. The Parti Québécois helped legitimize less polite strains of Quebec separatism, which drew on ancient themes of French Canadian nationalism and had a lunatic fringe (not at all supported by Lévesque) that kidnapped the British diplomat James Cross and assassinated the Quebec labour minister, Pierre Laporte.

The PQ effectively mobilized primeval French Canadian grievances against the historic regime of la Conquête in British North America. It became the political arm of a much broader cultural movement, which transformed many old Canadiens into new Québécois, in an aspiring new nation of Quebec. And when René Lévesque won the Quebec provincial election of 1976, it was unmistakably clear that the diverse destiny in the northern half of North America had reached a point of high crisis.

O Trudeau

Lévesque and the Parti Québécois stood for one definition of Quebec society, with deep roots in the past and an increasingly undeniable place of some sort in the future of the Confederation. Yet the victory of the "Non" side in the 1980 Quebec referendum on sovereignty-association implied that this was not the only definition of French Canada.

In the tradition of La Vérendrye and the transcontinental fur trade, and of Louis Hippolyte LaFontaine, George-Etienne Cartier, Wilfrid Laurier, Henri Bourassa, Ernest Lapointe, and even Louis St. Laurent, there was also a French-speaking Quebec that looked beyond the banks of the lower St. Lawrence River — at least as far as the Canadian national capital at Ottawa.

Similarly, there were two sides to the traditional "English Canada." One had hanged Louis Riel, repealed Manitoba's French language rights, passed assorted Manitoba Schools Acts in the 1890s, repressed French-language education elsewhere in the West and in Ontario, reminded French Canadians that they were a "conquered people" in the Maritimes, and conscripted isolationist North American sons of the ancient habitants in 1917 and 1944 for imperial wars in Europe. The other side, an English-speaking Canadian nativist sentiment, from ocean to ocean, increasingly appreciated how the French, and even the Indians, had pioneered the country's diverse destiny.

At least as a matter of hard pragmatism, this English-speaking Canadian nativism equally understood that embracing the deepest roots of the diverse destiny with a new conviction was crucial to keeping the modern Confederation together after the now inexorable fall of the British Empire. Since the age of Wilfrid Laurier, it had found its strongest national political home in the federal Liberal Party, honed to a fine and subtle instrument by the wizard

Mackenzie King and his indispensable French Canadian lieutenant Ernest Lapointe in the 1920s, 1930s, and 1940s.

The Conservatives under John Diefenbaker, the populist "Chief" from Saskatchewan, defeated St. Laurent's extension of King's Liberal regime in 1957 — signalling another quiet revolution in other parts of the country, one that would finally find its focus in a new debate on Senate reform. But, somewhat like the Red Tory George Grant who had great empathy for Diefenbaker's plight, the Chief could only grieve over the waning of the Empire and of the particular exotic brand of English Canadian nationalism it had sustained.

The Liberals returned to power in 1963 under Lester Pearson, an Ontario-born former Canadian diplomat who had won the Nobel Peace Prize for his international role in resolving the Suez Crisis of 1956. Pearson had been a favoured young bureaucrat under the long regime of Mackenzie King in Ottawa, where he had learned about the importance of Quebec in Canada. In a spirit of moderation, compromise, and regional accommodation, his regime carried on with the development of at least a version of the Canadian federal-provincial welfare state envisioned by the Rowell-Sirois Commission. Yet the Pearson government also appointed a new Royal Commission for the 1960s, on "Bilingualism and Biculturalism." In 1965 it at last delivered on Mackenzie King's promise of a distinctive Canadian national flag. (In 1967 "O Canada!", composed by the French Canadian Calixa Lavallée in 1880, was approved by Parliament as a Canadian national anthem, though it would not be adopted officially until the National Anthem Act of June 1980.)

In 1965 Pearson convinced Gérard Pelletier, Jean Marchand, and Pierre Trudeau, the "three wise men" from the side of la révolution tranquille that still believed in Canadian federalism, to join his government at Ottawa. In April 1968 "Mike" Pearson retired, and Pierre Trudeau was elected leader of the federal Liberal Party. His resulting status as prime minister was confirmed by the people of Canada in a June election, dominated by "Trudeaumania." It seemed that the diverse destiny, a mari usque ad mare, at last had the leadership it needed, to survive the challenge of Quebec separatism. Through many trials and tribulations, and with the exception of nine months in 1979 and 1980, Trudeau would remain in power until 1984.

We are still too close to Trudeau's more than 15 years as prime minister of Canada to understand their deepest long-term significance. What can be said is that, even for brilliant politicians, democratic politics is in the end a learning experience. No political leader in a democracy can genuinely impose an abstract design on events.

It is equally true that in a country as diverse and varied as the modern Canadian Confederation, no one leader can have a vision that integrates all parts of the nation. Despite his world travels and cosmopolitan education, Trudeau's grasp of and empathy for what was actually on the ground in Canada grew progressively weaker as one moved progressively west of the Ottawa River.

Yet, while Mackenzie King might be said to have succeeded where Trudeau failed in this respect, the complaint about King was that he had no vision at all. In a way that was rare or even unique among Canadian politicians of his or any other era, Trudeau did bring a vision to his leadership of Canada at a time when this was sorely needed. Gérard Pelletier has reported that as early as the 1940s, Trudeau was in the midst of "a highly personal search for a political line of thought appropriate to the Canadian situation." Even among his fellow future quiet revolutionaries inside Quebec, at that point Trudeau was "the only one to have already begun reflecting on the evolution of politics in Quebec and Canada."

The vision was challenging (and, as time would eventually show, it had utopian overtones). Trudeau would ask English-speaking Canadians to be Canadians before they spoke English, and French-speaking Canadians to be Canadians before they spoke French. It was also his regime that declared Canada a "multicultural" country, and asked the increasing numbers of Canadians of neither English nor French-speaking descent to respect the heritages of those who were. In the end Trudeau would even ask the Indians, Inuit, and Métis to acknowledge that they too were Canadians.

Trudeau believed in a strong federal government for Canada, but he also believed in strong provincial governments. He was an opponent of Quebec separatism, but the price of his opposition was an officially bilingual federal government, from the Atlantic to the Pacific to the Arctic Oceans. Even at the provincial level, one of his last unsuccessful crusades was for official bilin-

Pierre Trudeau, on the left, confers with Jean Marchand.

gualism in Ontario. Trudeau declared that "the foundation of the nation is will," but he had no more use for a parochial Canadian nationalism than he had for a parochial Quebec nationalism.

Even inside his native province of Quebec, Trudeau was highly unusual. His background as the son of a wealthy French Canadian businessman was rare for his generation, because French Canadian businessmen were so rare. (Ironically, one of the seminal practical achievements of Trudeau's Quebec separatist opponents would be to create the conditions for making this kind of background much less rare in the future.) In Canada at large, Trudeau's background as the son of a wealthy businessman who was also a cosmopolitan French and even English intellectual, was rarer still.

Trudeau himself could not be, as he sometimes seemed to imagine, a model for individual Canadian aspirations for the future. It could be said that he left almost as many new problems as he solved. His two undeniable Canadian national achievements, however, were to turn aside the challenge of Quebec separatism in the late 1970s and early 1980s, and at last to achieve enough federal-provincial consensus on a constitutional amending formula to permit the final "patriation" of Canada's Constitution from the United Kingdom.

It is clear at the edge of the 1990s that he did not conclusively resolve the problem of Quebec separatism once and for all. But who can say what might have happened if Pierre Trudeau had not been prime minister of Canada in the early 1980s? Similarly, although patriating the Constitution was only a bare beginning for coming to grips with the constitutional dilemmas of Canada in the twenty-first century, it was something no one else, including Mackenzie King, had been able to do through more than half a century of vain effort. Whatever else, under Pierre Trudeau, the diverse Canadian Confederation survived the death of the British Empire in the late twentieth century intact. At some point between 1968 and 1984, the old cocoon of the Dominion of Canada had been shed forever, and the post-colonial future of a new Canadian federation had finally begun.

11

THE NEW WEST

It has been bemoaned often enough that Canada, unlike the United States, is a country without heroes. Like so much else in the place, this too can be attributed to its vast diversity and abiding regionalism.

In one way or another, a national hero personifies some central image of the nation. Yet in Canada acceptance of pluralism and democracy means that there is no central image of the nation. As George-Etienne Cartier declared in 1865, "diversity is the order of the physical, moral, and political world." The most vital element in Canada's diverse destiny, the Anglo-American economist Kenneth Boulding quipped in 1977, is that "anything can exist."

Thus, at Trudeau's last election, in February 1980, his federal Liberal Party won five of the seven seats in Newfoundland, two of the four seats in P.E.I., five of the 11 seats in Nova Scotia, and seven of the ten seats in New Brunswick. It won 74 of the 75 seats in Quebec, and 52 of the 95 seats in Ontario. But it won only two of the 16 seats in Manitoba, and no seats at all in Saskatchewan, Alberta, British Columbia, and the territories.

This was not an altogether unprecedented situation for the historic Canadian federal governing party in the first three-quarters of the twentieth century. When Mackenzie King narrowly won his inaugural election as prime minister, in December 1921, the Liberals had garnered 16 of the 16 seats in Nova Scotia, five of the 11 seats in New Brunswick, and four of the four seats in Prince Edward Island. They had taken all 65 of the 65 seats in Quebec, and 21 of the 82 seats in Ontario. But they had won only one of the 15 seats in Manitoba, only one of the 16 seats in Saskatchewan, three of the 13 seats in British Columbia, and none at all in Alberta and the territories.

In Western Canada and, to a lesser extent, even in that part of Ontario that was a kind of precursor to Western Canada, the federal electoral victories of 1921 had gone not to the Conservative heirs of John A. Macdonald and Robert Borden, but to a new Canadian Progressive Party. Mackenzie King shrewdly viewed the Progressives as "a sort of advanced Liberal group" and gradually co-opted many among them into a new national dispensation. By the federal election of 1935, King's Liberal supporters had managed to win 37, or some 52%, of the 71 seats in Western Canada.

During Trudeau's regime the New Democrats had come to play a role in the West similar to that of the Progressives during the early years of Mackenzie King. After the federal election of 1972, Trudeau governed for two years through what amounted to an informal alliance with the NDP. Yet, toward the end of his career as prime minister, when journalists pressed him on the reasons for his continuing lack of support west of Ontario, he did not pretend to have an answer.

In fact, during the long focusing of the Canadian national agenda on the agony of Quebec in the Confederation, Western Canada grew increasingly preoccupied with its own alienation from the federal government at Ottawa. But that, according to Trudeau, was not something he could do anything about. It was a problem for someone else, someone who understood the issue from the inside in the way that Trudeau himself understood *Federalism and the French Canadians*, the title of a book of his essays published in English in 1968.

The difficulty was not that Trudeau lacked an intellectual awareness of Canada's historic regionalism outside Quebec. He had read the Rowell-Sirois report. On the emotional issue of John A. Macdonald's old National Policy, he even agreed that, as he wrote in 1965, "in the past, Canadian tariff regulations have on the whole worked against the West and the Maritimes." In 1973, when three of the four western provinces were under NDP governments, he convened a Western Economic Opportunities Conference at Calgary, to explore "potentials for economic and social development and specifically, to consider concrete programs for stimulating and broadening the economic and industrial base of western Canada."

As Trudeau's own ultimate response to western grievances implied, the crucial problem was more visceral. In 1962 he informed readers of *Cité libre*, an influential organ of the early Quiet Revolution in Quebec: "I have no intention of closing my eyes to how much Canadians of British origin have to do — or rather, undo — before a pluralist state can become a reality in Canada. But I am inclined to add that that is their problem."

Like many French Canadians from Quebec, Pierre Elliott Trudeau, when he listened to what he once called "the fire in your belly," tended to see "English Canada" as an essentially monolithic opposing force. The fundamental point about the Confederation was its French and English "dualism" (though Trudeau has stressed that he himself prefers the term "bilingualism"). He also wrote in 1962:

> The die is cast in Canada: there are two main ethnic and linguistic groups; each is too strong and too deeply rooted in the past, too firmly bound to a mother-culture, to be able to engulf the other. But if the two will collaborate at the hub of a truly pluralistic state, Canada could become the envied seat of a form of federalism that belongs to tomorrow's world.

To the archetypal Western Canadian, however, there were indeed two fundamental parts to Canada, but the dualism was geographic, not linguistic. At bottom, the country was divided into Western Canada and Eastern Canada. To the most rigorous exponents of the philosophy, French and English dualism, or bilingualism — or whatever it was — was largely an Eastern Canadian affair.

A related trouble at the visceral level was that, again like many French Canadians from Quebec, Trudeau tended to see the West as the place that had hanged the French Catholic Louis Riel in the 1880s — and the place where "English-speaking Canadians ... quashed bilingualism in the Manitoba legislature" in 1890. The fundamental point about the role of the West in the new Confederation for French Canadians was that it should become more open to Canada's French fact, whose history in the West stretched back to La Vérendrye's journey to the Rocky Mountains in the 1740s.

To Western Canada, there were far more fundamental points about its role in the Confederation than this. The modern region did have many people whose backgrounds were not "British," or even "English." But in 1961 the strictly "French" population was less than 1% in all western provinces. Even the bilingual "French and English" population amounted to only 7.4% in Manitoba, 4.5% in Saskatchewan, 4.3% in Alberta, and 3.5% in British Columbia. (By 1986, on the other hand, the bilingual numbers had increased to, respectively, 8.8, 4.7, 6.4 and 6.2%. And there still were more Indian and Métis heirs of the ancient fur trade in the West than in any other part of the Confederation — something that Trudeau himself especially seemed to begin to appreciate during his last years in power.)

What's more, like the Quebec of the Quiet Revolution, Western Canada too was changing, borne along by the continuing wider evolution of twentieth century industrialism. In the end it too would develop its own doubts about the Rowell-Sirois solution to the problems of Canadian regionalism, already opposed by British Columbia and Alberta in the early 1940s. It would even develop its own version of separatism.

English-speaking Canada may have seemed monolithic to the French-speaking quiet revolutionaries — at best made up of minor variations on the same bland "Anglo-Canadian" theme that, as Trudeau once suggested, "has never had much of an edge." But such appearances were deceiving. Times were changing everywhere. Quebec may have begun the transformation from the old Dominion to the new Confederation, but it could not finish everything that had to be done by itself.

From the Last Best to the New West

One fundamental change in Western Canada after the Second World War was that its economic centre of gravity moved west. The "Last Best West" of the early twentieth century had been dominated by Saskatchewan and Manitoba, and its largest city was Winnipeg, in a cold climate that looked out on the flat grandeur of the open prairie. The "New West" of the late twentieth century would be dominated by British Columbia and Alberta. Its largest city would be Vancouver, set among the mountains in the lotus land of the Pacific Northwest Coast.

Even in 1941 Saskatchewan was still the most populous province in Western Canada, and the third largest in all the Confederation. But by this time both Alberta and British Columbia were larger than Manitoba, and Vancouver had already replaced Winnipeg as Canada's third-largest city in

1931. By 1951 British Columbia had replaced Saskatchewan as Canada's third-largest province, and there were more people in Alberta than in either Saskatchewan or Manitoba.

These changes in population statistics reflected deeper changes afoot in the regional economic base. The wheat economy had dominated the Last Best West of Manitoba and Saskatchewan. The New West of Alberta and British Columbia would still have a regional economy dominated by natural resources, but the western resource sector became increasingly more diversified.

Insofar as there was a successor to wheat as a symbol of a new western economic dynamism, it was oil and natural gas. And, like the old wheat economy, the new oil economy revived an earlier era in the history of Central Canada. *Canadian Economic History*, a standard text of the 1950s by W.T. Easterbrook of the University of Toronto and Hugh G. J. Aitken of the University of California, explained:

> It is sometimes forgotten that the first producing oil well in the American continent was drilled in Canada — in Lambton County, Ontario, in 1858 — and that the oil-fields in the southwestern peninsula of Ontario, between Lake Huron and Lake Erie, were successfully exploited throughout most of the second half of the nineteenth century.

This old oil country in southwestern Ontario was also the birthplace of Imperial Oil, a Canadian enterprise inspired by Macdonald's old National Policy. And it was Imperial Oil that discovered the Leduc oil field near Edmonton in 1947, the event customarily said to have begun the Western Canadian oil boom in the second half of the twentieth century. The Leduc field, as Easterbrook and Aitken related, "was found to lie in a type of geological formation — a Devonian coral reef — very similar to the formations in the West Texas and New Mexico oil-fields, with which American oil companies were already very familiar." In an era when the superhighway and the automobile increasingly superseded the railway throughout North America, the Western Canadian oil boom would increasingly be presided over by multinational corporations headquartered in the United States. Imperial Oil in Toronto would come to be 70% owned by Exxon in New York. (There is a parallel of sorts to this modern continentalism, in the wave of Anglo-American wheat farmers who had driven the last covered wagons into Western Canada during the early twentieth century. There was equally a somewhat different sort of parallel, in the Canadian automobile industry, concentrated in Ontario and, by the Second World War, more or less completely dominated by branch enterprises of American multinational corporations.)

Oil, or gas, or both were eventually discovered in all four provinces of Western Canada, as well as the northern territories. But the oil boom would be centred in Alberta. An increasingly diversified grain-growing economy

There's everything to see in the

CANADIAN

WEST...

MAJESTIC MOUNT ROBSON, *tallest peak in the Canadian Rockies, soars 12,972 feet into the clouds.*

Canadian National will take you there!

You don't know Canada until you've visited the West... There's something to see every minute...and your way there is as pleasant as your stay there when you travel Canadian National. It's a fascinating journey on the Continental Limited in smart modern equipment and a friendly relaxing atmosphere.

What would you like in a vacation?...For a lakeland background, choose Minaki...Cities...visit Winnipeg, Saskatoon, Edmonton, Vancouver, Victoria, Prince Rupert...Mountains... Jasper, Maligne Lake, Mount Robson.

You'll enjoy Canadian National hospitality in gracious resort hotels, Jasper Park Lodge, Minaki Lodge, and in all-year hotels at cities en route. Regular sailings of Canadian National's S.S. Prince George from Vancouver to Alaska.

Visit any Canadian National ticket office or Travel Agent and plan that western vacation *now.*

FOR ANY GIFT OCCASION

Canadian National now offers an attractive Gift Certificate covering Train Travel anywhere...to any rail destination...for any amount you wish...on sale at all Canadian National ticket offices. Easy to buy, easy to use. A gift that's sure to please.

CANADIAN NATIONAL

THE ONLY RAILWAY SERVING ALL TEN PROVINCES

An early 1950s print media ad run by the Canadian National Railways, whose passenger services would be taken over by Via Rail in the 1970s. At some point during this period the phrase "Canadian West" would be rendered virtually obsolete by the phrase "Western Canada" — a subtle but significant enough difference.

remained important in Saskatchewan and Manitoba, and even parts of Alberta. The postwar boom in British Columbia continued to lean on forestry and mining, which were important in some other parts of the West, and on Vancouver's growing eminence as a Pacific seaport in North America.

British Columbia also benefited from a growing wider realization that Vancouver, once a home to Diamond Jenness's exotic tribes of the Pacific Coast, was easily the most physically beautiful city in all of Canada, or even all of North America. In the late 1940s the Vancouverite Eric Nicol had complained about "the common belief," even among "some Eastern Canadians," that "British Columbia is a steaming colony in the heart of the South American jungle," with "a tattered Union Jack fluttering over a few square miles of monkeys and malaria." But by the 1980s even many Eastern Canadians had migrated to Vancouver. On national television in the United States, the former Vancouverite Michael J. Fox — a star of the Hollywood TV series "Family Ties" — diplomatically explained that the city where his own family still lived was certainly not a place that anyone would ever want to leave.

Innovation in the Old Culture of Saskatchewan and Manitoba

In the 1940s George Orwell, living in the old British Canadian mother country of the United Kingdom, had drawn attention to the "slowness of historical change, the fact that any epoch always contains a great deal of the last epoch." In real history, "abrupt transitions don't happen .... Each age lives on into the next." In Canada itself the West of the 1950s, 1960s, and 1970s was increasingly dominated by Alberta and British Columbia. But the West that had been dominated by Manitoba and Saskatchewan in the 1920s, 1930s, and 1940s did anything but disappear.

From the late 1940s, to the early 1960s, for instance, Saskatchewan, site of the most dramatic chapter in the story of western drought and the Great Depression, also became the site of what the Prairie journalist Robert Tyre would call "the first experiment in Socialism on the North American continent."

In 1944 the Co-operative Commonwealth Federation, under T.C. "Tommy" Douglas, acquired command of the Saskatchewan provincial government — in a wartime surge of popular support for the CCF that also affected Ontario and other parts of the West. (There were, as well, metropolitan analogues in the British Labour Party's 1945 defeat of Winston Churchill in the United Kingdom, and in Harry Truman's surprise 1948 presidential victory in the United States.) Douglas would remain premier of Saskatchewan until 1961, when he resigned to become leader of the federal wing of the CCF's successor, the New Democratic Party. And the "agrarian socialists" of Saskatchewan would remain in power until 1964.

As it happened, the socialist experiment was not as dramatic as some had feared and others had hoped. A serious beginning to any real assault on the citadel of New World capitalism, the radical theorists of the CCF came to believe, would require command of at least the Canadian federal government in Ottawa — not one mere hinterland province, still recovering from an especially intense regional dose of the ravages of the 1930s.

By the time the CCF had reincarnated itself as the NDP in the early 1960s, all its mainstream wanted to be was a North American variation on the "social democratic" (or "democratic socialist") political parties of postwar Western Europe. Much of what the Douglas regime's critics in Saskatchewan most often complained about — such as a dramatic expansion in the size of the provincial public sector — also took place, to one degree or another, in all other Canadian provinces and even in the states of the American Union.

All the same, in at least North America, the 20-year CCF/NDP regime in Saskatchewan was at the leading edge of the international postwar trend toward government intervention in social and economic life. In Canada it spawned innovations that would be models for government programs in other provinces and in the Confederation at large. By the end of the 1960s, a public health insurance and ultimately complete "medicare" program, which began in Saskatchewan, had spread across the country, part of a complicated version of the federal-provincial structure envisioned by the Rowell-Sirois Commission.

Douglas's successor as Saskatchewan's NDP premier, Woodrow Lloyd, was defeated by the Liberal Ross Thatcher in 1964. This convinced some opponents of the socialist experiment that the pioneering CCF regime had been held together only by the political magic of "the spellbinder" Tommy Douglas — a blend of Anglo-American populist wit and the Scottish poetry of Robert Burns. (Douglas, like John A. Macdonald and William Lyon Mackenzie, had been born in Scotland, an asset in a still somewhat colonial political culture of the British Empire where "British" had acquired overtones of Celtic dominance distinctly not present in the mother country. The frequency with which the spellbinder presided over the opening of new blessings for the people of Saskatchewan prompted the story of the Regina housewife who, having trouble opening a jar of pickles, observed: "I should get Tommy Douglas to open this. He's opened everything else in the province today.")

Yet in 1969 Edward Schreyer brought the New Democrats to power in the province of Manitoba. Sterling Lyon's Conservatives defeated Schreyer in the late 1970s, but the New Democrats returned to office in the early 1980s, under Howard Pawley. Meanwhile, by 1971 the NDP was ruling again in Saskatchewan itself, under Allan Blakeney, who had moved west from the Maritimes after the Second World War.

Even confirmed critics of socialism had to concede that, whatever else, the new Confederation now had — partly as a result of the country's historic ties to the United Kingdom — a North American variation on the Western European theme of the social democratic political party, at least capable of forming provincial governments in Western Canada.

"The spellbinder" Tommy Douglas, premier of Saskatchewan, 1944–61; leader of the federal New Democrats in Ottawa, 1961–71.

The Chief's Brief Renegade Regime at Ottawa

The side of the old Last Best West that pioneered Canadian social democracy also made direct contributions to Canadian national politics, when Tommy Douglas became the federal leader of the NDP in 1961, and when Trudeau, partly as a bow to western sentiment, appointed Ed Schreyer as governor general of Canada in 1979, just over a year after Schreyer's electoral defeat in Manitoba.

With somewhat greater practical consequences, a not altogether different side of the old western culture made the supreme national contribution in 1957, when John Diefenbaker, the Conservative *Renegade in Power* from Saskatchewan (the title of the later book by the Central Canadian journalist Peter C. Newman) defeated Louis St. Laurent's Liberals at Ottawa.

The 1957 election took place in the wake of a controversy over the construction of a pipeline to ship Alberta gas to markets in Central Canada. Diefenbaker's initial victory was very narrow, and he called a fresh election in 1958. In this contest he dramatically proclaimed a new "northern vision " and won the largest majority of any prime minister in the Canadian House of Commons (78.5% of all seats), before or since.

"The Chief's" prairie populist rhetoric was in the tradition of John Bracken, the former Progressive premier of Manitoba who had become leader of a new federal "Progressive Conservative" party in 1942. But, though he appealed to such eastern Red Tory intellectuals as George Grant, Diefenbaker was at odds with the clubby old Tory side of the business establishment in English-speaking Central Canada — as well as with the establishment's democratic old Ontario Grit side in the federal Liberal party.

What the renegade did share with his eastern fellow Conservatives was an attachment to the waning traditions of the British Dominion, all the more sincere in a person of German descent who had been born in southwestern Ontario. This made Diefenbaker's relations with French Canada difficult — even though the Quebec electorate, spurred on by one of the last requests of le Chef, Maurice Duplessis, had joined the massive Conservative federal majority of 1958. With the start of the Quiet Revolution in 1960, Duplessis's earlier support only made matters worse.

In the 1963 federal election that finally defeated him, Diefenbaker managed to win well over half the seats in Nova Scotia, Manitoba, Saskatchewan, and Alberta, and he made a notably respectable showing in New Brunswick and Prince Edward Island. In all these places, his northern vision was still shining. But it had tarnished quickly, or had begun to seem not at all well enough thought-out, in Ontario and Quebec — and in Newfoundland and British Columbia.

Nonetheless, in his brief federal regime the Chief did make some characteristic contributions to the new Confederation. The progress of the Rowell-Sirois National Adjustments Grants philosophy in the federal bureaucracy was accelerated (though the modern Canadian federal-provincial system of equalization payments to less affluent provinces had actually begun during

John Diefenbaker, prime minister of Canada, 1957–63: "the Chief" from Saskatchewan, who was helped to the largest parliamentary majority in the Confederation's history by Maurice Duplessis, "le Chef" from Quebec.

the late St. Laurent era). In the late 1950s and early 1960s John Diefenbaker presided over the early modern Canadian federal enthusiasm for "regional development" programs that would blossom in the late 1960s and 1970s.

This too was in the tradition of Bracken, whose Manitoba government had been the strongest provincial supporter of the Rowell-Sirois report in the early 1940s. The Chief also had an instinct for another aspect of the western approach to the country at large — the one that had prompted Emily Murphy of Alberta to campaign so hard for a woman senator. Early in 1958 the Western Canadian renegade, only briefly in power at that point, had caused James Gladstone, a Blood Indian and former president of the Indian Association of Alberta, to become what Gladstone's mid-1980s biographer would call "the first treaty Indian to be appointed to the Senate of Canada." Here as elsewhere, the Chief had not managed to clothe his political thoughts in real substance. But he had hinted at some other dimensions in the new northern vision.

The New Regional Culture in Alberta and British Columbia

The 1950s and 1960s were a great boom era in Canada at large — a worthy successor to the buoyancy of the early twentieth century and the pre-Confederation bliss of the 1850s and even 1860s. Yet, as in the past, the blessings of the business cycle were not spread evenly across the country. All regions and provinces grew, but some grew faster than others.

Ontario and (until the mid-1960s) Quebec, in the old opportunistic Central Canada, were two notable provincial cases of especially rapid population growth. Another two were Alberta and British Columbia in a new and at least somewhat opportunistic Western Canada. British Columbia and Alberta were also — not accidentally, it could be said — the two western provinces that had joined Central Canada's staunch opposition to the Rowell-Sirois report in the early 1940s.

In Manitoba and Saskatchewan, provincial shares of the national population actually declined progressively throughout the generation from 1951 to 1981. The result was that, despite the rising prosperity in Alberta and British Columbia, down to 1971 Western Canada at large remained stuck at just above 26% of the national population, still below its more than 29% high point of 1931.

Nevertheless, in the 1970s, when the boom would bust in Ontario, having already busted in Quebec, it hung on in British Columbia. And it grew greater still in Alberta. By 1981 Western Canada had still not quite recovered its peak 1931 share of the national population, but it had come close.

The West's increasing prosperity and demographic weight in the wider Confederation was accompanied by an increasing emphasis on the regionalism of provincial aspirations, a phenomenon already well developed in Alberta and especially British Columbia. The Vancouver Stock Exchange gradually turned Vancouver into a distinctly "junior" and somewhat wild but nonetheless undeniable financial centre in Canada. By the late 1970s the oil boom in Alberta had built Calgary into a bustling regional service and financial centre, and Edmonton into an aggressive provincial capital, whose detractors sometimes said that it was too much like an earlier Toronto.

WESTERN CANADA IN CONFEDERATION, 1951–1981

Province/Region	% of Total Canadian Population			
	1951	1961	1971	1981
Manitoba	5.6	5.1	4.6	4.2
Saskatchewan	5.9	5.1	4.3	4.0
Alberta	6.7	7.3	7.6	9.2
British Columbia	8.3	8.9	10.1	11.3
Western Canada	26.5	26.4	26.6	28.7
Total Canadian Population (000s)	14,009	18,238	21,568	24,343

In this atmosphere, provincial governments on both sides of the Mountain Barrier revived the English-speaking Canadian traditions of "province building" begun by Oliver Mowat of Ontario in the late nineteenth century. (George Woodcock, the friend of George Orwell who gradually fashioned a revised and updated British Columbian regional variation on Goldwin Smith's old role in Ontario, would gallantly acknowledge Mowat's historic contribution to the cause in *Faces from History: Canadian Profiles & Portraits*, published in 1978.)

For a time after the Second World War, Alberta and British Columbia shared another distinction in the emerging new Confederation. In the 1950s and 1960s they were the only two of all Canada's provinces to enjoy the blessings of Social Credit provincial governments, though a Quebec Créditiste wing of the federal party, under Réal Caouette, also basked in a brief burst of prominence in the 1960s.

From one angle, Social Credit was the right-wing version of the left-wing British-American populist hybrid created by the agrarian socialist pioneers of the CCF/NDP. Like the much more intellectually respectable postwar American economist Milton Friedman, the founder of Social Credit doctrine in the United Kingdom, Major Clifford Hugh Douglas had believed that the secret to the successful management of capitalism lay in the money supply. But, after federal-provincial wrangles prompted by William Aberhart's late 1930s regime in Alberta, Social Credit became even less interested in any systematic implementation of abstract philosophy than the CCF/NDP.

It was more significant that Aberhart in Alberta, premier from 1935 to 1943, had established a variation on the regional populism of Duplessis in

Quebec — or on that of the provincial Liberal populists of the same era in Ontario and British Columbia, Mitch Hepburn and T.D. Pattullo. Ernest C. Manning would carry on this side of Aberhart's crusade in Alberta down to 1968. In 1952, W.A.C. ("Wacky") Bennett brought a related variety of regional Social Credit regime to the Canadian Pacific Coast, where, as George Woodcock declared in the late 1970s, "British Columbia man is a populist." As much as anything else, postwar Social Credit in both Alberta and British Columbia became a political ideology for populists who could reasonably aspire to at least some forms of prosperity.

As what Woodcock would call a "peculiarly fabricated" populist politician of the increasingly prosperous Canadian Pacific, the Maritimes-born Wacky Bennett was also carrying on a uniquely provincial tradition, stretching all the way back to Amor De Cosmos in the Confederation era. (In 1958 Bennett actually wrote a foreword to a biography of De Cosmos. The text, the modern premier pointed out, disproved the claims of those "who contend that the history of British Columbia is not a colourful story.")

Bennett's right-wing impulses had some uniquely Canadian dimensions. In the spirit of the quiet revolutionaries in Quebec and of the much earlier "small-p" progressive Conservatives in Ontario, in the early 1960s his Social Credit regime brought the province's private hydro corporation, B.C. Electric, under public ownership. By this time the Government of British Columbia was also in the midst of a major program of road and railway building, which opened up many neglected parts of the province's vast wilderness geography. The province operated the public ferry service between Vancouver Island and the B.C. mainland as well. And Wacky Bennett could plausibly enough boast that

> the Social Credit government is more conservative than the Conservatives in financial matters, more liberal than the Liberals in terms of providing the nation's highest old age and social assistance benefits, and even more in favour of public ownership than the CCF because of our ferry system and hydro program.

"Western Separatism" and the Crisis of the Early 1980s

Despite the growing cleavage between the dynamism of the mountain provinces and the slow growth on the prairies, the New West led by Alberta and British Columbia cultivated its earlier regional ties with the old Last Best West of Manitoba and Saskatchewan.

Even among its western brothers and sisters, British Columbia remained something of a region in its own right. Yet Pacific Coast communicators were among those who invented the new Louis Riel, who was neither the defender of French Catholic rights nor the Indian protestor against the Anglo-American frontier, but the first modern patriot of the wider, predominantly English-speaking region of Western Canada, from the Lake of the Woods to the Pacific Ocean.

The New Democrats provided another link between the old West of Manitoba and Saskatchewan, and the new West of British Columbia. In 1972 the spirit of the age (and the prosperous but still quite volatile B.C. resource economy) finally let the NDP under David Barrett, a stocky former social worker with another kind of populist politician's common touch, defeat W.A.C. Bennett's long Social Credit regime in Victoria.

British Columbia thus became the third province of Western Canada to join the social democratic experiment in North America. Here the experiment did not work so well, and Wacky Bennett's son, Bill, led Social Credit back to office in 1975. But British Columbia had confirmed that it now enjoyed a provincial political system whose two major parties — Social Credit on the right and the New Democrats on the left — were both new parties that had been created by the old culture of the Dominion of Canada and the Last Best West.

As if to show that, even in the West, British Columbia nonetheless remained unique, by 1971 the more mature Social Credit regime in Alberta was about to disappear. It would be replaced by a new provincial Progressive Conservative Party, under the gentlemanly but still tough and angry leadership of Peter Lougheed, whose grandfather had been R.B. Bennett's Calgary law partner, and one of the the few distinguished members of the Senate of Canada during the first half century of the Confederation.

Here, lubricated by the new wealth of the oil economy — especially after the Organization of Petroleum Exporting Countries (OPEC) crisis of 1973 — the regional leadership of the New West would set down its strongest roots. As the pressures of the quiet revolution in the wider Confederation increased, a few western separatist groups set up camp on the fringes of practical politics, funded, it was sometimes said back east, by American oil companies.

In the political mainstream Peter Lougheed, premier of a now resoundingly booming Alberta, became Western Canada's answer to René Lévesque in Quebec. Beyond the borders of the emerging new Confederation, in 1981 Joel Garreau, the American author of *The Nine Nations of North America*, told viewers of William F. Buckley's highbrow U.S. television program that Alberta was "another secessionist area" in Canada — which had much in common with Colorado to the south.

Beyond the issue of French and English dualism or bilingualism, in the 1970s and early 1980s oil also became the leading symbol of regional conflict between Western Canada and "Eastern Canada." The most practical side of the argument was largely between Alberta and Ontario. But this more narrow conflict came to symbolize a wider regional cause in both Western and Atlantic Canada.

In 1952 C.D. Howe, the American-born Canadian "Minister of Everything" in St. Laurent's federal regime, had told Alberta's premier, E.C. Manning, in the presence of Ontario's prime minister, Leslie Frost, that Ottawa would not allow any gas exports to the Midwest United States "unless the needs of central and eastern Canada were provided for first." This principle set in motion a long conflict that would finally come to a head with the Trudeau regime's National Energy Program (NEP) of the early 1980s.

To many in Ontario, if the nation meant anything it must mean that Canadians ensured they had enough of their own natural resources for themselves before they sold them to Americans or any other foreign nationals. To many in Alberta, if it was in the national interest for branch operations of American multinational corporations to produce automobiles in Ontario for sale in the United States, it was also in the national interest for branch operations of American multinational corporations to produce oil and gas in Alberta for sale in the United States. And exactly such an arrangement for automobiles produced in Ontario had been established by the federal Liberals' 1965 Canada-U.S. Auto Pact — the first major departure from the rhetoric of Macdonald's National Policy since the 1911 reciprocity election, and a signal of a still more major departure to come.

Trudeau, however, was not fundamentally the heir of the Canadian liberalism that had created the Canada-U.S. Auto Pact, the liberalism of Lester Pearson or Mackenzie King or even Wilfrid Laurier. If anything, he seemed to be proving the heir of the late nineteenth century liberal-conservatism of George-Etienne Cartier. In some respects, his regime's National Energy Program seemed to signal some kind of neo-nationalist return to the principles of Cartier's old partner, John A. Macdonald.

Whatever the historical parallels, the NEP amounted to an explicit public declaration and permanent implementation of the point that C.D. Howe had made privately to Ernest Manning in 1952. It involved several sweeping schemes of federal government intervention in Canadian energy industries. These were perceived by influential figures in Alberta and other parts of Western Canada as an attack on both provincial governments and the private sector of the regional economy. And Donald Smiley, a leading academic expert on Canadian federalism, had already accused Trudeau of promoting a doctrine of "federal majoritarianism" — which was not something that had been articulated in the future prime minister's intellectual musings of the 1950s and 1960s.

The implementation of the NEP in the early 1980s coincided with a sudden international bust in oil-based regional economies everywhere. This affected such places as Texas, Oklahoma, New Mexico, and Colorado in the United States, as well as Alberta in Canada. To many in Alberta the NEP only made the situation worse. Despite an ultimately successful resolution of some particular disagreements between Alberta and Ottawa, it brought the New West's increasing dissatisfaction with the way "national" decisions were made in the Confederation to a new height.

As W.A.C. Bennett had explained in the late 1970s, from his retirement on the other side of the mountains, he "would never want to see British Columbia leave confederation." But the politicians and bureaucrats of the

> have centralized everything and this is very, very danger-
> ous in a country like ours. In the United States where the
> Senate has power, you have two Senators from each state,
> but in Canada we do it by population. Central Canada has
> the population and so it dominates Canada.

In 1981 the Canada West Foundation in Calgary (a name redolent of an earlier era in the history of Central Canada) published a "Task Force Report" that pursued this particular logic. The task force was made up of Peter McCormick, chairman of the Department of Political Science at the University of Lethbridge; Ernest C. Manning, former Social Credit premier of Alberta; and Gordon Gibson, former leader of the provincial Liberal Party in British Columbia. It recommended that "the resolution of the problem of effective regional representation in Canada be sought by establishing an elected Senate in Canada."

Peter Lougheed, both the premier of Alberta and increasingly the leading spokesman for a much broader array of provincial grievances against the Trudeau regime in Ottawa, was not initially convinced by the specific recommendations of the 1981 Task Force Report. But, like many others in his region, he had come to agree that Harold Innis's Canadian "Senate, that unique institution" was the strategic focal point for Western Canadian concerns about the structure of the new Confederation — the undeniable arrival of which had been announced by Trudeau's "New Constitution" of 1981–82.

In August 1982 the Government of Alberta published what it described as a "discussion paper on strengthening Western representation in national institutions." The paper was entitled *A Provincially-Appointed Senate: A New Federalism for Canada.*

The long era of conceiving the political problems of Canadian regionalism principally in the terms outlined by the Rowell-Sirois report, so strongly supported by John Bracken of Manitoba in the early 1940s, had come to an end. And the long journey to Senate reform in Canada had reached a point that virtually no one, in Western Canada or Eastern Canada, French Canada or English Canada, or any other part of Canada, had anticipated a generation before.

12
ATLANTIC ADVENTURE

In the 1860s the editor of the *Daily British Whig* in Kingston, Canada West, had complained that "the generality of Canadian readers admire nonsense and bosh ... like the Yankees with whose domestic habits they assimilate." Put another way, the history of economic development frontiers in North America has bred a strain of robust boosterism in the English-speaking culture of the New World.

The classic modern literary critique of the phenomenon can be found in such early twentieth century novels as Sinclair Lewis's *Main Street, Babbitt, Arrowsmith, Elmer Gantry,* and *Dodsworth.* The Nova Scotian Thomas Chandler Haliburton's adventures of Sam Slick, on the other hand, constitute a gentler, warmer, more admiring satire of what is involved. Something similar could be said about *Sunshine Sketches of a Little Town* and *Arcadian Adventures with the Idle Rich* by the McGill University professor of political science Stephen Leacock.

It is arguable that in the late twentieth century the old North American culture of boosterism has remained somewhat warmer and less out of date in Canada than in the United States. (Though the reputation of Mark Twain, much closer to Haliburton or Leacock than Sinclair Lewis, still has defenders in the Republic today.) Whatever the case, the phenomenon has retained some importance in all parts of the Confederation. It remains, however, at its highest expression in the West — the region with the most recent direct experience of an economic development frontier, making allowances for the still unclear future of Canada's Far North.

In any part of the country, to have some respect for the culture of boosterism is to appreciate that, like their critics, those who use it most successfully do not take it seriously. To admire nonsense and bosh is not the same as believing that it is true. The value of the culture of boosterism lies in its capacity to motivate people faced with arduous tasks of economic development.

Western Canadians, for example, who stress the geographic dualism of Canada — East and West — understand that this does not exactly reflect the country as it actually exists on the ground. Western Canada knows that its antagonist at the other end of the real geographic dualism is merely "Central Canada." The real "Eastern Canada" — the four provinces of the Canadian Atlantic Coast, and perhaps even Quebec east of Trois Rivières — is in fact an ally in the continuing struggle for the right national policy for all parts of the country.

In the new Confederation, Atlantic Canada sees Western Canada in a similar light. Thus, Premier Joe Ghiz of Prince Edward Island told the Canadian Club of Montreal early in 1987: "From our perspective in the

A "down-east" variation on the early 1950s "Canadian West" ad, run by Canadian National Railways. The "romantic playground by the Sea," as viewed by the copy writer in English-speaking Montreal, now included "picturesque fishing villages" in Newfoundland as well as Nova Scotia, and there were at last "all ten provinces" from ocean to ocean.

Atlantic region the political scales are weighted in favour of Central Canada. That perspective is shared by the Western provinces."

Yet, as noted earlier, Ghiz also made it clear that the most fundamental "reality of Canada is that the perspective changes depending where you are." And to be in the Atlantic region is not the same as to be in the West. At the very bottom of the new Confederation, Atlantic Canada knows that it is not what Central Canada thinks it is. But it knows as well that it is not what Western Canada thinks it is either. From the 1950s through the 1970s, it too had some quiet revolutions of its own.

"The Only Living Father of Confederation"

The first great change in Atlantic Canada after the Second World War was the admission of Newfoundland into the Canadian Confederation in 1949. This was an event whose full complexities have only recently begun to appear in most Canadian national history books.

Geologically, it could be said, Newfoundland and Labrador have always been part of Canada. "The Rock" was only the eastern-most extension of the Canadian Shield. Among other things, this meant that it never quite escaped the rocky economic troubles of the late nineteenth century. Like the Canadian Confederation, what would gradually evolve into the Dominion of Newfoundland built a railway from coast to coast. But, as a provincial elementary school textbook of the early 1980s would explain, "it was hoped that the railway would lead Newfoundlanders to build new mines, factories, and towns in the interior .... Unfortunately, this did not happen."

After the failure of negotiations to join Canada in the 1890s, and then the First World War era, the flinty resolve of Newfoundlanders sustained the evolution of their own version of a self-governing British dominion until the Great Depression. When the Rock went bankrupt in the 1930s, however, the British government assumed its debt. As a kind of security, it abolished the elected responsible government granted in the 1850s, and established a six-member "Commission of Government," appointed in the United Kingdom. The Rock returned to the status of a mere colony of the mother country.

By the 1940s the Second World War had brought British, Canadian, and American military bases to Newfoundland, and at least a degree of new prosperity. The Commission of Government reformed the civil service and, for the first time in the region's history, made the education of children compulsory — even for those who, as the textbook of the early 1980s put it, "were old enough to help their fathers fish."

At the end of the war, the United Kingdom announced that the people of Newfoundland would be given an opportunity to choose their own ultimate destiny. As it happened, some wanted to keep the British-appointed Commission, in which case Newfoundland would have become like the residual fishing colony of St. Pierre et Miquelon, which retains its status as a piece of France in the Gulf of St. Lawrence down to the present. Others wanted to return to the self-government that had been lost in 1933. This group included one faction that saw self-government merely as a prelude to joining the Canadian Confederation, and another that saw it as a prelude to joining the United States.

Those strongly in favour of joining the United States, whose free-spending soldiers had made an impression during the war, included Chesley Crosbie, father of John Crosbie, who would become a Conservative federal Cabinet minister in the 1980s, and Don Jamieson, who would become a Liberal federal Cabinet minister in the 1960s and 1970s. But in the late 1940s Andrew Foster, a spokesman for the State Department in Washington, indicated that, with regard to Newfoundland

> any manifestation of interest by officials of the United States Government would obviously be received with considerable misgivings in Canada and the United Kingdom and might be considered as undue interference in the domestic political affairs of a foreign country.

The Newfoundland crusade to join Canada at last was led by Joseph R. "Joey" Smallwood, an enormously shrewd and energetic journalist and radio broadcaster (rumoured to have once known Leon Trotsky), who later liked to call himself "the only living Father of Confederation." Mackenzie King's Canadian federal government had some reservations about the generous financial terms that were required to bring the Rock into the country, but it could not help acknowledging the geopolitical fulfilment that Newfoundland and Labrador would add to an emerging new Canadian nation. While it would have been improper for the federal government itself to support Smallwood actively, the Canadian federal Liberal Party did help finance the activities of his "Confederate Association."

As in the original Confederation of the 1860s and 1870s, the Government of the United Kingdom finally concluded: "It is in our interest and Newfoundland's that she should accept the very reasonable offers from Canada .... U.K. policy is to try to get Newfoundland to join Canada." Thus, the referendum on the future of the Rock that was finally held in June 1948 placed three options on the ballot: retain the Commission of Government; return to self-government; join the Canadian Confederation.

Two ballots, on 3 June and 28 July, actually proved necessary to arrive at an unambiguous result. The 3 June ballot showed 44.5% of the Newfoundland electorate in favour of returning to self-government, 41.13% for joining Canada, and 14.32% for keeping the Commission of Government. A run-off ballot between the two most popular options on 28 July showed 52.34% for joining Canada and 47.66% for returning to self-government.

Mackenzie King's original view had been that Newfoundland probably should return to self-government before it entered Confederation, and that unless the join-Canada option won overwhelming support in the 1948 referendum, it might be wise for Canada itself to demur. But his valued senior civil servant, and subsequent Liberal federal Cabinet minister, Jack

Newfoundland's Joey Smallwood, "the only living Father of Confederation" (on the left) confers with federal Cabinet minister Paul Martin Sr. (father of Paul Martin Jr., who would seek the leadership of the Liberal Party of Canada at the start of the 1990s).

Pickersgill, calculated that King's own Liberal Party had never won a Canadian federal election by more than 52% of the popular vote. As Pickersgill has reported, when King "asked my opinion of the vote, I was able to tell him how favourably the vote for Confederation compared with the support he had received in successive elections which he had regarded as clear expressions of the will of the Canadian people."

In the end King announced that Newfoundland would be welcomed into the Confederation by all its peoples and regions, and invited "authorized representatives" to come to Ottawa to negotiate final terms. Joey Smallwood telegraphed that King himself would "go down in history as the greatest Newfoundlander since John Cabot."

Ottawa's side of the negotiations, intriguingly enough, was co-ordinated by a steering committee under the chairmanship of R.A. MacKay, who had published *The Unreformed Senate of Canada* in the 1920s, served on the Rowell-Sirois Commission in the 1930s, and joined the federal civil service after the war in the 1940s. When the negotiations were complete, Newfoundland became, on 1 April 1949, what Mackenzie King had earlier described as Canada's "10th province and quite clearly the last."

Heartland of Regional Development, Phase I

Initially, Newfoundland's entry into the Confederation in 1949 did have the effect of boosting Atlantic Canada's share of the total Canadian population

— from 9.8% in 1941 to 11.6% in 1951. As in Newfoundland, the Second World War had stimulated economic growth in Nova Scotia, New Brunswick, and even Prince Edward Island. There was as well an ever so gentle boost for Atlantic Canada in the initial postwar boom; regional population growth was more rapid in the 1950s than it would be in the 1960s and 1970s.

Yet the problems of lagging development in the region proved frustratingly persistent. As before the war, Atlantic incomes remained well below the national average.

After 1951 Atlantic Canada's regional share of the national population returned to its pattern of progressive decline. By 1971, even with the addition of Newfoundland, the region had a smaller proportion of the people of Canada than in 1941 (without Newfoundland), and by 1981 its share was somewhat smaller still.

Despite such statistics, however, by the 1970s it could no longer be said that Atlantic Canada's growth problems flowed fundamentally from a lack of interest or effort on the part of the Canadian federal government. By the 1960s, the renegotiation of Nova Scotia's financial terms for admission to the Confederation in the late 1860s, the Royal Commission on Maritime Claims in the 1920s, the Rowell-Sirois Commission of the 1930s, and related impulses released by John Diefenbaker's renegade regime at Ottawa in the late 1950s, had evolved into one major new Atlantic industry. Strongly supported by assorted federal, provincial, and municipal government organizations, it was generically known as "regional development."

ATLANTIC CANADA IN CONFEDERATION, 1951–1981

Province/Region	% of Total Canadian Population			
	1951	1961	1971	1981
Nova Scotia	4.6	4.0	3.7	3.5
New Brunswick	3.7	3.3	2.9	2.9
Newfoundland	2.6	2.5	2.4	2.3
Prince Edward Island	0.7	0.6	0.5	0.5
Atlantic Canada	11.6	10.4	9.5	9.2
Total Canadian Population (000s)	14,009	18,238	21,568	24,243

To start with, Atlantic Canada regularly benefited from the federal-provincial system of equalization payments, in place by the late 1950s and more or less modelled on the Rowell-Sirois conception of National Adjustment Grants. It benefited as well from a federal government decision to extend the national unemployment insurance system to the seasonal pursuits of inshore fishermen. And it was in a unique position to profit from such alphabet-soup innovations of the Diefenbaker era as ADA (the Area Development Agency), ARDA (the Agricultural Rehabilitation and Development Agency), and FRED (the Fund for Rural Economic Development).

None of these federal programs were unique to Atlantic Canada. It benefited from them because its four provinces invariably qualified for special assistance under more general criteria, as did, often enough, Manitoba, Saskatchewan, and Quebec.

In 1954 public and private regional interests established the Atlantic Provinces Economic Council (APEC), a non-profit, non-political organization to promote the economic and social development of the Atlantic region. As explained by T.N. Brewis, pioneering analyst of Canadian regional development in the 1960s, APEC came to believe that there was also a need for "a federal authority which could serve as a focal point for all matters pertaining to the economy of the Atlantic region."

This belief helped prompt the Diefenbaker regime to establish, in 1962, the Atlantic Development Board (ADB). This was, according to the federal minister of national revenue who introduced its implementing legislation, "the most forward step ever taken in his lifetime for the benefit of the Atlantic provinces." It could "very properly" be considered to involve "the development of the national economy, with special reference to the difficulties peculiar to the Atlantic region."

By 1968 the ADB had committed some $188 million in federal funds to the provision of new hydroelectric power plants, water and sewage systems, highway developments, industrial parks, and research facilities in the four provinces of Atlantic Canada.

The New French Fact in Old Acadia

The historic fishing rights of France, on Newfoundland's "French shore," had been a historic problem for the Rock. The place itself had only a few French-speaking people when it joined Canada in 1949. The new Atlantic region at large, however, was the latest expression of ancient Acadia, and it was more directly affected than Western Canada by the resurgence of the French fact in the wider Confederation during the 1950s and 1960s.

By 1961 Newfoundland actually had a smaller proportion of French-only and bilingual French and English-speaking people (1.3%) than any other Canadian province. The proportion in Nova Scotia (6.9%), however, though somewhat smaller than in Manitoba, was larger than in any province west of Manitoba. The proportion in Prince Edward Island (8.8%), on the other hand, was larger than in any province west of Ontario. And the proportion in New Brunswick (37.7%) was larger than in any province except Quebec, and even above the national average of 31.3%.

The northern part of New Brunswick, closest to the border with Quebec, had in fact become the warmest refuge for the heirs of les Acadiens in the seventeenth and eighteenth centuries. The majority of people in this region of what had traditionally called itself "The Loyalist Province" were French speaking, as they remain today.

Given these demographics, both the Quiet Revolution and the separatist movement in Quebec raised some unsettling prospects, even for New Brunswick's English-speaking majority. In the mid-1960s Trudeau hinted at the worst case in a discussion of traditional nationalist theorizing in Europe:

> Danton ... pointed out in 1793 that the frontiers of France were designated by Nature .... Fortunately for German-speaking peoples, however, Fichte was soon to discover that the natural frontiers were in reality the linguistic ones; thus the German nation could will itself towards its proper size.

Serious prospects of quite this sort in Canada — of a new Quebec nation's annexing northern New Brunswick, for instance — were somewhat remote. (And what the most radical Acadians wanted was a province of their own in northern New Brunswick that would stay in the Confederation.) Nevertheless, psychologically, all this helped prepare the ground for the provincial regime of Louis Robichaud, who was elected Liberal premier of New Brunswick in the summer of 1960, just one week after Jean Lesage had been elected Liberal premier of Quebec.

For the next decade Robichaud presided over an Atlantic or Acadian version of Quebec's Quiet Revolution, culminating in 1969 with a provincial

Louis Robichaud, premier of New Brunswick, 1960–70, and founding father of Canada's first and as yet only officially bilingual provincial government, in the strongest modern refuge of the ancient Acadiens.

Official Languages Act that granted equal status to English and French in the public life of New Brunswick. The resulting concept of provincial official bilingualism, where numbers warranted, would become an ingredient in Pierre Trudeau's recipe for the wider new Confederation.

Robichaud's defeat at the hands of the Conservative Richard Hatfield in 1970 signalled a mild English-speaking backlash against the resurgence of New Brunswick's historic Acadian fact. The ebullient Hatfield would remain in power, through assorted scandals and lapses of good taste, down to 1987. In the ancient tradition of Maritime gentlemen, the backlash was notably polite. Hatfield never turned his back on official bilingualism and largely continued with the gradual strengthening of the French presence in New Brunswick that Robichaud had begun. By 1986 the combined French-only and bilingual French and English share of the province's population had risen to 41.2%, though the French-only share had actually declined from 1961 and the bilingual share had risen a great deal.

When the national constitutional crisis reached its climax in the late 1970s and early 1980s, New Brunswick was the one province that most unreservedly supported Trudeau and the federal government. To top the record off with an example of even deeper historical sensitivity, Richard Hatfield became a notably sympathetic supporter of the rights of the Indians, Inuit, and Métis in the new Confederation.

Beyond the special circumstances of New Brunswick, Quebec's increasingly articulate agonies in the Confederation of the 1960s and 1970s raised other grim prospects for Atlantic Canada. While René Lévesque and the Parti Québécois in the 1970s were not exactly suggesting that Quebec would leave Canada altogether, more extreme Quebec voices were advocating just that. And if it did happen, Atlantic Canada would be cut off from the other predominantly English-speaking parts of the country. Canada itself would become the kind of unstable, territorially bifurcated national state that its fellow Commonwealth state of Pakistan had been until the creation of Bangladesh in 1971.

Concerns of this sort blended with the continuing struggle for survival of old French Acadia in Nova Scotia and especially Prince Edward Island, as well as in New Brunswick. They helped give the three traditional Maritime provinces of Atlantic Canada rather more sympathy for Quebec's struggles to define a new place for itself in the new Confederation than was typical in Western Canada — or even, to a lesser degree, in Ontario.

Thus, although Jean Lesage had complained in the early 1960s that "French Canadians do not have the feeling that they belong to Canada to the same extent that their English-speaking fellow countrymen do," he had stressed that Quebec did nonetheless find more understanding of its situation in "the older provinces." And, beyond Quebec itself, the oldest provinces were on the Atlantic Coast. In the very end, at the decisive federal-provincial constitutional conference of 1981, it would be Angus MacLean, premier of Prince Edward Island, who would pay the heartfelt gentleman's tribute to the bowed-but-unconquered René Lévesque.

Regional Development, Phases II and III

By the late 1960s, the initial regional development efforts in Atlantic Canada had not really had time to produce dramatic results. Yet a new regional impatience had arisen, fed both by the apparent dynamic prosperity elsewhere in Canada and by new insecurities rooted in the resurgence of the French fact. In October 1969 the Atlantic Provinces Economic Council convened a conference that revived the ancient regional concept of Maritime Union.

Some even said that the new Atlantic region should return to the old name of Acadia. But by this point, the Maritime Union concept no longer had overt separatist overtones: it was merely about the organization of provinces inside Canada. A federal representative told the APEC conference that

> the future organization of your government or governments ... will be decided only by the people of the region. What you decide does not affect, either way, the responsibility of the federal government to do its best, to make its contribution to the economic and social progress of the people of this region.

In the end, enthusiasm for Maritime Union subsided in the face of all the old objections. It nonetheless reflected a fresh determination to do something dramatic about Atlantic Canada's continuing development problems. And the new Trudeau Liberal regime at Ottawa shared this determination. Regional development more generally, in all parts of the country, became a continuing Trudeau enthusiasm, partly, English-speaking cynics sometimes suggested, because it was also a good excuse for giving federal money to Quebec.

In 1969, not long before the APEC conference on Maritime Union, the Trudeau regime had established the Department of Regional Economic Expansion (DREE), with a mandate "to see that economic growth is dispersed widely enough across the country to provide equal access to opportunities of productive employment for Canadians everywhere."

As a sign of the political weight behind this commitment, the Cabinet minister responsible for DREE was Jean Marchand, a former labour organizer and one of Trudeau's fellow wise men from quiet revolutionary Quebec. The senior civil servant in charge was Tom Kent, a Canadian born in the United Kingdom. Kent had already helped mastermind the federal-provincial medicare program, inspired by Saskatchewan and brought in throughout the country by the Pearson government.

With particular reference to Atlantic Canada, Marchand and Kent reorganized the Atlantic Development Board into the Atlantic Development Council (ADC). They charged it with devising a "strategy for economic development" in the region, to be implemented through "two main instruments." The first, as Kent explained to APEC's conference on Maritime

Union in 1969, was a "new industrial incentives program," which "means that we can greatly reduce the capital on which a new plant in a slow-growth region has to show a return during the life of its original capital assets." The second was a "special area" program, through which the federal government could "help your provincial governments to provide the facilities and services essential for the industrial and commercial growth of urban centres."

In comparatively short order, the new ADC prepared *A Strategy for the Economic Development of the Atlantic Region, 1971–1981*, that reflected these new priorities, which at first seem to have been shared by both the federal government in Ottawa and many interested parties in the region itself. The fundamental problem of Atlantic Canada, in this view, was that it was still so much more "rural" than the rest of the country. The new objective was to promote urban growth, and the "key target" in the strategy was "an increase in total manufacturing employment in the Atlantic Provinces of 50,000 by 1981."

By the early 1980s, it was clear enough that, on any meaningful definition of manufacturing employment, the target had not been met. And, as described by Anthony Careless, an Ontario civil servant who published a leading second-generation contribution to a developing academic literature in the later 1970s: "Unavoidably some efforts led to irrational ventures in peripheral areas ... in Nova Scotia a goodly number of industries attracted ... failed."

Of still greater importance for politics if not economics, as another contributor to the developing literature, Donald Savoie, would put the point in 1981, the Trudeau regime's initial strong approach to regional development was "highly centralized in Ottawa," and "a handful of federal personalities like Marchand and Kent had been able to exercise considerable influence on the provinces' priority determining processes." Against the background of the growing constitutional crisis in the Confederation at large, this only helped give Atlantic Canada new grievances against the same doctrine of federal majoritarianism that increasingly irked the West.

By the mid-1970s the federal government had itself moved to take account of such complaints in at least this particular context. DREE was decentralized, and the leading vehicle for federal regional development policy became the General Development Agreement (GDA), negotiated separately with each province. With particular reference to the experience in New Brunswick, Donald Savoie observed: "In decentralizing decision making ... the federal government appears to have fragmented the process to such an extent that, under the GDA approach, it is incapable of providing regional leadership in the field of economic development."

In Atlantic Canada, as elsewhere, this had some obvious attractions for provincial governments, traditionally concerned to protect their constitutional status and authority, as even the ebbing enthusiasm for Maritime Union had once again made clear. The GDA approach also made, as Savoie reported, "for a less combative form of federalism." At the same time, it seemed to pass some new power on from elected politicians to appointed civil servants, further complicating an already complicated world of federal-provincial relations.

A New Atlantic Mood

Ultimately, the 1980s witnessed a somewhat muted Canadian variation on the international Anglo-American revival of enthusiasm for the ancient principles of the market economy, first clearly enunciated by Adam Smith at the time of the American War of Independence. In the midst of all this, there were some; especially in Central and Western Canada, who began to voice profound doubts about the federal government and regional development. Under Brian Mulroney's post-1984 federal regime, "DREE" would be pared down to "DRIE" (the Department of Regional Industrial Expansion).

All provinces, and especially Quebec, Manitoba, and Saskatchewan, had slow-growth areas that benefited from federal regional expansion largesse. Atlantic Canada, however, was the geographic heartland of the national experience with the concept. By the last year of the Trudeau regime in 1984, after a quarter of a century of various federal policies and much federal taxpayers' money, the four provinces of Atlantic Canada still had the lowest average incomes in all the Confederation. The region's share of the national population was lower than it had ever been before. (In fact, average Atlantic family income had been about 75% of average family income nationally in 1951, but was closer to 80% in 1984. Similarly, the decline of the region's share in the national population between 1951 and 1981 was smaller than it had been between 1911 and 1941, or 1871 and 1901. Yet even such marginal improvements, it was reported by sceptical professional economists, were almost all attributable to federal equalization payments and related direct government transfers of tax money into the region.)

At bottom, the market solution to Atlantic Canada's regional economic problems was for individual Canadians who could not find work in the region to migrate to some other part of the country (or even, from some points of view, "the continent"), where work was available. This kind of "labour mobility" had indeed been practised for generations. In 1957, how-ever, gentle hints that still more labour mobility might be one possible element in a healthier Atlantic economic future had found their way into the report of the federal Royal Commission on Canada's Economic Prospects, chaired by the Toronto businessman Walter Gordon. In Atlantic Canada itself this had, as T.N. Brewis reported from Ottawa in the 1960s, "triggered off an outburst of criticism."

By the early 1980s, there was new frustration in Atlantic Canada over the "dependency" relationships that federal equalization and regional develop-ment policies too often generated. There was also hope that offshore Atlantic Canadian oil development would bring new, more independent regional wealth and enhance regional and provincial autonomy. There were even more than a few Atlantic Canadians who felt that the region might prosper best with a rigorous dose of market economics.

Yet there was as well some apparent modest agreement that regional development and the growth of the new Canadian Confederation after the Second World War had, perhaps, brought somewhat more to the Atlantic region than met the eye of a too casual observer. In 1981, for instance, Newfoundland had the highest unemployment rate of all Canadian provinces. But, despite the attractions of labour mobility, some 80% of individual Canadians born in Newfoundland were still living there — a proportion exceeded only in British Columbia (88%), Ontario (90%), and Quebec (92%). In 1985 Prince Edward Island had the second lowest average provincial family income in Canada. But it also had a smaller percentage of its population below the Statistics Canada "low income cutoff" (10.9%) than any province except Ontario (10.2%).

In New Brunswick the rate of growth in average family income between 1975 and 1984 was actually somewhat above the national average. And in Nova Scotia, Halifax was slowly but unmistakably starting to become a regional metropolis for Atlantic Canada. It had 12.4% of the region's total population in 1981, up from 8.6% in 1951; over the same period it had grown faster than either of its two nearest rivals — Saint John, New Brunswick, and St. John's, Newfoundland.

THE REGIONAL RESULTS OF LABOUR MOBILITY IN CANADA, 1981

% Persons born in a Canadian province or territory still resident in that province or territory, June 1981		#Persons born in a Canadian province or territory resident in some other province or territory, June 1981 (000s).	
Quebec	92.2	Ontario	634.6
Ontario	89.9	Saskatchewan	535.8
British Columbia	88.4	Quebec	471.0
Newfoundland	80.1	Manitoba	370.7
Alberta	79.2	Alberta	313.4
Nova Scotia	74.1	Nova Scotia	239.6
New Brunswick	73.8	New Brunswick	202.6
Northwest Territories	73.5	British Columbia	164.6
Prince Edward Island	67.7	Newfoundland	132.1
Manitoba	66.2	Prince Edward Island	47.0
Saskatchewan	58.2	Northwest Territories	9.3
Yukon Territory	46.4	Yukon Territory	8.1
ALL CANADA	84.5	ALL CANADA	3,128.8

In the late 1980s the economist Michael Bradfield, at Dalhousie University in Halifax, allowed that the "intractability of regional disparities after 25 years and several billions of dollars of subsidies and concessions from all levels of government could be taken as evidence of the futility of fighting market forces." On the other hand, "both the imperfect nature of markets and the non-material aspirations of people may lead to different assumptions about what is an efficient set of policies with respect to regional disparities."

Not long before, the Nova Scotian Elmer MacKay, Brian Mulroney's minister for a new Atlantic Canada Opportunities Agency, had suggested something similar. Nature and geography had made Atlantic Canada a hard place that bred crusty people with flinty souls. Though they seldom voted for the New Democratic Party, all Atlantic Canadians were, in at least some degree, "natural social democrats," who looked to public as well as private enterprise because they had no other choice.

In the very late 1980s, a few new Atlantic voices began to revive some very old arguments. The Atlantic Provinces Economic Council, still very much in business, published a controversial study in 1989. It showed that in 1980 federal government grants to businesses in the Atlantic region had amounted to some $125 per person, compared with only $89 per person in all other parts of the country. But in 1987 federal grants to businesses in all other parts of the country amounted to $152 per person, compared with only $121 per person in Atlantic Canada.

In the midst of both old and new controversies, it was clear enough that a new kind of mood was finally beginning to settle in on Canada's Atlantic Coast. Some would still argue that, especially in the new province of Newfoundland, Atlantic Canadians were still not enthusiastic about calling themselves Canadians. George Rawlyk, regional historian of the old Maritime provinces, believed otherwise: "By the late 1970s the Maritimes had undergone a remarkable transformation of collective identity ... they had become, in an ironic twist of historical development, ardently Canadian."

Whatever else, individuals from all parts of Atlantic Canada were making important contributions to the new Confederation that had at last emerged from the old cocoon of the Dominion of Canada. Joey Smallwood, premier of Newfoundland from 1949 to 1972, was the only living father of Confederation and, in his day, reliable copy for much Canadian national news. Robert Stanfield of Nova Scotia served as the much-respected leader of the federal Progressive Conservative Party and of the loyal opposition in Ottawa, from 1967 to 1976.

In the 1960s and 1970s Louis Robichaud and Richard Hatfield of New Brunswick cut figures in the Canadian federal-provincial arena out of all proportion to their province's natural population weight. By the late 1970s Allan MacEachen of Nova Scotia had become what amounted to Pierre Trudeau's English Canadian lieutenant — in a kind of historic revival of the much earlier relationship between Wilfrid Laurier and W.S. Fielding.

(It could also be said that without MacEachen, Canada might not have made it through the late 1970s and early 1980s intact. The federal Conservatives under Joe Clark from Alberta had narrowly defeated Trudeau in 1979. This struck René Lévesque as an opportune occasion for the long-planned Quebec referendum on sovereignty-association. But MacEachen, an heir of Maritimes gentlemen who remembered Sam Slick, engineered a surprise defeat of Clark's slender majority government in the Canadian House of Commons. And this precipitated a new federal election in 1980, which returned Trudeau to power, just in time to inspire the "Non" forces in René Lévesque's referendum.)

One particular key to the new Atlantic Canadian mood in the new Confederation was reflected in a late 1983 presentation by James Lee, premier of Prince Edward Island, to yet another federal Royal Commission, this time on "the Economic Union and Development Prospects for Canada" and appointed by Trudeau himself. Premier Lee's concern was not to express a grievance. It was to focus on the "future for Canada ... so torn by competing visions of nationalism, regionalism and federalism." The central problem for the Atlantic region, in his view, was no longer better financial terms, Maritime Union, regional development, or provincial autonomy. Rather it centred on how to bring the Confederation at large closer together — how "to establish truly national decision-making in the country."

The solution that this particular Atlantic premier advocated had much in common with new arguments being advanced in Western Canada. It was strikingly similar to a solution that other representatives of Prince Edward Island had advocated almost 120 years before. And it picked up on the advice that Harold Innis, author of *The Cod Fisheries* as well as *The Fur Trade*, had offered some 40 years earlier:

> The complex problems of regionalization in the recent development of Canada render the political structure obsolete and necessitate concentration on the problem of machinery by which interests can become more vocal and their demands be met more efficiently ... the political scientist ... can best make a contribution to economic development by suggested modifications to political machinery.

Thus, Premier Lee urged the Royal Commissioners of 1983 to reflect that

> mechanisms for expression of all national interests at the federal level of government are weak and ineffective .... The Canadian Senate cannot play this role because the provinces are not equally represented, and therefore the federal government lacks the legitimacy that would come from such representation .... If Senate reform were to take place, such that the equality of the provinces (not regions) was estab-

13
DECLINE AND FALL?

Neither the more journalistic history of Canadian political punditry, nor the academic literature of Canadian political science, has as yet arrived at any firm consensus on the exact sequence of centralizing and decentralizing impulses in the new Confederation of the era after the Second World War.

It is clear that there was considerable centralization and strengthening of the federal government during the war itself. This carried on to some degree after 1945, partly aided and abetted by the Rowell-Sirois vision of federal-provincial financial and other relations. And, apparently against the advice offered in his own early writings, Pierre Trudeau felt increasingly obliged to stand up for the federal government in an unusually abrasive way, when what amounted to a national constitutional crisis boiled over in the late 1970s and early 1980s.

It is equally clear that, from some point in the 1950s, the Quiet Revolution and the separatist movement in Quebec, and the increasing new prosperity of Alberta and British Columbia in Western Canada, helped promote considerable decentralization and strengthening of provincial governments. And, even with the Rowell-Sirois vision, the rise of the postwar welfare state, many of the responsibilities for which were constitutionally rooted at the provincial level of government, stiffened this trend.

Thus by the late 1970s many, especially in Western Canada, Atlantic Canada, and Quebec, could agree with W.A.C. Bennett that the "federal government ... have centralized everything and this is very, very dangerous in a country like ours." At the same time, by the late 1980s many would also have agreed with what the Toronto business leader Conrad Black told an audience of his peers in Vancouver: "It is a platitude to point out that Canada is a difficult country to govern. It is already more politically decentralized than any other important country in the world except Switzerland."

Especially in Western and Atlantic Canada, and even Quebec, there were those who still argued that one crucial reason for political decentralization was the need to counter continuing economic centralization in English-speaking Central Canada. Even this, however, seemed not at all clear in the late 1970s and early 1980s. But, with allowances for the still imponderable impact of the 1988 Canada-U.S. Free Trade Agreement, by the late 1980s old regionalist complaints about the economic dominance of Central Canada in the Confederation had recovered at least some of their earlier grains of truth.

For those who lived in English-speaking Central Canada, by fate or by choice, the 1950s, 1960s, and 1970s were, almost as much as for those who lived in French-speaking Central Canada, an era of quiet revolution, and of occasionally somewhat noisy and often unsettling change.

By the time the "new Constitution" was proclaimed in 1982, it was unmistakably clear that one historic bastion of economic centralization in the metropolitan heartland had fallen. At some point between 1945 and 1976, English-speaking Montreal's *Empire of the St. Lawrence* (in the language of Donald Creighton, enthusiastic 1950s biographer of John A. Macdonald) had come to the end of its long and controversial economic reign over, to borrow another of Creighton's epithets, the *Dominion of the North*.

It can be seen as part of Central Canada's continuing perfidy, however, that no sooner had one imperialist metropolis been duly knocked down than another popped up. As a centre of civilization, Toronto, Harold Innis's "second largest city" of the 1920s, was no Montreal. And for a few brief, wild moments, at the peak of the Western Canadian boom in the late 1970s and early 1980s, Ontario — old fat-cat, central, English-speaking province of opportunity and opportunism alike — actually qualified technically for federal equalization payments. But Ontario did not take the payments, and soon enough it ceased to qualify even technically.

By 1989 Peter C. Newman, the Austrian-born, best-selling Canadian author of such books as *Renegade in Power*, *The Distemper of Our Times*, *The Canadian Establishment*, and *Company of Adventurers*, could inform his readers: "The fact that most of the dominant Canadian capital pools operate out of Toronto is no accident." There had been a "brief flowering of Calgary as a serious money centre." But "once oil prices slipped, the West's influence diminished and power flowed back into Toronto which has since firmly entrenched itself as Canada's economic centre."

A Tale of Two Cities

The westward shift of the economic centre of gravity in Central Canada after the Second World War can be seen as a kind of companion to the parallel westward shift of economic dynamism in Western Canada.

Both these shifts can be linked up with a wider international evolution, involving the metropolitan centres of London in the United Kingdom, and New York City in the United States. It captures something of what happened to say that, in the twentieth century, economic dominance in Canada gradually shifted from London, Montreal, and Winnipeg to New York, Toronto, and Vancouver.

Of course, propositions of this sort represent enormous over simplifications of complicated human realities and need to be qualified in various ways. For instance, in the 1960s and 1970s, Canada has also been affected by a continental shift of economic energy from New York City to Los Angeles. (On some readings of the data, by the late 1980s Los Angeles had actually surpassed New York as America's largest metropolis.) It has been affected as well by continental decentralizing trends that promoted new economic strength in such places as Miami, Atlanta, Dallas, and Denver in the United States, or Edmonton and Calgary in Canada itself.

Pride in the Past...
Confidence in the Future

Confederation was still more than three decades distant when Toronto was born. But even then, in 1834, the city—having grown from a tribal meeting place—was bursting with myriad evidences of future greatness.

Today, of course, Toronto has more than fulfilled that promise, having taken its place as the fastest growing city in North America—a growth that has set the pace for the entire nation.

We at The Toronto-Dominion Bank are proud that our progress and growth has paralleled that of the city. Indeed, the first train from Toronto to Montreal, in October of 1856, made its historic journey just three months after "The Bank" opened its doors for business.

On the occasion of its 125th birthday, we join with Toronto in looking with pride to the past, and with confidence to the future.

THE TORONTO-DOMINION BANK
THE BANK THAT LOOKS AHEAD

An ad from the official volume published to commemorate the 125th anniversary of the city of Toronto in 1959. Only a few years before, the Bank of Toronto had merged with the Dominion Bank, to form the Toronto-Dominion. Within a decade, work would be under way on the Toronto-Dominion Centre, an early entry in an array of new head office and other structures that would transform the late 1950s skyline of "the fastest growing city in North America."

Similarly, shifts in dominance do not imply any inevitable diminution of economic vigour and great continuing influence in such older centres as Montreal or Boston or Chicago, or London in the United Kingdom. In the late twentieth century, Canada is also being affected by much wider international shifts in economic dominance, involving such places as Tokyo and Singapore, and the still uncertain future of a new European Community.

Even historically, Toronto has had a relationship with London as well as a more dominant relationship with New York, and Montreal with New York as well as London. Montreal and Toronto have been national partners in Canada, as well as rivals for economic dominance. Winnipeg, which has its own trans border relations with such places as Minneapolis, was and is more than a western satellite of Montreal (or Toronto). Vancouver, which has its own relations with San Francisco and the West Coast in the United States, is even less enthusiastic about any connections it may or may not have with Toronto (or Montreal) today.

All this having been said, it is a straightforward fact that, after the Second World War, the economic centre of Central Canada did move west from Montreal, which had traditional strong ties with London, England, to Toronto, which had traditional strong ties with New York City. And, as in Western Canada, the change is ultimately reflected in population statistics.

Even before the population evidence was all in, an official volume, published to commemorate the 125th anniversary of the city of Toronto in 1959, enthused that the rising metropolis on the northwestern shore of Lake Ontario was already "the Economic Capital of Canada." It also reported: " 'Toronto is America's gateway to Canada,' an editor from Montreal said this past winter. He thought that explained what was to him the unnatural pre-eminence of Toronto. But does it?" The real truth was that Toronto had become "Canada's bridge (not door) to the culture of the United States."

The more neutral story told by population statistics stretches well back into the twentieth century, and does not reach its climax until the 1970s. At the start of the century, the population of the metropolitan region in Toronto was only 73% of the population in the metropolitan region of Montreal, and this fell to only 70% in 1911. The headquarters for Canada's transcontinental railways on the St. Lawrence River profited somewhat more from the great boom of the western wheat economy than the old English Canadian "Hogtown" in the Great Lakes interior.

Toronto's early twentieth century burst of population dynamism did not arise until the First World War decade, between 1911 and 1921. And in a subtle way this points to the London–New York side of the story.

It is true that in 1911 a slim majority of the Canadian electorate rejected Laurier's Reciprocity Treaty with the United States. This majority was especially concentrated in Ontario and British Columbia — and financed by the British Canadian merchants of both Montreal and Toronto. But in 1913 the U.S. Congress, via the first low American tariff bill in decades, known as the Underwood Bill, unilaterally gave Canada, and all other parts of the world, almost as much enhanced access to U.S. markets as Laurier's Reciprocity

Treaty would have brought. Toronto, which had traditionally looked first to New York, gained ground on Montreal, which looked first to the old imperial metropolis in London. And, by 1918, as the Hungarian-born American historian John Lukacs has recently explained, the "financial center of the world had gone from London to New York."

THE CHANGING POPULATION GROWTH OF MONTREAL
AND TORONTO 1901–1986

| Year | Population (000s)* | | Toronto/ |
	Montreal	Toronto	Montreal
1901	415	303	.73
1911	616	478	.70
1921	796	686	.86
1931	1,086	901	.83
1941	1,216	1,002	.82
1951	1,539	1,262	.82
1961	2,216	1,919	.87
1971	2,743	2,628	.96
1976	2,802	2,803	1.00
1981	2,828	2,999	1.06
1986	2,921	3,427	1.17

* Data for 1901–41 are from Leroy Stone, *Urban Development in Canada* (Ottawa: Dominion Bureau of Statistics, 1967). Data for 1951–86 are from Statistics Canada.

On the other hand, by the 1920s, when Toronto's gains on Montreal fell back somewhat, U.S. tariffs were once again rising. They peaked in the early 1930s, when Canada negotiated new imperial trade agreements with the United Kingdom and other parts of the British Empire. The late 1930s were marked by new trade agreements among all three of Canada, the United Kingdom, and the United States. But the Second World War kept up the modest inter war revival of Canadian economic ties with the United Kingdom. In both English-speaking Montreal and Toronto, the war focused attention on what a late 1930s Ontario elementary school textbook called "the Heart of the Empire," nobly standing up to the siege of Hitler's Reich.

Not much more than a decade after the end of the war, the Suez Crisis of 1956, which led to Lester Pearson's Nobel Peace Prize, may well have finally signalled, as Lukacs has suggested, the twentieth century Anglo-American "turning point ... the end of the British Empire and the end of the rise of the American one." Whatever else, for Canada it meant that the British Empire could no longer be used as a shield in the Confederation's always difficult relationship with the colossus to the south. The happy side of the story for Toronto was that in the 1950s it once again began to gain ground on Montreal.

The rise in Toronto's population, from 82% of Montreal's in 1951 to 87% in 1961, was the hardest evidence for the sense of triumph expressed in the official publication of 1959 commemorating Toronto's 125th anniversary. (The evidence the publication itself pointed to was the comparative performance of the Toronto and Montreal stock exchanges. Thanks in part to mining in Northern Ontario for such precious metals as silver and gold, the Toronto Stock Exchange had weathered the 1930s and 1940s with an expanding glow; the old transcontinental Canadian railway headquarters in Montreal had not.)

In the 1960s and 1970s, population data continued to confirm the sense of triumph felt by the burghers of Toronto as early as the late 1950s. By 1965 the Canada-U.S. Auto Pact had brought free trade in automotive products between Canada and the United States, and fresh energy to Ontario's manufacturing sector. This time, unlike in the 1920s, there would be no falling back. By the quinquennial Canadian census of 1976, the verdict was indisputable. The Census Metropolitan Area in Montreal now had 2,802,485 people. In Toronto, the comparable statistic was 2,803,101.

The Hard Fate of the English Fact in Quebec

The year 1976 marked the triumph of René Lévesque's Parti Québécois in Quebec. And, though this was certainly not meant to benefit the regional economy of Toronto, it did — in the short to mid-term at least.

Early in 1978 the Sun Life Assurance Company, whose headquarters building was an ancient ornament of Dominion Square in the heart of the city of the British Canadian merchants of Montreal, announced that it was moving to Toronto. The decision symbolized a much broader trend that had begun some time before and would continue for some time after 1976. The postwar business community in Toronto would not only grow bigger and stronger than that of the merchants of Montreal but some of these merchants would actually move themselves and their businesses to Toronto.

It was said that the fundamental problem was language, and this was certainly important. In Quebec the majority language was still French, as it had been since the later seventeenth century. But, virtually since the days of la Conquête, the commercial life of Montreal had been run as if the majority language were English. From a French Canadian standpoint, the British merchants of Montreal were not unlike "the British merchants of Buenos Aires," who had built and run the railways and much else in Argentina, for much of the nineteenth and twentieth centuries.

By the middle of the 1980s the Quebec separatist or neo-nationalist movement had still not taken Quebec out of the Confederation, but it had changed all this. Quebec, like the rest of Canada, was a democracy now. The majority language in the province was French, and all parts of the provincial society, including the commercial life of Montreal, would be run with respect for this democratic fact. Of at least equal importance, a related and not widely anticipated achievement of the neo-nationalist movement was the creation of what amounted to a new French-speaking business class, determined to find a place for itself in the commercial metropolis of its own region.

The Quiet Revolution and its more noisy sequel under the Parti Québécois fundamentally changed the cultural parameters of survival for both the Montreal business community and the somewhat wider English-speaking minority in Quebec at large. Montreal became what a book by the English-speaking journalist Gerald Clark dubbed *The New Cité*. Some old English enterprises, along with some old English-speaking people, adjusted to the new regime. Even in 1988 four of the 10 largest Canadian industrial corporations (BCE Inc., Canadian Pacific Ltd., Alcan Aluminum Ltd., and Provigo Inc.) were still headquartered in Montreal.

Others, like Sun Life, chose not to adjust. They moved to Toronto, or to other parts of English-speaking Canada, or in some cases to the United States. Both corporate and more popular decision- making of this sort had its demographic reflections. The proportion of the Quebec population reporting English as its official language fell from 11.6% in 1961 to 5.7% in 1986.

In either case, the final result was that the English-speaking imperialism of the St. Lawrence, which had begun in the late eighteenth century and flourished until the middle of the twentieth, ended forever. This brought

René Lévesque, the television journalist who in 1976 finally brought "sovereignty association" and the Parti Québécois to power in the predominantly French-speaking province of Central Canada.

some sorrow to many of those most directly involved. In their own eyes, the biological and sociological heirs of what Donald Creighton had called the "British Canadian merchants" of Montreal were not at all like the British merchants of Buenos Aires. They too were Canadians who had made a historic contribution to the diverse destiny in the northern half of North America.

Creighton's roll call of the late eighteenth century charter group suggests something of the legend that once seemed compelling — all the more impressive since Creighton himself was not a native Montrealer, but merely an admirer from Toronto:

> There were a few foreigners, Wentzel, Ermatinger and Wadden and the Jews, Solomons and Levy. John Askin and William Holmes were natives of Ireland. Allsopp, Oakes, Gregory, Lees, Molson, the Frobisher brothers and many others were English. From Scotland came George McBeath, Simon McTavish, Richard Dobie, the McGills, Finlays, Grants, Lymburners, and Mackenzies. A certain number of merchants were natives of the Thirteen Colonies and among these were Price, Heywood, Alexander Henry, the German-American Pangman and the illiterate, indomitable Pond.

Ultimately, the contribution of the English-speaking community became more than strictly economic. Stephen Leacock, described by Innis in 1938 as "the best known Canadian in the English-speaking world," moved from Ontario to McGill University in Montreal. Hugh MacLennan went to Montreal from Nova Scotia, to write about the *Two Solitudes* of French and English Canada. After the Second World War, the culturally vigorous Montreal Jewish community brought forth the English-language writers A.M. Klein, Irving Layton, Leonard Cohen, and Mordecai Richler, the last also distinguished by a successful apprenticeship in the old imperial metropolis of London, England.

It seems the fate of declining imperialisms, even in small colonial approximations, that few outside their inner circles shed real tears over their demise. In any case, as those least inclined to crying liked to point out, in the late 1980s there was still a rather more than modest, late twentieth century version of English-speaking Montreal, even if you could no longer tell from the signs on the streets.

The Quiet Revolution in Ontario

The English-speaking merchants of Montreal who moved to Toronto brought more than their businesses to Ontario. Something similar could be said, with still greater conviction, about those who stayed behind in Montreal.

Since the era of the United Province in the middle of the nineteenth century, the old "Two Canadas" had played a recurrent political game around the sociological fact of a French-speaking majority and English-speaking minority in Quebec living beside an English-speaking majority and French-speaking minority in Ontario.

In its original form, the game was cleverly mixed in with the historic debate over public (Protestant) and separate (Catholic) schools in the old Canada West. (The Roman Catholic Church in Canada East had controlled education, and the Vatican in Rome had looked kindly on its French Canadian flock in North America. In both Canadas, the cleavage between Catholics and Protestants drew the "Southern Irish" toward the side of the French.)

Over time, the strictly Canadian national principle that reasonable people from all camps were urged to agree on (if the game were to be played more or less fairly) was that the rights of the French (Catholic) minority in Ontario should be equal to the rights of the English (Protestant) minority in Quebec. This, of course, was diametrically opposed to the order of cultural relationships that flowed from the new regime of economic power established by la Conquête — and from the continuing international might of the British Empire. It was, instead, an early assertion of the principles of a bicultural Canadian nativism.

In the middle of the nineteenth century, the real democratic political energy for the Ontario Catholic side of the game had come not so much from the relatively few French in old Canada West, as from the increasingly more numerous Irish. It was their effective alliance with the French majority of Canada East in the old United Canada Assembly which finally assured that Ontario would begin its career after 1867 with at least an attenuated version of a tax-supported Catholic separate school system, as well as a tax-supported public school system on the model of the Anglo-American frontier.

By the late nineteenth century, however, Ontario was starting to acquire its modern French-speaking minority, as new waves of French Canadians migrated from Quebec to the old Loyalist bastion of Eastern Ontario and, later, to the eastern part of New or Northern Ontario. From the 1890s down to the 1930s, and even after the Second World War, one side of the Ontario Protestant majority, as in Manitoba, and other parts of Western Canada, staunchly resisted any serious efforts to approximate the fair-minded principle, for either the Catholics or the French.

In the 1960s, 1970s, and 1980s, the Quiet Revolution and the Parti Québécois and, above all else, Pierre Trudeau changed all this too, but in complicated ways.

The modernizing and sometimes genuinely Progressive Conservative provincial regime that ruled Ontario without interruption from 1943 to 1984, began to reflect quietly on its own French and Indian regional roots as early as the 1950s, under Leslie Frost. Under John Robarts in the 1960s, French language education in Ontario was dramatically strengthened, as in other English-speaking provinces. Under William Davis in the 1970s and early 1980s, French began to acquire a kind of semi-official status in the institutions of the Ontario provincial government, a trend confirmed and strengthened still more under the Liberal regime of David Peterson after 1984. The combined French-only and bilingual French and English share of the Ontario population increased from 9.4% in 1961 to 12.3% in 1986.

In 1984, his last year in power, Davis announced that "full funding" would be extended through to the end of the secondary level in the tax-supported Ontario separate school system. This at last met a demand that Ontario Catholics had been struggling for virtually since Confederation, and that had almost been won under the volatile Liberal populist Mitch Hepburn, in the 1930s. By the 1980s full funding was popular with newer Ontario Italians, Portuguese, Poles, and Filipinos, as well as with older Ontario Irish and French. At this point, close to one-half of all Canadians were reporting themselves as Catholics, compared with less than one-quarter of all citizens in the neighbouring American Republic.

At the same time, there were those in both Ontario and Quebec who felt that the Government of Ontario ought to stand up and be counted for the newly besieged ancient rights of the English Protestants in Quebec. This was a role that the Ontario provincial government had been not altogether loath to play at in the past. But it grew increasingly unwilling to touch the issue in the new atmosphere of the 1960s, 1970s, and 1980s.

At bottom, to play the role at all convincingly in the changing world of the new Confederation, Ontario itself would have had to become officially bilingual. As Pierre Trudeau discovered, to his disappointment, this was something that even the self-consciously enlightened, nationally minded, polyethnic mainstream of Canada's most populous province in the late twentieth century was not quite prepared to do.

Trudeau's argument about official bilingualism in Ontario was straightforward enough. While it was true that a much greater share of the provincial population was French-speaking in officially bilingual New Brunswick, Ontario's much greater demographic weight meant that in absolute numbers it had the largest concentration of French-speaking Canadians outside Quebec. In fact, in absolute numbers, Ontario had more than twice as many people reporting French as their mother tongue as New Brunswick.

This argument carried enough force in Ontario itself to prompt what might be described as an increasingly pronounced provincial policy of "unofficial bilingualism." Federally, official bilingualism rightly enough had taken on the conventional meaning that the prime minister of Canada and senior civil servants ought to be able to get by, more or less convincingly, in both official languages in, for example, televised election debates among federal party leaders. Was it fair, or even democratic, to impose similar linguistic rigours on premiers of Ontario and their senior civil servants — when less than 1% of the provincial population spoke only French, less than 12% reported themselves as bilingual, and more than 86% reported their official language as English? (And if provincial official bilingualism did not mean this, what did it mean?)

Besides, by the 1980s it was clear that the new Quebec that was beginning to emerge from the constitutional restructuring struggles was not itself officially bilingual, but officially unilingual French. By the time of Quebec's renewed determination to have French-only outdoor signs in the late 1980s, it could be said that, taking account of everything that had transpired since the election of Jean Lesage in 1960, the rights of the French-speaking minority in Ontario were now at last equal to the rights of the English-speaking minority in Quebec.

Whatever else, Central Canada's English-speaking province had at last lived up to the historic fair-minded Canadian national principle, for both French and Catholic Canadians who chose to dwell within its borders. The trend was officially confirmed by the proclamation of the Peterson regime's "Bill 8," which extended French-language government services in designated areas and declared some 6,000 provincial civil service positions bilingual, in the late fall of 1989. For the foreseeable future, the limits of high-minded progress had been reached on Canada's perpetually divisive but nonetheless stimulating bilingualism and biculturalism issue, in Central Canada and no doubt in every other part of the Confederation.

The Confederation of Tomorrow (and "Central Canada" Today)

It cannot be entirely an accident that Toronto's ultimate replacement of Montreal as Canada's largest metropolitan region was accompanied by an equally historic shift in Ontario's approach to federal-provincial relations in the wider Confederation.

Even in the late nineteenth century, there had been a side to Ontario that agreed with John A. Macdonald about the insignificance of provincial politics and the primacy of the federal government in Canadian public life. Part of Trudeau's continuing electoral appeal in Ontario related to the survival of this particular element in the regional imagination of English-speaking Central Canada. Given the national demographics, this played an important part in keeping Trudeau in power for more than 15 years.

Yet, more than anyone else, it was Oliver Mowat, Liberal premier of Ontario for 24 uninterrupted years in the era immediately after Confederation (and a proponent of an elected Canadian Senate in 1864), who successfully established the tradition of province building and the regional state in English-speaking Canada. With virtually no major exception, the tradition was faithfully carried forward by every Ontario premier who succeeded Mowat, down to the 1950s, when Toronto began to sense that it had supplanted Montreal as the economic capital of Canada.

Under Leslie Frost (the "Silver Fox") in the 1950s Ontario began to take more of a nation-building approach to its role in the emerging new Confederation. Turning its back on the Mitch Hepburn who had contemptuously dismissed the Dominion-Provincial Conference of 1941, Frost's regime finally made a guarded peace with Ottawa over federal-provincial taxation and the Rowell-Sirois principle of National Adjustment Grants.

Other provinces have pointedly seen Ontario's new postwar concern for the nation at large as simply a continuation of its old, self-interested regional policies under new social, economic, and geographic circumstances. There can be no doubt that modern Ontario's federal-provincial strategies, like those of every other province, flow from conceptions of provincial interest. The tradition of the old Ontario regional state has never altogether faded, and in the very late twentieth century there have been signs of a modest revival.

Yet Ontario's postwar urge toward nation building carried on into the 1980s, and enjoyed a few brief moments on what at least Ontario itself conceived as higher ground. In 1967 Leslie Frost's successor, John Robarts, convened the Confederation of Tomorrow Conference in Toronto, during the first wave of deepening concern over the questions Quebec was raising for the new Confederation. This helped launch the federal-provincial "constitutional review" process of 1968–71.

In the late 1970s and early 1980s John Robarts's successor, William Davis, stood up for national unity with Trudeau's federal government at Ottawa when the national constitutional crisis at last boiled over. (Jean Chrétien, Trudeau's justice minister from 1980 to 1982, has reported that Ontario was something of an irascible ally; only New Brunswick kept the faith unconditionally. Yet, whatever else, the Ontario provincial government's official public support for Pierre Trudeau's late twentieth century nation-building policies played an important part, in enabling the visionary prime minister to at least begin responding to the Quebec referendum of 1980 with the renewed Canadian Constitution of 1982.)

By the late 1980s the term "Central Canada" itself had virtually been reduced to a synonym for Ontario. The old United Province of Ontario and Quebec still had more than 60% of the total population, but now, even in what was once the overwhelmingly English world of commerce and finance, the somewhat different cultural instincts of francophones and anglophones divided the two provinces more than ever before.

Since the end of the Second World War, Ontario had also developed into a place rather different from the edgeless ethnic heartland of Anglo-Canadianism, bemoaned by the founders of the Quiet Revolution in Quebec. To start with, it was not just the merchants of Montreal who moved to Toronto, but people from virtually every part of the world. The movement included much more diverse migrations from Europe than in the past, and increasing numbers from the "non-white" Commonwealth and especially from Asia (said to be the original homeland of the ancient Indians of Canada).

By 1981 one out of every four residents of Ontario had been born outside Canada, and only a distinct minority were from the United Kingdom or the United States. In the city of Toronto the proportion was more than four out of every 10 residents. In Canada at large the proportion was only four out of every 25 residents. The only other place in the Confederation where the relative size of the recent immigrant population approached that of Toronto was Vancouver, at the western end of the New York–Toronto–Vancouver axis.

Trudeau played a part in all this when his federal government adopted a national policy of multiculturalism in the early 1970s. To Trudeau himself, it sometimes seems, the uniquely Canadian precedent was the early polyethnic history of Canada since the sixteenth century; the heartland of this

John Robarts, premier of the predominantly English-speaking province of Central Canada, 1961–71: a man who had been born in Banff, Alberta, who liked to go hunting, and who convened the Confederation of Tomorrow Conference in Toronto, during the centennial year of the Confederation in 1967.

history was not so much Quebec or even the old Atlantic Acadia of the cod fisheries, as the ancient transcontinental French and Indian fur trade of Ontario and the West.

PERCENTAGE OF CANADIANS AND CANADIAN RESIDENTS BORN OUTSIDE CANADA, 1981

Toronto, Ontario	43
Vancouver, British Columbia	39
Hamilton, Ontario	29
Victoria, British Columbia	27
Windsor, Ontario	24
St. Catharines, Ontario	23
Kitchener, Ontario	23
Montreal, Quebec	22
Edmonton, Alberta	21
Calgary, Alberta	21
London, Ontario	21
Winnipeg, Manitoba	20
Ottawa	19
Thunder Bay, Ontario	17
ALL CANADA	**16**
Saskatoon, Saskatchewan	12
Regina, Saskatchewan	11
Halifax, Nova Scotia	9
Saint John, New Brunswick	5
Charlottetown, Prince Edward Island	5
St. John's, Newfoundland	4
Quebec City, Quebec	2

Even the Toronto of the late 1980s that had, in Peter C. Newman's words, "firmly entrenched itself as Canada's economic centre" was different from the Toronto that had sensed its coming triumph over Montreal in the late 1950s. In the late 1960s, journalist Barbara Moon reported that "dark hose, the tab collar, the vest, the English wide-pant tailoring, the chaste cufflinks, the garters" were still part of what it took to succeed in old Toronto's corporate culture. In 1989 Newman declared:

Power and influence are no longer passed on; they must be earned. Family ties no longer bind; they must be overcome. Performance, judged mainly by bottom-line dollars, has become the test supreme. It matters very little who you are, who your father or grandfather may have been; or where you went to school .... Only what you've actually done ... that's what counts.

What Western and other Canadians of an earlier era had called "Tory Toronto" had given way to "the city with the heart of a loan shark." And in the wider world of Ontario beyond Toronto, the Western Canadian resource boom in the late 1970s and early 1980s shook some other ancient assumptions about Central Canada.

In the early 1970s Canada's most populous province had already acknowledged that it had its own regional development problems in Eastern and Northern Ontario. By the late 1970s assorted statistical series studied by economists and bureaucrats — that in the past (almost forever it seemed) had regularly shown Ontario at the top of the Canadian provincial heap — had also begun to suggest new problems, even in the central and southwestern parts of the province.

In 1982 the Canadian province with the highest average family income was not Ontario, but Alberta. Ontario was not even the province with the second-highest average family income; this honour belonged to British Columbia. Ontario's coincidental brief eligibility for federal equalization payments was not widely discussed and debated or even reported in public. But it sent quiet alarms throughout the provincial government bureaucracy and political system.

The events of the 1980s through which Ontario regained its accustomed primacy in such matters had similarities with regional developments in the United States. There, economic energy in the 1960s and 1970s moved from the old manufacturing "Rustbelt" in the Northeast to the new resource-dominated "Sunbelt" in the Southwest, only to move back toward the Rustbelt as the 1980s progressed. In Canada the great resource boom in the West suddenly collapsed. By 1984 Ontario once again had the highest average family income in the country. Alberta and British Columbia returned to their accustomed second and third places in the inter provincial economic hierarchy.

For a brief wild moment, however, the concept that the primacy of Ontario had been built into the structure of the Confederation had been tested, and found wanting. The thought that perhaps Ontario was not forever destined to receive the most of everything that Canada had to offer had entered even the Central Canadian regional imagination.

In the early 1940s the Ontario-born Canadian historian Arthur Lower had told an audience in Montreal: "En Canada il est certain que Montréal a été notre centre métropole pendant toute notre histoire, dominant le Canada jusqu'au Pacifique." By the late 1980s Toronto was secure for the moment at least, in its position as the new kingpin of Canadian cities — just as Montreal had been in the 1920s after Toronto's first twentieth century burst of dynamic growth. But the deepest long-term truth may have been expressed in the early 1970s by Jacob Spelt, the pioneering Dutch-born Canadian student of *Urban Development in South-Central Ontario*: "Toronto's emergence as a worthy rival to Montreal destroyed the possibility of a truly primate centre in Canada."

Peter C. Newman expressed vaguely related thoughts in 1989. "Canada's new Meritocracy" in Toronto, he reported, "may be very different from their patrician predecessors, but one thought binds them: they know that any elite which fails to renew itself is bound for extinction."

14

THE RENEWED CONSTITUTION

If the legacy of Pierre Trudeau to the Canada of the twenty-first century is still somewhat unclear, the legacy of René Lévesque remains almost completely shrouded in mystery. Yet, however Lévesque's career is finally understood, it is a simple truth that his Quebec referendum on sovereignty-association marked both the culmination of the postwar transition from the old Dominion to the new Canada of the late twentieth century, and the beginning of the modern history of an at last utterly independent Canadian national democracy.

The referendum was held on 20 May 1980, just over three months after the surprise resurrection of Trudeau himself in the federal election of 18 February 1980. ("Guardian angels," the pundit Dalton Camp suggested, "must be rooting for Canada.") The exact question put to the people of Quebec was:

> The government of Quebec has made public its proposal to negotiate a new agreement with the rest of Canada, based on the equality of nations.
>
> This agreement would enable Quebec to acquire exclusive power to make laws, levy taxes and establish relations abroad — in other words, sovereignty — and at the same time to maintain with Canada an economic association including a common currency.
>
> No change in political status resulting from these negotiations will be effected without approval by the people through another referendum.
>
> On these terms, do you give the government of Quebec the mandate to negotiate the proposed agreement between Quebec and Canada?

When all the ballots were counted 40.5% of the Quebec electorate had voted "Oui" and 59.5% had voted "Non".

Various subtle interpretations of these results have been offered. Even before the referendum the Quebec sociologist Pierre Drouilly had argued that, given the demographics of the non-French minority in Quebec, including recent "allophone" immigrants as well as more traditional anglophones, the Oui side would be able to claim at least a victory among the French majority if it won not too much more than 40% of the vote.

Arguments of this sort would have an impact on the longer-term future. For almost all immediate practical political purposes, however, it was indisputable enough that the Non side had won the referendum — "a symbol of the continuity," as Trudeau put it, "which from LaFontaine to Cartier, from

Mercier to Laurier, and Taschereau to Lapointe, and from St. Laurent to Lesage, has always been that of the majority of Quebecers."

On the other hand, during the campaign Trudeau had promised the people of Quebec that if they voted Non,

> we will take in hand immediately the mechanisms for re-newing the constitution, and we will not stop until it is done .... We will say to you, Canadians in other provinces, we will not allow you to interpret this No as an indication that everything is going all right here and can stay the way it was.

Several premiers of other provinces had voiced similar commitments to a "renewed federalism " if the people of Quebec voted Non in the referendum, and, like Trudeau, made it clear as well that they were not prepared to negotiate sovereignty-association. Afterwards, Trudeau singled out "individual speeches made by premiers Davis, Blakeney and Bennett " of, respectively, Ontario, Saskatchewan, and British Columbia. Claude Ryan, who had led the Non forces for the provincial Liberal Party in Quebec, especially stressed the role of Blakeney and Peter Lougheed of Alberta.

For the next year and a half, negotiations for at least a start to this renewed federalism, among the leaders of the federal government of Canada and the governments of its ten provinces, dominated Canadian politics. As almost always happens in such cases, only a distinct minority of the Canadian electorate followed the lawyers' arguments with anything that approached sustained attention. Yet in the end, Trudeau lived up to his promise to "not stop until it is done," in at least a few historic respects.

The "Patriation" Debate

The single most important long-term achievement of Trudeau and the provincial premiers between late May 1980 and early November 1981 was to at last actually do what both their own and earlier generations of Canadian federal and provincial politicians had been repeatedly trying to do — from the late 1920s through to the late 1970s.

On the other hand, though it is still too early for confident judgements, one striking point is how much of what the Trudeau era finally put into the "new Constitution" had its origins in the early 1960s federal regime of the populist Chief from Saskatchewan, John Diefenbaker.

No kind of renewal of Canadian federalism could take place until Canada had "patriated" the power to amend its Constitution from the Queen and Parliament of the United Kingdom. Since the late 1920s, the problem had not been that the Queen and Parliament were at all reluctant, but that the Canadian provincial and federal governments could not agree on an "amending formula."

Led by among others the province-building Ontario of the late 1920s and early 1930s, the provinces had insisted that the federal government alone could not amend those parts of the British North America Act, 1867, that involved provincial powers. Yet, despite fresh attempts under Mackenzie King in 1935 and Louis St. Laurent in 1950, Ottawa and the provinces could not agree on the exact extent of provincial approval required.

In the early 1960s Diefenbaker's justice minister from British Columbia, Davie Fulton, picked up the discussions of 1950. Though patriating the Constitution was a logical part of the Chief's new northern vision, however, in the midst of his other troubles, he never had time to do it.

Then Lester Pearson's justice minister, Guy Favreau, picked up Fulton's initiative. An arrangement known as the Fulton-Favreau Formula was almost accepted at a federal-provincial conference in Charlottetown in 1964 — 100 years after the 1864 Charlottetown Conference. Broadly, Fulton-Favreau had divided the Constitution into two main elements. For amendments to a few "entrenched" parts, such as the existing rights and privileges of provincial governments and the use of the English or French languages, unanimous consent of all provinces would be required. For other parts, excepting some special provisions regarding education and matters affecting some but not all provinces, amendments required approval by two-thirds of the provincial legislatures, representing at least 50% of the national population.

This arrangement, along with various other provisions on more complex matters, was finally defeated by objections from the province of Quebec. By the late 1960s, however, Trudeau, first as Pearson's justice minister, then as prime minister himself, had linked his own particular views on federalism and the French Canadians with the patriation debate that continued after the failure of the Fulton-Favreau proposal— and with Diefenbaker's earlier separate enthusiasm for a Canadian bill of rights. (In the early 1960s, intriguingly enough, the lack of some form of bill of rights in the Fulton-Favreau Formula had brought complaints from the provincial government of Saskatchewan.)

By 1971 Trudeau's initial constitutional exertions finally seemed to win unanimous support for a new amending formula at a federal-provincial conference held in Victoria, B.C. This so-called Victoria Charter Formula has been succinctly described by Richard Simeon, the early 1970s analyst of *Federal-Provincial Diplomacy:*

> For most changes passage would require the approval of the federal government, plus: all provinces with 25 per cent or more of the population (assuring Quebec and Ontario a veto, even if Quebec's population were later to fall below 25 per cent); at least two of the Atlantic provinces; and at least two of the western provinces, with at least 50 per cent of the region's population (thus assuring British Columbia a strong position).

Along with various other arrangements embodied in the Victoria Charter, this too, however, was ultimately rejected by the provincial government of Quebec, even under the first political incarnation of the Liberal Robert Bourassa. In the late 1970s, after the 1976 election of the Parti Québécois, Trudeau tried to revive the same process of "constitutional review" at two more federal-provincial conferences in Ottawa. As he himself once stressed, however, timing is everything in politics. It would take the May 1980 Quebec referendum to present the decisive opportunity.

Grown Up at Last (Almost?)

Given all this background, the shortest version of what happened after May 1980 is that Trudeau called a federal-provincial conference at Ottawa in September. Here he proposed to patriate the old British North America Act, and more broadly, Canada's "written and unwritten" constitution from the United Kingdom, based essentially on the amending arrangements embodied in the Victoria Charter Formula.

Only Ontario and New Brunswick supported the federal position. René Lévesque was still premier of Quebec. He allied with the premiers of the other seven predominantly English-speaking provinces to form what the perfidious Central Canadian mass media dubbed "the Gang of Eight" — a group seeking, from another point of view, an extreme "provincialization" of Canadian federalism. The September 1980 conference broke up in disarray.

Trudeau now announced that the federal government was prepared to patriate the Constitution unilaterally by asking Margaret Thatcher's government in the United Kingdom simply to pass the required legislation without Canadian provincial approval, or at least with only the approval of Ontario and New Brunswick. Thatcher seemed willing enough. The federal government and various provincial governments asked the Supreme Court of Canada to rule on the constitutionality of such a procedure from a Canadian point of view.

The Supreme Court brought down its rulings in September 1981. These demonstrated that it was a Canadian Supreme Court, and not any other kind. On the one hand, seven of the nine judges offered the majority opinion that it would not be technically "illegal" for the Canadian federal government at Ottawa to patriate the Constitution unilaterally. On the other hand, six judges offered the majority opinion that it would violate an unwritten Canadian "convention" for the Constitution to be patriated without some more substantial degree of provincial approval than two provinces. (And by a now 114-year-old tradition, Canada's Constitution was both partly unwritten, as in the United Kingdom, and partly written, as in the United States.)

This ambiguous judgement prompted another federal-provincial constitutional conference at Ottawa, early in November 1981. By this point Lévesque had called a post-referendum provincial election in Quebec, and despite his defeat in the referendum, he had been returned to power, with 80 of the 122 seats in what was now known as the National Assembly in Quebec City. Trudeau, however, made a Machiavellian offer to Lévesque, his old rival and one-time colleague. Lévesque's reaction had the effect of shattering the unity of the Gang of Eight.

This cleared the way for the federal government and nine provinces — all except Quebec — to agree at last on patriation, with an amending formula essentially based on the old Fulton-Favreau principles: approval by two-thirds of the provinces, or seven of the present 10, representing 50% of the population for most matters and unanimous provincial approval for a very few basic structural arrangements. The agreement included a provision allowing individual provinces to opt out of amendments affecting provincial powers, rights, or privileges. It included as well a variety of provisions regarding French- and English-language and other rights, in what would be the start of a renewed Constitution for a now thoroughly independent Canada.

All of this was subsequently ratified by the federal Senate and House of Commons and nine provincial legislatures. It took formal effect on 17 April 1982 — not after the Parliament of the United Kingdom passed its required legislation, but when Elizabeth II came to "our City of Ottawa" to proclaim the Constitution Act, 1982, which, among other things, changed the name of the British North America Act, 1867 to the Constitution Act, 1867.

When she signed the proclamation Queen Elizabeth also signed away the last remaining constitutional connections between Canada and the United Kingdom. She ended a long era that had begun with the first British fishermen in Newfoundland as early as the sixteenth century, had blossomed with the Hudson's Bay Company in the seventeenth century, and had endured the ancient grievance of la Conquête in the eighteenth century. She did not, however, sign away all of the connections between Canada and her own family. Canada was still not a republic — as Quebec had urged it ought to be, in constitutional discussions stretching back to the late 1960s.

Yet even here the new Confederation would be different from the old Dominion. The destiny first crystallized in the sixteenth and seventeenth centuries could be said to have had the last word. Trudeau's "Canadians in other provinces" had to realize that the Non vote in the Quebec referendum did not mean "that everything is going all right here and can stay the way it was." The Queen of Canada, apparently, was still a head but no longer necessarily the head of the Canadian state. Put another way, a non-Canadian who carefully reads the Constitution Act, 1982 — and the Proclamation and Canada Act, 1982 in which it is technically embedded, as well as the subsequent Constitution Amendment Proclamation, 1983 — might reasonably come away with the impression that late twentieth century Canada has alternative constitutional personifications.

On the one hand, for those who prefer this, it is a constitutional monarchy, ultimately presided over by "Elizabeth the Second, by the Grace of God of the United Kingdom, Canada and Her other Realms and Territories Queen, Head of the Commonwealth, Defender of the Faith." On the other, for those who prefer this, it is a federal parliamentary democracy presided over by "the Governor General and Commander-in-Chief of Canada" (who, in the case of the Constitution Amendment Proclamation, 1983, happened to be "Her Excellency the Right Honourable Jeanne Sauvé" — herself a representative of that rarest and most exotic sub-species among the national citizenry, a French Canadian born in Western Canada).

The Canadian Charter of Rights and Freedoms

When it was all over, an aging Tommy Douglas from Saskatchewan agreed on national television that a great deed had been done. And, he suggested, it could only have been done by Pierre Trudeau.

There is a cynical sense in which this seems true enough. To some extent, the most fundamental difference between the 1981 Ottawa conference and the second Charlottetown conference in 1964 was that in 1981 a French Canadian prime minister, who enjoyed overwhelming support from the regional branch of the federal electorate in Quebec, was prepared to patriate the Constitution even without the agreement of the government of the province of Quebec.

In a related sense, Trudeau succeeded in patriating the Canadian Constitution only at the price of giving up on most of his personal substantive goals for constitutional reform. Canada is a diverse country, and no one person can be equipped to come up with comprehensive concrete answers to the questions that it so regularly seems to pose. Substantively, many hands from many places, over many years, were involved in creating the deal that finally worked.

At the same time, in yet another sense, Trudeau wielded a controversial but undeniable influence over the Canadian nation building of the late twentieth century, somewhat like that wielded by John A. Macdonald over the nation building of the late nineteenth century. Trudeau himself appeared to see the original Confederation of the 1860s and 1870s more from the standpoint of George-Etienne Cartier. Yet the analogy with Macdonald is striking in at least the sense that, in both cases, the deepest source of influence was the same: among all the major actors of their eras, only Macdonald and Trudeau had really thought the matter through.

One strong expression of Trudeau's influence is that the renewed Canadian Constitution, or the Constitution Act, 1982, effectively begins with 34 sections collectively known as the "Canadian Charter of Rights and Freedoms." This had precedents in Diefenbaker's Canadian Bill of Rights, passed by a simple majority of the federal Parliament in 1960 and subsequently viewed as not altogether enforceable by the courts, especially with regard to provincial law. By the early 1980s, however, some among the old Gang of Eight, and especially the western provinces — despite Saskatchewan's views of the early 1960s — feared that Trudeau's variation on the Chief's earlier theme would be only another device to thwart provincial powers, Canada's ancient British traditions of parliamentary democracy, or both.

To win agreement from nine provinces, Trudeau finally had to qualify the new Charter with a "notwithstanding clause." This allows federal and provincial governments to violate certain Charter rights simply by recurrently passing a law every five years that says they are going to do so, notwithstanding what the Charter says. To some the clause is absurd; to others it only reflects the unique profundity of Canada's particular democratic tradition of moderation and compromise.

Beyond all this, the Canadian Charter of Rights and Freedoms did give the renewed Canadian Constitution a more elegant and logical beginning than the old British North America Act. Even so, there were those who stressed that its mere existence reflected a certain Americanization of Canadian constitutional practices, an unhappy departure from the more strictly British traditions of the old Dominion. There is something to this in a formal sense. In a general way, Trudeau can fairly be described as a constitutional Americanizer, like those who now support the "Charter 88" movement for a bill of rights in the United Kingdom itself. Yet the substance of the Charter can equally be described as uniquely or even incredibly Canadian.

Still reflecting something of the spiritual conservatism of the ancient French and British, and of the still more ancient Indians, it begins with a notably brief and simple preamble: "Whereas Canada is founded upon principles that recognize the supremacy of God and the rule of law .... "

It then goes on to guarantee, "subject only to such reasonable limits prescribed by law as can be demonstrably justified in a free and democratic society": "Fundamental Freedoms"; "Democratic Rights"; "Mobility Rights"; "Legal Rights"; "Equality Rights"; rights regarding the "Official Languages of Canada"; and "Minority Language Educational Rights."

It notes as well that its guarantees do not "abrogate or derogate from" the "rights and freedoms" of "the aboriginal peoples of Canada," including "any rights or freedoms that have been recognized by the Royal Proclamation of October 7, 1763" — a historic document prompted, in great measure, by the Conspiracy of Pontiac, war chief of the Ottawa Indians, in the primeval Great Lakes wilderness of the eighteenth century.

A Revised Version of the French Fact?

Whatever Trudeau's more diffuse influence on the symbolic elegance and logical thrust of late twentieth century Canadian nation building, the failure of the Quebec provincial government to endorse, or "sign," the Constitution Act, 1982 ultimately added up to a failure for at least this part of his particular solution to the modern problems of federalism and the French Canadians.

Trudeau's own plausible enough rhetoric was that, while certainly regrettable, the attitude of the Quebec provincial government did not fundamentally matter. He himself, a French-speaking native of Quebec, who had won 74 of the province's 75 federal seats in 1980 and had played a key part in the Non victory in the referendum, was proof enough of that. On the actual Proclamation signed by Queen Elizabeth on 17 April 1982 there also appeared the signatures of Jean Chrétien, attorney general of Canada, André Ouellet, registrar general of Canada, and Pierre Trudeau, prime minister of Canada — all three, natives of Quebec.

At the same time, the Quebec provincial government had not signed the renewed Constitution. At bottom the reason was that the people of Quebec had quite comfortably returned René Lévesque and the Parti Québécois to power in the provincial election of 1981, even after they had defeated Lévesque's particular proposal for sovereignty-association in the 1980 referendum. As the Quebec entertainer Yvon Deschamps quipped, the 1981 provincial election showed that what Quebec really wanted was "an independent Quebec in a united Canada." However it was interpreted, in the world of the continuing unwritten parts of the Canadian Constitution, the electoral verdict had important implications.

Moreover, the Constitution Act, 1982 was, in effect, arranged to accommodate any subsequent progress Trudeau might have made in bringing the most rigorous side of his personal vision to fruition. Yet, during his final two years as prime minister, he could not persuade Ontario to become officially bilingual like New Brunswick, even after a strong last effort during his, and William Davis's, last year in power, in 1984. Despite a 1979 Supreme Court of Canada decision, it became clear, as well, that there were democratic limits on Manitoba's willingness to reverse altogether the cultural assumptions behind its pro-English legislation of the late nineteenth century.

All this kept the way open for the federal-provincial Meech Lake Accord of 1987. Under this tentative arrangement, which still remained to be ratified by 23 June 1990, the second incarnation of Robert Bourassa agreed that Quebec would endorse the renewed Constitution provided that, among other things, Quebec secured constitutional recognition as a "distinct society" within the Confederation.

This phrase had appeared in Quebec provincial government documents as early as the 1960s, but some in English-speaking Canada still wondered aloud just what it meant. Almost as if to help explain, and despite another Supreme Court of Canada decision, early in 1989 Bourassa's government passed legislation confirming that it was illegal for outside signs in Quebec to be in a language other than French.

Bourassa subsequently stressed that this legislation does not actually relate to the Meech Lake Accord (and its technical justification is in fact the notwithstanding clause in the Constitution Act, 1982). Whatever the case, it only capped an extended recent history, involving both the Quebec Liberals and the Parti Québécois. This history demonstrated that the Quebec provincial government, whatever its partisan political colouring, was unalterably determined to secure Quebec as a geographic region that was not officially bilingual, as it could be said to have been in the ancient past, but officially unilingual French.

Whatever would finally happen to the Meech Lake Accord, by the late 1980s it seemed clear enough that, under any effective renewed Constitution the new Confederation might have, Quebec in fact was and would remain a distinct society in at least one crucial sense. Any Canadian, or any other person, who wished to exercise his or her "mobility rights" and move to Quebec had to be willing to speak French, or to learn how to speak French, in ordinary public life.

As Trudeau had long prophesied, this ultimate resolution of Quebec's role in the new Confederation also implied less utopian efforts at promoting French language and culture outside Quebec, from the Atlantic to the Pacific to the Arctic Ocean. The federal government was now officially bilingual, and so was the provincial government of New Brunswick. Quebec was unilingual French. All the other provinces were unilingual English, hedged by varying degrees of unofficial bilingualism in Ontario and Manitoba and by various special commitments to French-language education in virtually all the English-speaking provinces.

All this amounted to a much stronger French political presence in the Confederation, both inside Quebec and in the country at large, than had prevailed in the old Dominion of Canada. There were still many pockets of English-speaking Canada that had trouble accepting the change. Late in 1989, when the Meech Lake Accord stumbled into deep trouble, unanticipated less than a year before, Premier Clyde Wells from Newfoundland put himself at the head of a new Canadian national questioning of "the distinct society clause," stressing Trudeau's earlier reservations about a "special status" for Quebec.

Were the Meech Lake Accord to proceed in its original form, one might reasonably guess, the result would indeed be still some considerable distance from Trudeau's early 1960s vision of the "two main ethnic and linguistic groups" collaborating "at the hub of a truly pluralistic state" as "the envied seat of a form of federalism that belongs to tomorrow's world." Yet what French-speaking Canada would achieve in the new Confederation would be a kind of compromise, somewhere between the competing visions of Pierre Trudeau and René Lévesque.

What English-speaking Canada would achieve would be another kind of compromise — a bilingual and multicultural country that still did not place unprecedented linguistic burdens on English-speaking Canadians who lived outside Quebec or New Brunswick, or who neither worked for the federal bureaucracy, nor seriously aspired to become a federal prime minister.

The Rights of the Canadian Indians, Inuit, and Métis

It was not just the French who had begun the history of Canada, but the French and the Indians and their Métis children of the northern wilderness. From a standpoint closer to practical politics in the late twentieth century, beyond the question of French and English dualism (or bilingualism), the Canadian constitutional renewal process that started in the early 1960s and ended in the early 1980s became a magnet for many of the more general democratic causes that flourished during the same two decades in many different parts of North America and Western Europe, and even the world at large.

In a particular North American setting, and with a particular historic justice in the Canadian case, the process became a key focus for the political impulse represented in the United States by the postwar American Indian Movement. In Canada, with only one-tenth of the general American population but with probably well over one-half the U.S. Indian population, the impulse ultimately came to be represented by four different groups: the Assembly of First Nations, for so-called status Indians; the Native Council of Canada, for non-status Indians and Métis outside the West; the Métis National Council, for the Western Canadian Métis who especially looked back to Louis Riel; and the Inuit Committee on National Issues, for the Inuit of the far north.

The more or less uniform demand of all four groups finally came to be "aboriginal self-government." In effect, this concept reflected a modernization and democratization of a special legal status that at least some descendants of the Confederation's original inhabitants enjoyed as a result of

The Red Lake chief making a speech to the governor of Red River at Fort Douglas, in what is now Manitoba, 1825. Attributed to the British draftsman H. Jones, after an earlier drawing by the Swiss American Peter Rindisbacher.

Councils between Indians and Europeans — the earliest expressions of multiculturalism — have been a recurrent feature of Canadian history. Four updated versions of such gatherings, in 1983, 1984, 1985, and 1987, formed the most exotic and in some ways most interesting (if also, alas, least successful) elements in the Canadian constitutional renewal process of the 1980s.

The first amendments to the renewed Constitution of 1982 deal with the rights of "the Indian, Inuit, and Métis peoples of Canada." Along with much else, there are bound to be other such amendments in the late twentieth and early twenty-first centuries.

attempts by British imperial officialdom and then the Dominion of Canada to reconcile them to the new colonial society of European settlement — thus, the significance, for example of the Royal Proclamation of 1763.

For many in the late twentieth century English-speaking mainstream, aboriginal self-government has proved even harder to swallow than the distinct society in Quebec. Even by the late 1980s it would remain a still to be fulfilled demand.

Yet, beyond the references in the Charter of Rights and Freedoms, the Constitution Act, 1982 did take care to note that the "existing aboriginal and treaty rights of the aboriginal peoples of Canada are hereby recognized and affirmed." It clarified that "'aboriginal peoples of Canada' includes the Indian, Inuit and Métis peoples of Canada." And it provided for another federal-provincial conference within one year, to which representatives of these peoples would be invited, to discuss "constitutional matters that directly affect the aboriginal peoples of Canada."

This conference, which also included representation from the governments of the Yukon and Northwest Territories, was held in March 1983. It produced the first amendments to the renewed Constitution under the new amending formula, and given effect by the Constitution Amendment Proclamation, 1983. These amendments said nothing about aboriginal self-government, but they did specify that the existing aboriginal and treaty rights could include potential new "land claims agreements" and applied equally to "male and female persons." They also provided for additional conferences on aboriginal constitutional matters.

The next conference, held in March 1984, marked Trudeau's last official appearance in the continuing drama of Canadian constitutional renewal. He was under considerable (if not exactly decisive) pressure from the leaders of the Assembly of First Nations, the Native Council of Canada, the Métis National Council, and the Inuit Committee on National Issues, for whom he had come to evince a somewhat guarded admiration. In the wake of his own recent decision to resign as prime minister of Canada by June, he announced a dramatic reversal in his own and the federal government's position on aboriginal self-government.

Up to this point, the great political difficulty of the concept had been reflected in a fundamental lack of serious support from both provincial and federal governments in the Confederation.

Trudeau's own traditional view had been that there was no more place for special status for Indians, Inuit, and Métis in Canada than there was for special status for the province of Quebec. All Canadians were equal, in the same way. In March 1984 he proved that even brilliant old politicians are sometimes capable of intellectual growth, and changed his mind.

The federal government now offered to "entrench" the principle of aboriginal self-government in the Constitution, and set in motion a federal-provincial-aboriginal process for gradually negotiating what aboriginal self-government actually meant.

This was considerably less than aboriginal leaders wanted, and considerably more than any combination of the required seven provincial governments felt able to accept. It did, however, win support from New Brunswick, Ontario, and Manitoba — three provinces collectively representing just under 43% of the national population. At the end of the conference, Trudeau told the representatives of the four Canadian aboriginal groups: "I am proud to have walked the first mile of this journey with you .... Others will take my place and continue ... for there can be no turning back."

This too recalled the earlier federal regime of the white Chief from Saskatchewan who had appointed James Gladstone "the first treaty Indian" in the Senate of Canada, and had at last given status Indians on reserves the right to vote in federal elections. René Lévesque, with some apparent justice, complained that while Trudeau finally seemed prepared to concede special status to some people in the Confederation, he was still not prepared to concede it to the predominantly French-speaking people of Quebec. (For his part, Lévesque had invited a representative of those historic Great Lakes–St. Lawrence Mohawks who still do not recognize the sovereignty of either Canada or the United States, to speak on Quebec's behalf.)

Down to the end of the 1980s, two more federal-provincial conferences on aboriginal constitutional issues were held, under Brian Mulroney's new Progressive Conservative federal regime, in 1985 and 1987. In 1987 Mulroney actually managed to secure agreement from the required seven provinces representing 50% of the population, on an even weaker version of the aboriginal self-government concept than in Trudeau's 1984 proposal. But, except for some Métis representatives, the deal was too watered-down to win significant support from aboriginal leaders.

Richard Hatfield of New Brunswick argued that it was time for aboriginal leaders to promote their visions of the role of Indians, Inuit, and Métis in the new Confederation more vigorously among the mainstream of the national population. The new premier of Alberta, Don Getty, a former Edmonton Eskimos football star who had been born in Montreal, acknowledged that aboriginal self-government was important unfinished business on the Canadian national agenda. But he argued that it had to be much more clearly defined, in a way "that maintains the basic historic fabric of our Canadian system."

It could at least be said that the political leadership of the new Confederation had at last begun to recognize what Harold Innis had understood more than half a century before: that "the Indian and his culture have been fundamental to the growth of Canadian institutions."

"The Atlantic and Western regions ..."

In the late twentieth century, it was not just the French, Indians and the Métis who made up the Confederation, but also a highly diverse assortment of people whose official language was English. Just after the May 1980 Quebec referendum, when the urgency of the negotiations that finally led to the Constitution Act, 1982, at last had become undeniable, Alberta's Premier Peter Lougheed had declared: "I hope that we aren't going to a constitutional conference where the whole conference is revolving around Quebec, as important as they are." There were, he pointed out, "aspirations of the people in the Atlantic and western regions" as well.

Two elements in the Constitution Act, 1982 expressed the barest beginnings of movement in this direction:

(1) Part III (section 36) was headed "Equalization and Regional Disparities". This flowed from a proposal put forward by Nova Scotia, during the earlier negotiations leading to the ill-fated Victoria Charter of 1971. It expressed the commitment of "the government of Canada and the provincial governments" to such objectives as "furthering economic development to reduce disparity in opportunities," and "making equalization payments to ensure that provincial governments have sufficient revenues to provide reasonably comparable levels of public services at reasonably comparable levels of taxation." If the early 1940s Rowell-Sirois vision of Canadian federalism had shown some decisive weaknesses by the early 1980s, at least some of it nonetheless found its way into the written parts of the new Constitution.

(2) Part VI of the Constitution Act, 1982 (sections 50 and 51) was an amendment to what was now the Constitution Act, 1867, dealing with "Non-Renewable Natural Resources, Forestry Resources and Electrical Energy." With special symbolic reference to an ancient concern of the three prairie provinces, which, unlike the others, had only acquired control over their natural resources in 1930, this amendment tried to make more precise exactly how, in the new Confederation, each of all ten provinces, as the *Canada Year Book 1988* puts it, "administers its own natural resources."

Especially in Western Canada, these two elements in the new Constitution only flagged much more diffuse, long-standing regional grievances that had nothing directly to do with ancient antagonisms between French and English Canadians. By the summer of 1982, however, a new and tighter focus for debate about a still broader conception of renewed federalism had at last arrived.

In August Alberta published its discussion paper on *A Provincially-Appointed Senate: A New Federalism for Canada*. It allowed that the "Alberta Government was pleased with the results of The Constitution Act, 1982 in that it contained Alberta's major constitutional proposals: the amending formula and the legislative override provision of the Charter of Rights and Freedoms" (or the so-called notwithstanding clause). Yet: "Despite the significant achievement in the area of the Constitution, the problems of regional discontent continue to cause considerable tension and strain throughout our federal system."

The document continued:

Under the provisions of *The Constitution Act, 1982* a

constitutional conference must be held within a year of patriation .... In addition to discussing aboriginal rights, governments will probably wish to resolve other constitutional questions. It is the intention of the Alberta Government to propose that the subject of Senate reform be one of the other matters addressed by governments.

The Central Canadian mass media had grasped the rising new issue on the agenda of constitutional reform in Canada even before the problems of "Quebec, as important as they are," had been truly confronted. On 22 May 1980, two days after the Quebec referendum, the *Toronto Star* had ran article headlined "West, not Quebec is the problem now." And, as it happened, the renewed Constitution in place at the end of Trudeau's regime in the early summer of 1984 was only the beginning of yet another urge to step forward, in the continually challenging world of the new Confederation.

15

AT THE LIMITS OF FEDERAL-PROVINCIAL DIPLOMACY

During the constitutional crisis in the late 1970s and early 1980s, there were some Canadians, in all parts of the country, who argued that it should be dealt with by a special popular convention. Then the results of this convention should be ratified in a national referendum. Similar concerns for rooting the Confederation's fundamental design more firmly in the will of the people had been voiced in the 1860s and 1870s. In both cases they were ignored.

Instead, what finally became the Constitution Act, 1982, was hammered out at meetings of elected officials of the federal and provincial governments, and ratified by votes in federal and provincial elected legislatures. Essentially the same arrangements had also been used to develop what is now known as the Constitution Act, 1867, except that in the mid-1860s there was no federal government, (though the "Great Coalition" of Macdonald, Cartier, and Brown in the old United Province, newly headquartered at the Central Canadian lumbering town of Ottawa, could be viewed as the aspiring germ of such a thing). This was, it seemed, a traditional Canadian way of managing constitutional issues.

Since the early twentieth century, and especially since the Rowell-Sirois report and the Second World War, this approach had also become a traditional Canadian way of managing a wide variety of non-constitutional issues, rooted in the abiding regionalism of the Confederation. Between the end of the war in Europe in May 1945 and the signing of the Meech Lake Accord in Canada in June 1987, there were an even 50 Canadian federal-provincial conferences of premiers and prime ministers (First Ministers' Conferences, or FMCs, in the most recent technical jargon).

As time went by, problems gradually developed in the evolution of this Canadian "executive federalism" (as Donald Smiley would put it) or *Federal-Provincial Diplomacy* (the title of the early 1970s book by Smiley's colleague Richard Simeon). This points to an important reason for the rather sudden appearance of the most recent and most serious stage on the long journey to Senate reform in Canada.

In the late 1980s, Stuart MacKinnon, secretary of the Canadian Intergovernmental Conference Secretariat, which has arisen to provide support services for federal-provincial meetings, observed:

> It may well be that if the *Constitution Act, 1867* had provided
> for an effective upper house in Parliament, similar to the

U.S. Senate, for resolution of regional differences within the institutions of the central government, it would have inhibited the growth and development of the FMC.

Similarly, Alberta's 1982 discussion paper *A Provincially-Appointed Senate*, did not actually strike the first blows in the late twentieth century campaign for just this kind of Canadian Senate. When Trudeau revived the federal-provincial constitutional review process in the late 1970s, British Columbia, the Canadian Bar Association, and the Canada West Foundation had made proposals for a provincially appointed Senate. The Trudeau regime itself had tested a somewhat different kind of Senate reform proposal in the Supreme Court of Canada. Other organizations and individuals had made different suggestions again. In 1981 the Canada West Foundation published a new proposal for an elected Senate, in a report called *Regional Representation*.

Alberta's 1982 paper stood out among the various proposals because in the 1970s Canada's fourth most populous province had come to inspire and

Ernest C. Manning in his prime. He had been premier of Alberta without interruption from 1943 to 1968. When he retired he had just edged out the late nineteenth century Ontario premier Oliver Mowat's earlier record as the longest-serving provincial first minister in Canadian history.

Even after his retirement Manning retained a strong interest in both provincial and national politics. As late as the early 1980s he served as a co-author of the Canada West Foundation's elected-Senate proposal, Regional Representation.

In the late 1980s Ernest Manning's son, Preston, became leader of a new federal Reform Party, based in Western Canada, and urging, among other things, a notably uncompromising approach to the reform of the federal Senate in Ottawa.

represent a diffuse Western Canadian, and even more generally, English-speaking "regional" protest, against the federal government at Ottawa. In the 1980s Alberta took the lead in a more focused campaign for a new and quite profound version of Canadian Senate reform, flowing fundamentally from staunch concerns for the more effective expression of regional and provincial interests in the national political culture of the new Confederation.

In 1982 the Alberta government explained why it had not raised the question in the late 1970s, as others had done. The province had been "silent on the issue of reform of the Canadian Senate because up to that time the First Ministers' Conference had evolved as an effective institution for representing provincial interests."

The Failure of the Federal Nature of the Federal Cabinet

Viewed from Canada's specific historical experience, the gradual rise of the First Ministers' Conference in the twentieth century had not really been, in the most direct sense, a reaction to the original weaknesses of the Canadian Senate. It had been more a response to the gradual erosion of the alternate institutional convention meant to compensate for the more or less deliberate failures of regional representation through the Senate — what Christopher Dunkin had put his finger on in the 1860s, when he complained that the "Cabinet here must discharge that kind of function which in the United States is performed in the federal sense by the Senate."

In the early twentieth century, the particular Canadian doctrine of "the federal nature of the Cabinet" as the "first great check on the central government" had been unambiguously articulated in R.A. MacKay's *The Unreformed Senate of Canada*, first published in 1926 and published again in a revised version in 1963. Even a new book on the subject, published in 1965 by F.A. Kunz (*The Modern Senate of Canada 1925–1963: A Re-Appraisal*), reaffirmed that the fundamental vehicle of regional representation in Canadian federalism was "the closely observed constitutional convention that the federal Cabinet must mirror in its composition all the provinces of the country."

Kunz also deftly characterized the parallel Senate strategy of Macdonald, Cartier, and other like-minded fathers of the Confederation of the 1860s and 1870s. The "assertion of the federal function of the Senate at the time of Confederation" had been merely "a well-calculated political device used as a constitutional tranquillizer to palliate the sectional fears of the weaker partners to federalism from the numerical majorities of the House of Commons." The original voice of region "was essentially a rhetorical device, a psychological rather than a political remedy."

With the benefit of a longer hindsight, we can see somewhat more clearly still. Given Kunz's description of what the Canadian Senate had become in practice, the twentieth century rise of, in his words, "the use of Dominion-provincial conferences as clearing-houses for all sorts of disputed questions," reflected the increasing failure of the "closely observed constitutional convention" of provincial representation in the federal Cabinet.

Even the first Interprovincial Conference of 1887 could be read as evidence that John A. Macdonald himself had some trouble making the federal nature of the Cabinet work. So could Goldwin Smith's *Canada and the Canadian Question*, first published in 1891. So could a partisan speech by Wilfrid Laurier at an 1887 political picnic in Megantic, Quebec:

> The truth is that after twenty years' trial of the system, the Maritime Provinces submit to Confederation but do not love it. The province of Manitoba is in open revolt against the Dominion Government .... The province of Nova Scotia demands its separation.

Laurier's own convening of the first of what are now known as First Ministers' Conferences in 1906 suggests that the federal nature of the Cabinet equally had some limitations, even in his revised version of Macdonald's federal governing regime. The same could be said about additional Interprovincial Conferences in 1902 and 1910. Another First Ministers' Conference was held in 1918, and another Interprovincial Conference in 1913, during the federal regime of Robert Borden from Nova Scotia.

The wizard Mackenzie King worked the convention of the federal nature of the federal Cabinet with more skill and subtlety than any other Canadian prime minister. He also showed that the convention included much more than mere concern for choosing Cabinet ministers who could represent provinces. It equally meant being blessed with the supreme good luck of a French Canadian lieutenant, such as King's "most loyal and truest of colleagues and friends," Ernest Lapointe, to represent Quebec. Sometimes it even involved deft and cynical appointments to a suitably humble federal Senate.

Yet the early 1940s recommendation of the Rowell-Sirois report for regular Dominion-provincial conferences implied that even King's success was not good enough, especially with the growing complexities of modern liberal democratic government, nourished by the 1930s Depression. All told, five conferences were held during King's more than 21 years in power. And four conferences were held during R.B. Bennett's much less skilful interregnum, from August 1930 to October 1935.

Following Mackenzie King, Louis St. Laurent held six conferences between 1949 and 1957. Then Diefenbaker held four between 1957 and 1963. "Mike" Pearson — an international diplomat by profession, and a beleaguered enthusiast for "co-operative federalism" inside Canada — held nine conferences, between 1963 and 1968. In 1968 the Canadian Broadcasting Corporation (and Radio-Canada), held in trust by the federal government for the people of Canada, began to televise the public portions of these now quite regular high councils of the nation's highest leaders.

By this point, on the eve of Trudeau's accession to power — which had itself been assisted by his nationally televised appearance as Pearson's justice minister at a February 1968 federal-provincial conference in Ottawa — the new Confederation's late twentieth century tradition of federal-provincial diplomacy was in full flower. Under Trudeau it became, in effect, a part of the unwritten constitution. Between 1968 and 1984, Trudeau held 23 First Ministers' Conferences, and Joe Clark held one more, for an even two dozen in the space of some 16 years. The phrase "conference composed of the Prime Minister of Canada and the first ministers of the provinces" finally appeared in constitutional writing, in section 37 of the Constitution Act, 1982.

Participants in the Dominion-Provincial Conference of 1935. The 1930s witnessed the first blossoming of such gatherings. Only three had been held during the history of the Confederation up to the start of the decade, but there would be a conference each year between 1931 and 1935.

In this photograph of participants in the 1935 gathering, Mackenzie King is seated in the centre of the first row. This was his second conference, and he would host three more in the 1940s. Then there would be seven conferences in the 1950s, and an average of well over one conference each year throughout the 1960s, 1970s, and 1980s.

The symbolism of having the conferees pose beneath a portrait of the nineteenth century fathers of Confederation has some distressing implications for an institution that would become such a regular part of Canadian national life. (In the Canada of the late twentieth century, it could be said, aspiring new fathers of the Confederation now get together at least once every year.)

Under Trudeau, the failure of the federal nature of the federal Cabinet became virtually complete. His federal Liberal Party finally left office in 1984 as a national political organization that had almost no seats, let alone elected Cabinet ministers, west of Ontario. (Even though, in the 1980 federal election, it did win 28% of the popular vote in Manitoba, 24% in Saskatchewan, and 22% in each of Alberta and British Columbia.)

In the early 1980s Richard Simeon argued that, in Canada's late twentieth century parliamentary democracy, extremely tight conventions of party discipline and Cabinet solidarity made it exceedingly difficult for any Cabinet minister to act as an effective spokesman for regional and provincial interests in the Confederation. And Donald Smiley complained about the harsh consequences of a new doctrine of "federal majoritarianism" at Ottawa.

The Virtues of Federal-Provincial Diplomacy

Alberta's 1982 discussion paper made clear that the more recent failures of the First Ministers' Conference itself, "as an effective institution for representing provincial interests," was the best starting point for a new debate on serious Senate reform. On the other hand, the paper equally implied that the history of federal-provincial diplomacy in Canada since the end of the Second World War could claim some genuine achievements.

To start with, federal-provincial conferences had been the vehicle for the gradual implementation of at least the spirit underlying the Rowell-Sirois Commission's early 1940s vision of regional equalization and the federal-provincial Canadian welfare state.

Beyond the modern federal-provincial financial equalization system, First Ministers' Conferences have played one role or another in the creation of Canada's modern federal unemployment insurance system; federal or, in the case of Quebec, provincial pension plans; federally funded provincial medicare programs; and federally funded provincial social assistance programs. (It is intriguing to note that the federal-provincial negotiations that created two virtually identical Canada and Quebec pension plans, as Richard Simeon has put the point, "implied a special status for Quebec" as early as 1965.)

More broadly, First Ministers' Conferences have been and will no doubt remain the primary arena for the management of federal-provincial financial relations. This must be an especially important subject under a judicially interpreted written national constitution that assigns great legislative authority to provincial governments and great financial resources to the federal government.

At some point, some systematic renegotiation of the terms of the division of federal-provincial powers and resources could conceivably become yet another item on the continuing agenda of Canadian constitutional reform. The clarification of provincial rights to "resource rents" in the amendment set out in sections 50 and 51 of the Constitution Act, 1982, could be read as a small step in this direction.

Another clear if ultimately stormy achievement of the Canadian First Ministers' Conference is the Constitution Act, 1982 itself. The new Confederation would not have been able to respond to the May 1980 Quebec referendum as quickly as it did without the two preceding decades of what sometimes seemed endless constitutional bickering at federal-provincial conferences.

The eventual fruition of the long journey to Senate reform itself must take the form of a constitutional amendment, and the fate of this amendment will finally be decided by some form of First Ministers' Conference. Many still complain about this approach to constitutional change. As Trudeau has subsequently stressed, one of his own unfulfilled constitutional objectives was to make some provision for popular referenda in the process. As matters stand, however, federal-provincial diplomacy remains at the centre of the Canadian tradition.

Much more generally, Australia has a system of government institutions that is, in many ways, closer to that of Canada than any other country in the world. Australia has as well an elected federal Senate, of the sort that Alberta and Western Canada at large have come to urge for Canada. Even so, to quote Richard Simeon again, in Australia, as in Canada, "conferences of premiers and prime ministers are an important mechanism for adjustment" of regional tensions. Lionel Bowen, the deputy prime minister of Australia in the late 1980s, also carried the title "Minister Assisting the Prime Minister for Commonwealth-State Relations" — a role played at the same time in Canada, by Lowell Murray, "Leader of the Government in the Senate."

As Trudeau has explained, "federal-provincial conferences are, per se, a good thing in a federation." By the late 1970s and early 1980s, the failures that Albertans and many other Canadians began to sense in the postwar tradition of federal-provincial diplomacy did not by any means argue for abandoning the tradition altogether. They pointed instead to the limitations of the tradition's capacity to resolve the abiding regional tensions of the Confederation by itself.

The problem with the continuing stream of First Ministers' Conferences in the 1980s was not that they could do nothing right. It was that increasingly they seemed to be doing some things wrong. They were trying to do other things that they were unable to do. And they were unable to do still other things that, with increasing urgency, needed to be done.

Federal-Provincial Diplomacy as an Arena for Regional Conflict

Part of the malaise of Canadian federal-provincial relations in the 1980s can be attributed to inevitable stresses and strains involved in any creation of such things as renewed constitutions for highly diverse countries. Another part, however, flows from a long-standing, particular, and even characteristically Canadian conflict. As the constitutional crisis of the late 1970s and early 1980s boiled over, this conflict was brought to a fevered pitch for those most directly involved. (One of the virtues of the great democratic mass in Canada is that it takes such things with an appropriate degree of more or less deserved disinterest, or even disdain.) The result was an atmosphere aptly described in December 1983 by Prince Edward Island's premier James Lee as "characterized primarily by an increasing degree of rancour between all levels of government, a lack of co-operation and an increasing degree of regionalism and centralism of an undesirable nature."

The conflict itself has equally aptly been characterized as a conflict between two visions of Canada. Yet Canadians can take some comfort from the durability of the phenomenom. It is, on any long and wide view of the national history, part of what keeps Canada Canadian.

Thus, notwithstanding the other profound differences between the late nineteenth and late twentieth centuries, the late twentieth century democratic warfare between Pierre Trudeau in Ottawa, and René Lévesque in Quebec City and Peter Lougheed in Edmonton, is close enough to the late nineteenth century warfare between John A. Macdonald in Ottawa, and Honoré Mercier in Quebec City and Oliver Mowat in Toronto.

In the late nineteenth century, it was "the centralizing proclivities of the Macdonald clique" that so irked Mercier, Mowat, and other provincial premiers. The parallel late twentieth century irritations felt by Lougheed are spelled out in the 1982 Alberta discussion paper on Senate reform. Up to the late 1970s,

> the First Ministers' Conference had evolved as an effective institution for representing provincial interests. However, the recent trend towards unilateralism and centralization has convinced the Alberta Government that a determined effort must be made to strengthen and protect further the rights of the provinces in the Confederation if we are to avoid the drift towards a unitary state.

Trudeau offered his own quite different assessment of what happened in the late 1970s, in his testimony on the 1987 Meech Lake Accord, before the House of Commons and the unreformed Senate:

> Throughout a certain period of our history, the pendulum swung towards a greater centralization, as was the case during the war and post-war periods; at other times the pendulum swung towards greater decentralization. And this has certainly been the case in Canada since at least 1955 or 1960, I would say ....

Trudeau himself had supported this most recent wave of decentralization in his Trudeau I incarnation, outside the partisan political arena. But Trudeau II (who had moved, as the wit Larry Zolf explained, "from philosopher king to Mackenzie King") had some sober second thoughts.

On his version of events, by the 1970s, under the spell of the Quebec of the Quiet Revolution and the separatist movement, healthy decentralization had mutated into neurotic regionalism and provincial "blackmail" of the

211

nation at large. The boil had burst with the 1980–81 designs of the Gang of Eight, led by Peter Lougheed and the Lévesque who had lost the Quebec referendum. The provinces' only solution to the problems of the new Confederation was to give the provinces everything. It was time to ask "who will speak for Canada?" and to show that there was still someone in Ottawa, and in Ontario and New Brunswick, who would.

Trying to assess, in any balanced way, the relative justice of the two sides to Canada's historic "nation-building vs. province-building" conflict of the late twentieth century would be an extremely difficult task. Sometimes, however, it is easiest for the least powerful player in a game to speak the simplest truth. James Lee's late 1983 observation about "an increasing degree" of both "regionalism and centralism of an undesirable nature" captured the fundamental point. The impact of the intensifying conflict on First Ministers' Conferences was that what was meant to be a forum for compromise, resolution, and reconciliation of regional tensions and federal-provincial differences, had become an arena for confrontation and polarization. At worst, federal-provincial diplomacy had shown that, when pushed to its limits, it was a bloodless battlefield for rancorous democratic civil war.

Trudeau's National Challenge: "Who will speak for Canada?"

From the standpoint of an abiding commitment to the bilingual and multicultural nation, only an unrepentantly partisan supporter of Pierre Trudeau could argue that the justice in the elemental constitutional conflict of the late 1970s and early 1980s was all on his side.

One kind of evidence was Donald Smiley's complaint about the new doctrine of "federal majoritarianism." James Lee stressed related evidence in 1983 — the number of more or less recent books published on Canada with such titles as: *Canada in Question* [in fact by Smiley himself]; *Option: Quebec; Must Canada Fail?; The Precarious Homestead; Unfulfilled Union; The Roots of Disunity; Canada and the Burden of Unity; Divided Loyalties; Western Separatism.*

From a long historical perspective, some argued that Trudeau had actually revived a version of John A. Macdonald's ancient arch-centralist doctrines, which viewed the provinces as no more than "glorified county councils." While this was too extreme on the other side, a good case could nonetheless be made for the argument that Trudeau II did revive much of the ghost of Macdonald's indispensable French Canadian Confederation partner, George-Etienne Cartier.

Like Cartier, Trudeau had a French-speaking Quebec native's convictions about the importance of provincial autonomy in Canadian federalism. Yet, like Cartier again, he came to share as well many of Macdonald's other instincts about the importance of centralizing impulses in the Confederation. Similarly, Trudeau was more than prepared to make concessions to the dramatic regional growth and development that had taken place in Canada since the 1860s and 1870s. But, in the heat of battle, he was also somewhat stridently concerned to stress some ancient "Macdonald-Cartier" understandings of Canada's Constitution.

This is reflected in his preferred Victoria Charter Formula for amendments to the Constitution, the ultimate defeat of which was, not surprisingly, led by Alberta. Under this arrangement, British Columbia would, in effect, have gained a veto over constitutional amendments, along with Ontario and Quebec. Put another way, in recognition of the growth of Western Canada since the nineteenth century, Vancouver would have been promoted to the ranks of "metropolitan" status, along with Toronto and Montreal. But Alberta, Saskatchewan, Manitoba, and the four provinces of Atlantic Canada would have remained in a kind of constitutional "hinterland." Under the variation on the Fulton-Favreau Formula that finally became law, on the other hand, all provinces are "equal," except that constitutional amendments must also, in effect, be approved by at least 50% of the national population.

Related impulses are reflected in the broad conception of Senate reform that Trudeau's regime began to ponder some considerable time before Alberta's 1982 discussion paper, or even before the 1978 proposals from the Canadian Bar Association and British Columbia. According to this conception, the Senate should indeed reflect provincial interests in the Confederation more strongly. Only half of it should be chosen by the federal government, and the other half by the provinces. Or, only half the "well-calculated ... constitutional tranquillizer," originally devised by an ancient Central Canadian imperialism, should survive in its original form.

Even the modified and modernized "Cartier," as opposed to "Macdonald," centralist principles behind all this were anathema to the late twentieth century followers of Lougheed and Lévesque, just as their more pristine versions had been to the like-minded followers of Mowat and Mercier in the late nineteenth century — a time when Montreal's *Empire of the St. Lawrence* still ruled the roost, even in Central Canada. For those who were not at bottom separatists of any variety, Trudeau's arguments were buttressed by one higher-minded principle that he could and did, however, assert with genuine conviction in all parts of the country. Not all the justice was on the "provincialist" side.

The most strident late twentieth century descendants of Mowat and Mercier seemed to be arguing not just that all ten provinces were equal, but that all 11 governments at the First Ministers' Conference table were equal as well. Even in the national arena, in other words, each province was equal to the federal government, and Ottawa's role was merely to implement some national consensus of provincial views on the policy of the Confederation.

At this point in the argument, Trudeau's question "Who will speak for Canada?" acquired claims to something that approached profundity.

Western Canada's National Response: An Elected, Equal, and Effective Senate

In the real world of practical politics, the federal government at Ottawa was never entirely alone in its concerns for the nation at large. Two of Canada's ten provinces supported the aggressive nation-building policies of Trudeau's early 1980s regime at Ottawa: officially bilingual New Brunswick, with 2.9% of the national population in 1981, and the Central Canadian heartland of Ontario, with 35.6%. In 1984 Manitoba, with an additional 4.2% of the national population, and now under Howard Pawley and the NDP, rather than Sterling Lyon and the Progressive Conservatives, would join Ontario and New Brunswick, in supporting Trudeau's Indian, Inuit, and Métis self-government proposal.

Ontario, for its part, was the place where English-speaking people had first begun to call themselves "Canadians," in the first half of the nineteenth century. Traditionally, a strident minority in Ontario had argued that Western Canadian complaints about Confederation were all too often animated by disloyal desires for annexation to the United States. In an earlier era the argument had been used against Oliver Mowat's Liberal "Great Reform Government " in Ontario itself.

In the late twentieth century democratic age of rampant opinion polling, it was not an easy argument to sustain. A Gallup Poll, for instance, was taken in June 1988, during the national debate on the ancient issue of Canada-U.S. free trade. It reported that the smallest proportion of Canadians in any region who would approve of "Canada becoming a part of the United States" was not in Ontario, but in the Prairie provinces of Manitoba, Saskatchewan, and Alberta.

GALLUP POLL JUNE 1988:
"Would you approve or disapprove of Canada becoming a part of the United States?"

Region	% Undecided	% Approve	% Disapprove
Prairies	7	6	87
Ontario	3	10	87
British Columbia	5	14	81
Atlantic	9	19	72
Quebec	8	23	69
ALL CANADA	5	14	81

Despite the prognostications of Goldwin Smith some 100 years before, there was not just east-west regionalism in Canada. There was a still more potent north-south regionalism in North America. In some ways, late twentieth century Western Canada was more enthusiastic about the diverse destiny of the northern half of the continent than Ontario (and certainly it was more enthusiastic than the Quebec that was still pondering the impact of the 1980 referendum).

The West had been the site of the last golden age of Harold Innis's trans-continental fur trade. It had been a homeland for the ancient romance of the Montreal-headquartered North West Company. It was the birthplace of the North West Mounted Police — one of the best-known symbols of Canada in the outside world. It was "Western," but it was also "Canadian." And when Pierre Trudeau asked "Who will speak for Canada?" some Western Canadians, even in Alberta, were impressed.

Other Western Canadians did have knotty feelings of populist alienation from an elitist federal government at Ottawa — and an equally elitist corporate culture in Toronto. The region was proud of its own pioneering heritage, and chronically concerned to defend itself from the ravages of Central Canadian imperialism. But, at bottom, as the new Saskatchewan NDP leader Roy Romanow would explain, Western Canada "wanted in." The deepest problem was that Central Canada seemed to want it to stay "out."

By the middle of the 1980s, the West had had some sober second thoughts of its own. On the long journey to Senate reform, the result was finally reflected in the March 1985 report of the Alberta Select Special Committee on Upper House Reform. In contrast to the title of Alberta's 1982 discussion paper, *A Provincially-Appointed Senate: A New Federalism for Canada*, the new report was entitled *Strengthening Canada: Reform of Canada's Senate* — and a maple leaf was prominently displayed on the cover.

This document picked up on earlier "major recommendations of the Government of Prince Edward Island and the position put forward in the last paper on this subject produced by the Canada West Foundation." The 1982 concept of a provincially appointed Senate was set aside. Alberta now advocated, with a respectful eye on the old North American culture of boosterism, a new "Triple E" or "elected, equal, and effective" Senate for Canada.

In this vision of the future, a provincially appointed Senate would do no more than give provincial bureaucrats and politicians one more arena for harassing or even immobilizing federal bureaucrats and politicians at Ottawa. A popularly elected Senate, on the other hand, with some form of "equal" representation for all parts of the new Confederation, would give regional and provincial interests a chance to collaborate in the actual management of the federal government itself.

As the University of Calgary political scientist Roger Gibbins had explained in 1983,

> Ottawa has been weakened in recent years not through a constitutional shift of powers to the provinces but rather by its loss of political legitimacy and authority. Because Ottawa is not seen as a truly national government by many Canadians it has trouble acting as such.

Even the federal government as presently constituted, in other words, could not credibly speak for Canada because it did not adequately represent all

Canadians, from the Atlantic to the Pacific to the Arctic Ocean. Its conception of the "national interest" was "little more than the regional interest of central Canada writ large."

An elected, equal, and effective Senate would change all this. In Gibbins's language, it "would bring in its wake a revitalization and strengthening of the national government." It would provide a new institutional answer to Pierre Trudeau's poignant question.

With the publication of *Strengthening Canada* in 1985, the Government of Alberta, the strongest spokesman for the Western Canadian regional cause, began to change directions with at least some degree of conviction. Like Quebec (and certainly British Columbia, and probably Saskatchewan, Manitoba, and the four Atlantic provinces as well), it still wanted to build a nation in which it could itself feel comfortable. In the somewhat ringing prose of *Strengthening Canada*:

> Alberta's proper place in Confederation can only be secured with a Senate constituted in a more credible manner .... Canada is currently the only free federal state that does not have an effective Upper House. Canada needs an effective Upper House in order to protect the diverse interests of Canadians.

But by the middle of the 1980s a new mood had set in on the eastern side of the Rocky Mountains. Canada's fourth-largest province had begun to set province building aside, and to take up the greater challenge of building the nation at large.

16

THE LATE TWENTIETH CENTURY DEBATE ON SENATE REFORM

In one important sense, the greatest obstacle to Alberta's or any other kind of credible Senate reform is the Senate that already exists at Ottawa.

Any movement for major change in the Canadian Senate in the late twentieth century must confront a long and deep tradition of academic, journalistic, and even, in some degree, popular scepticism, bred by the almost 125-year survival of the unreformed Senate of Canada. It is a simple historical fact that, despite much criticism, abuse, and ridicule, the Canadian Senate as it now exists has survived for as long as the modern Canadian Confederation itself. And, for good enough reasons, sheer survival is a virtue still admired in both English- and French-speaking Canada.

In 1986, about one year after the publication of Alberta's Triple E proposals, Senator Keith Davey ("The Rainmaker" in both Lester Pearson's and Pierre Trudeau's federal Liberal Party) spoke of "Canada's unreformable Senate." He personally supported a version of Senate reform rather different from Alberta's — one proposed in 1984 by a special joint committee of the federal House of Commons and the unreformed Senate itself. But his seasoned professional advice to anyone who might be interested was: "When will the Senate reform actually take place? We had better not hold our breath."

The Queen's University political scientist, C.E.S. Franks's *The Parliament of Canada*, published in 1987, observed:

> There are fashions in parliamentary reform as much as in clothes, pop music, and architecture ... the proposal for a "Triple E" Senate (elected, effective, equal) has been ardently pushed by the government of Alberta .... The problem with the kind of new upper chamber being proposed ... is not just that it is not likely to be created, but that it will not produce the results proponents hope for. It will not reduce federal-provincial conflicts, and could quite possibly be as unruly and ineffective a decision-maker as present federal-provincial conferences. It could make Canada more, not less, ungovernable.

In a 1988 article in the *Canadian Journal of Political Science*, Jennifer Smith from Dalhousie University in Halifax analyzed the original Confederation debates of the 1860s in the light of American traditions of federalism. She concluded that in Canada "it is quite possible that provincial governments today are immune to the alleged nationalizing effects of an elected Senate ...

those who are looking for ways of strengthening the federal government may well have to turn to ... the distribution of legislative powers" between the federal and provincial governments.

Objections and reservations of this sort flow from the considered opinions of analysts who are intimate with the historic practical machinery of Canadian national political life, and acutely conscious of the wisdom in Mackenzie King's injunction that "the difficulty of maintaining unity" in Canada "is very great indeed." There have never been simple solutions to the problems of governing Canada.

Nevertheless, the strongest reply of the Triple E Senate's staunchest proponents is that while remaining chained to the wisdom of the ages may or may not still work for a Canada that is content merely to continue to survive, it will certainly not work for a new Confederation that has already done some things the old Dominion could never do, and now wants to move beyond survival — into some democratic national future more of its own making than in the ancient past.

Even for these staunchest proponents, the long and deep traditions of scepticism ought to make clear that the quest for credible Senate reform must navigate many different kinds of troubled waters. Yet, a Canada content with mere survival may well not make it through the new challenges of the twenty-first century. And, here as elsewhere, there are also reasons to take confidence in a bold "leap of faith."

"Improving the existing Senate ..."

One reason is that, even without the 1985 proposals of the Alberta Select Special Committee, there has been more sustained discussion of serious Senate reform in the past few decades of Canadian history than during any preceding period since 1867. The pace and depth of the discussion has increased and thickened in the most recent past. There have been two modest actual reforms as well — one in the mid-1960s and one in connection with the renewed Constitution of the early 1980s.

Similarly, the traditional Canadian idea that the most sensible thing to do with the current unreformed Senate is simply to abolish it, has considerably less influence in the late twentieth century than it had at the end of the Second World War. Even the New Democratic Party, once the most secure home of abolitionist sentiment in the national political party system, seems to have had a few sober second thoughts more recently. Keith Davey has stressed that, according to Gallup Polls, only some 26% of the national population supported simply abolishing the Senate in the mid-1980s, down from some 36% in the mid-1940s. By 1989 only 19% of the national population wanted to abolish the Senate.

Viewed from this angle, as C.E.S. Franks has explained, "proposals for Senate reform divide into two distinct groups ... those concerned with improving the existing Senate" and those "tied in with questions of the federal system in Canada and its weaknesses" that, in effect, "propose a totally new second chamber." The Alberta Triple E proposal clearly belongs to the second group. Its ranks did not really start to fill until the 1970s. Before this the mainstream of Canadian Senate reform had more modest objectives, in the spirit of Franks's first group.

This "improving the existing Senate" tradition of reform could be traced back to even before Mackenzie King in the late 1920s, though it could claim few actual improvements until after the Second World War. Its objectives can be broadly characterized as: neutralizing the Senate's theoretical power to permanently thwart the wishes of the popularly elected House of Commons; removing what twentieth century popular opinion seems to regard as the unreformed Senate's most absurd features; and encouraging the Senate itself to focus on what is at least useful if not altogether significant work.

By the 1980s the tradition had two major modest reforms, and several minor ones, to its credit. The first major one was a 1965 constitutional amendment, via the old route of a request to the Parliament of the United Kingdom, stipulating that senators must retire when they are 75 years old. This at last threw out the old Tory heirloom of appointment for life. Among other things, it became harder for Canadian political science professors to amuse their students explaining how the Italian political theorist Gaetano Mosca's principle of "the representation of social forces" could be illustrated by the statement "The Canadian Senate represents the social force of senility."

The second major reform came with the Constitution Act, 1982. Section 47 of the act limits the Senate's powers to object to constitutional amendments approved by the House of Commons to a period of 180 days. After this period the amendment can proceed, once it is approved by the Commons a second time. The result is to give the Senate merely what is sometimes called a "suspensive veto" over constitutional amendments — in theory as well as in practice.

Two minor changes, if not quite reforms, in representation have also taken place since the Second World War. Newfoundland was assigned six senators when it joined Confederation in 1949 increasing the total number of Senate seats to 102, and giving the Atlantic Canadian section 30 seats, compared with only 24 seats for each of the Quebec, Ontario, and Western Canadian sections. Each of the Yukon and Northwest Territories was assigned one seat in 1975, bringing the total number of seats to 104.

Since at least the 1950s, both Liberal and Conservative federal prime ministers have made efforts to appoint more distinguished and energetic senators than was customary in earlier eras. Most recently, for instance, Senator Davey has noted such Trudeau appointees as Thérèse Casgrain, Jacques Hébert, Joyce Fairburn, and Michael Kirby, and such survivors of Joe Clark's brief Conservative regime as Lowell Murray and Nathan Nurgitz. Trudeau also appointed two Indian and two Inuit senators, following the precedent set by Diefenbaker in his appointment of James Gladstone in 1958.

As a consequence of all these changes, the modern unreformed Senate has also made some effort to reform itself, in the narrowest sense of the word.

Disinterested analysts have increasingly praised its technical role as a chamber of sober second thought about the details of House of Commons legislation. The deep background work of its special committees on such national public policy issues as poverty, divorce, the mass media, child abuse, and youth unemployment has won outside admirers.

In 1969 the Trudeau regime included the office of leader of the government in the Senate in the federal Cabinet — as a direct link between the Senate and the federal executive branch. Senator Lowell Murray, Brian Mulroney's Senate leader in the late 1980s, became as well minister of state for federal-provincial relations — point man, as it were, for the federal government's own evolving position in the new wider constitutional debate on Senate reform.

Despite all this technical improvement, the late twentieth century unreformed Senate of Canada has not been altogether able to resist periodically indulging in some of its more ancient bad habits.

Showing that he had indeed moved from philosopher king to Mackenzie King, Trudeau, and his immediate successor John Turner, made a number of cynical last-minute appointments in the dying days of the federal Liberal regime in 1984, to ensure that some available Senate seats would remain in Liberal Party hands. When Brian Mulroney's new Progressive Conservative government came to office, it complained, with at least some slight justice, of harassment by the continuing Liberal majority in the Senate. The then federal justice minister John Crosbie introduced a resolution in the House of Commons, never followed up, to "reduce the Senate's power over money bills ... to a 30-day veto" and to reduce the rest of the Senate's still great theoretical powers to "a 45-day suspensive veto over all other bills."

On the other hand, there are Canadians who still believe that the unreformed Senate, with its unelected Liberal majority, did indeed live up to its highest responsibilities as a body of sober second thought in 1988, when it helped precipitate a federal election over the Canada-U.S. Free Trade Agreement.

"A totally new second chamber ..."

The zenith of the "improving the existing Senate" tradition of reform came in 1973, when Senator David Croll, a much-respected former Cabinet minister from Mitch Hepburn's Ontario provincial regime of the 1930s, issued a 12-point "reform or perish" manifesto for internally induced change.

This triggered almost four months of debate in the Senate itself. But in the wider Canadian political arena, even aggressive proposals for modest internal reform had begun to be overwhelmed by more major proposals for some kind of "totally new second chamber." These new proposals flowed from the wider constitutional crisis mobilized at last by René Lévesque and the Parti Québécois, and focused on the need for stronger regional representation in federal institutions at Ottawa.

Interestingly enough, Quebec itself began to point vaguely in this direction in 1968, though its fundamental concerns of course lay elsewhere. Then in 1969 a white paper, prepared by the Trudeau federal government as a contribution to the new constitutional review process, introduced Pierre Trudeau's characteristic half-and-half federal-provincial appointment version of Senate reform. In 1972 a joint committee of the federal Senate and House of Commons endorsed a variation on the theme, whereby the federal government would appoint half the senators from lists submitted by the provinces.

In 1978 Trudeau's regime tested another variation in the Supreme Court to determine whether it was something the federal government might unilaterally implement itself. This variation prescribed half-and-half federal-provincial appointment by legislatures rather than executives, with each political party receiving a share of senators proportionate to its share of elected representatives. In 1979, however, the Supreme Court unanimously decided that this kind of major change in the Senate could certainly not be legislated by the federal Parliament alone.

At Premiers' Conferences held in 1976, the year of the PQ victory in Quebec, British Columbia had already introduced the still more fundamental theme that would eventually lead to Alberta's Triple E proposal of 1985. B.C. noted that from the standpoint of the third-largest province in the new Confederation, it was "no longer acceptable for the first and second of Canada's provinces to have 24 Senators each whereas the third-largest Province has only six." It pointed to the *Bundesrat* in the Federal Republic of Germany and to the Senate in the United States as examples that illustrated the need for still deeper reforms in the Senate of Canada, "to ensure that the point of view of the various regions of the federation are properly brought to bear on the federal law-making process."

By 1978 British Columbia had put together its more complete proposal for a provincially appointed Senate, more or less modelled on the West German *Bundesrat*. In the same year somewhat similar proposals, some of which suggested renaming the Canadian Senate the "House of the Provinces," were advanced by the Canada West Foundation, the Canadian Bar Association (in which a then not widely known Newfoundland politician, Clyde Wells, had a hand), the Ontario Advisory Committee on Confederation, and the Progressive Conservative Party of Canada. In 1979 more Senate reform proposals came from the Pepin-Roberts Task Force on Canadian Unity, appointed earlier by Trudeau, and from the Fédération des francophones hors Québec.

Others appeared in 1980. One was from the Standing Committee on Legal and Constitutional Affairs of the unreformed Senate in Ottawa. Another was from the Quebec Liberal Party, girding its loins for the May referendum. This latter, as a subsequent federal document would put it, "recommended an intergovernmental council that would not be part of the federal Parliament but would have some of the functions often proposed for a reformed Senate."

In 1981 the Canada West Foundation published its second report, *Regional Representation*, now advocating an elected, not a provincially appointed, Senate — and, along with the earlier similar proposal from the

Fédération des francophones hors Québec, marking an early turning point in the nation-building vs. province-building side of the debate. In 1982 Alberta released its *A Provincially-Appointed Senate*, still stuck for the moment in the province-building mode but putting the firm political commitment of a provincial government behind the movement for major Senate reform.

Getting to the Root of the Issue

At this point, the Senate and House of Commons at Ottawa established the Special Joint Committee on Senate Reform. In 1983 the Trudeau government offered a discussion paper called *Reform of the Senate* as a contribution to the Committee's deliberations. The paper noted that "an elected Senate scores higher than any other option in opinion polls."

In December 1983 the Government of Prince Edward Island added an Atlantic voice to the debate, stressing, as it had in the 1860s, that each province, not region in some broader sense, should have equal representation in any genuinely credible new version of major Senate reform.

In 1984 the Senate and House of Commons Special Joint Committee unveiled its major reform proposals. These called for an elected Senate, but not one with equal representation for each province, and with a merely suspensive veto over House of Commons legislation.

In 1985 the Alberta Select Special Committee published *Strengthening Canada*. This proposed, in effect, a much more rigorous and credible version of the 1984 Special Joint Committee themes that also embraced the historic concerns of Prince Edward Island: an elected Senate, equal representation from each province, and effective powers in the federal Parliament at Ottawa.

The international models for the Triple E Senate were the United States and — of still more direct relevance — Canada's fellow member of the Commonwealth of Nations, Australia. The United States had been electing two senators for each state since the Seventeenth Amendment of 1913. Australia has had its own version of an elected, equal, and effective Senate, in the British parliamentary tradition, since its creation in 1901.

Whatever else, *Strengthening Canada*'s Triple E Senate proposal crystallized the late twentieth century practical political debate on major Senate reform. In the particular historical context of Canada's complex and diverse political traditions of moderation and compromise, some saw the proposal as an unusually blunt and radical instrument. But it at last gave all parties to the debate a clear and bold point of reference, against which to test and measure their own thinking and opinion.

By the time of the Meech Lake Accord in the late spring of 1987, the new movement for major Senate reform in Canada had emerged from its report-writing phase to join the mainstream of the federal-provincial political process for continuing constitutional renewal. By May 1988 the broad principle of an elected, equal, and effective Senate had behind it the political weight of not just Canada's fourth-largest province of Alberta, but its third-largest province of British Columbia, and all four provinces of Western Canada at large, from the Lake of the Woods to the Pacific Ocean.

Reiterating the Nation-Building Logic of an Elected Senate

Among the plethora of major Canadian Senate reform documents and proposals that marked the last half of the 1970s and first half of the 1980s, Alberta's Triple E Senate proposal in *Strengthening Canada* has stood out and endured, while others, in one degree or another, have fallen by the wayside. More than anything else, it has been Alberta's proposal of 1985, and the Government of Alberta's subsequent political proselytizing on the issue, that finally made the debate more than a mere subject of discussion by pundits and academics.

The 1984 report of the federal Joint Committee of the Senate and House of Commons had made efforts in this direction earlier, but it was too "soft," too moderate and too compromising, to bring the debate that began with British Columbia's *Bundesrat*-model proposal of 1976 to a decisive focus. Put another way, in the mid-1980s it was still too early in the debate for anyone to strike a realistic compromise.

As implied earlier, one reason for the success of *Strengthening Canada* has been a hesitant but still unmistakable shift in Alberta's conception of its role in the wider Confederation, as the 1980s progressed. By the mid-1980s Alberta had begun to set aside province building for nation building.

This change is reflected in the quite striking differences between its 1982 provincially appointed Senate proposal and its 1985 elected, equal, and effective Senate proposal. Roughly the same ground had been covered earlier by the Canada West Foundation, in its 1978 and 1981 reports. The fundamental logic of the change in both cases can be related to Trudeau's critique of the excessively provincialist orientation of his regionalist critics in the late 1970s and early 1980s, and his ringing question: "Who will speak for Canada?"

Trudeau's own answer was that the federal Parliament, in particular the elected Canadian House of Commons at Ottawa, spoke for Canada. In 1980 he told the House of Commons, in a speech much remembered by critics of federal majoritarianism:

> We, who are here in Parliament, are the only group of men and women in this country who can speak for every Canadian. We are the only group, the only assembly in this country, which can speak for the whole nation, which can express the national will and the national interest.

This had also been essentially the answer of Mackenzie King, who had skilfully if often rather mysteriously sailed the old Dominion safely to the shores of the new Confederation. But for Alberta, for Prince Edward Island, and, in principle, for everyone in both Western and Atlantic Canada, this

W.A.C. Bennett: born in Nova Scotia and premier of British Columbia 1952 to 1972 — "Central Canada has the population and so it dominates Canada."

answer suggested a fundamental flaw that was just as important to rectify as the historic injustices sustained by the French Canadian fact. Here as elsewhere, the new Confederation had outgrown the habits of the old Dominion.

The elected House of Commons at Ottawa was based on representation by population in the nation at large. And, from the original Confederation of the 1860s and 1870s down to the present, the central provinces of Ontario and Quebec together, or the old mid-nineteenth century United Province of Canada, had always had and still had more than 60% of the national population.

CENTRAL CANADA IN CONFEDERATION

| Year | % Total Canadian Population | | |
	Quebec	Ontario	Ontario and Quebec
1871	32.3	43.9	76.2
1881	31.4	44.6	76.0
1891	30.8	43.7	74.5
1901	28.8	38.1	66.9
1911	27.8	35.1	62.9
1921	26.9	33.4	60.3
1931	27.7	33.1	60.8
1941	29.0	32.9	61.9
1951	29.0	32.8	61.8
1961	28.8	34.2	63.0
1971	27.9	35.7	63.6
1981	26.4	35.6	62.0
1986	25.8	35.9	61.7

Thus, as W.A.C. Bennett from British Columbia had explained in the late 1970s, "Central Canada has the population and so it dominates Canada." Or, given Canada's regional demographics, the federal majoritarian doctrine that, in Donald Smiley's language, "asserts that the government which controls the House of Commons is the sole repository of the Canadian common good" was fundamentally a recipe for having the Canadian common good commonly defined by Ontario and Quebec — even though, geographically, the largest part of the country was in the other eight provinces. Or, as Roger Gibbins had stressed in 1983, the "national interest" was "little more than the regional interest of central Canada writ large."

The genuinely logical solution was for the new Confederation, at long last, to follow the example of the other transcontinental "free and democratic" federal systems in the world, in Australia and the United States, and accommodate the less populous regional jurisdictions through equal representation in an elected Senate. Then the Parliament at Ottawa, made up of an elected House of Commons and an elected Senate, could speak both for the more populous central provinces in the Confederation and for the less populous Atlantic and Western provinces.

This was a rather different argument from the one for an appointed House of the Provinces that had been made in several quarters in the late 1970s, and by Alberta itself in the early 1980s. Both provincially appointed and elected models of major Senate reform were meant to, as British Columbia had urged in 1976, "ensure that the point of view of the various regions of the federation are properly brought to bear on the federal law-making process." Provincially appointed models, however, assumed that provincial governments would define the point of view in question. Elected models assumed that it would be defined by democratic regional electorates, or "the people" of the regions — perhaps even against the narrow institutional interests of provincial governments.

As Roger Gibbins also stressed in 1983, major Senate reform based on the principle of a popularly elected upper house was ultimately "a game in which provincial governments will be the clear losers." Residual concerns of this sort are in fact reflected in the details of Alberta's specific Triple E proposals in *Strengthening Canada*. Yet, as Gibbins predicted as well,

> particularly in the West, where concern over effective regional representation in the national political process is both chronic and acute, proposals for an elected Senate would be difficult to attack. In so doing, provincial governments could be seen to be acting in their own institutional self-interest rather than the regional interests of their provincial electorates.

What Jennifer Smith in 1988 called "the alleged nationalizing effects of an elected Senate" have subsequently been strongly questioned for betraying a too naive appreciation of the tenacity of provincial attachments in Canada. There is nonetheless enough in the details of Alberta's particular Triple E proposals to suggest that by 1985 the Government of Alberta did see itself as confronting something of a choice between province-building and nation-building aspirations in the quest for major Senate reform. And while it did what it could to protect its more narrow provincial interests, in the end it chose the nation.

Senate Reform and National Economic Development

One particular reason for the shift from province-building to nation-building priorities in the Senate reform debate during the first half of the 1980s was the increasingly profound failure of federal-provincial diplomacy on the critical issue of national economic, or economic development, policy. In the rapidly changing world economy of the late twentieth century, this was the bedrock, as it were, of any other national or provincial policy that federal and provincial governments might formulate.

Ontario, the province that many said profited most from the Canadian national economy, took something of a lead on the issue. At a First Ministers' Conference in February 1978, it released a discussion paper called *An Economic Development Policy for Canada*. Its major themes were "Price Stability," which included a subsection on "Public Sector Restraint"; "Improving the Business Climate and Increasing Private Investment"; "Increasing Exports and Replacing Imports"; and "Regional Development."

Premier William Davis signed a foreword to the document. It asserted that "with this Conference of First Ministers, there is an opportunity to begin mapping a strategy for the future growth and enrichment of our economy." It then pointed to an

> outline of the Ontario Government's views on some of the basic building blocks we need for a fresh beginning. I hope you will consider them, test them against your own opinions, and let your own thinking be known in this most important debate.

Over the next several years, many of Premier Davis's fellow premiers took this last part of his advice to heart. Alberta's bitter quarrel with the federal government, and Ontario as well, over the National Energy Program in the early 1980s did much to shape its own thinking on the subject. More traditional grievances over pressure on the federal government from the Montreal-headquartered national railways to reduce the ancient Crow's Nest freight rate subsidies, helped shape the thinking in other parts of Western Canada.

In Atlantic Canada there were disputes over offshore oil development on the Atlantic Coast. There was disappointment over the U.S. Congress's rejection of a new Canadian-American fishing agreement in 1981. In all parts of the country, there was growing business concern about the signs of a potential new protectionist trade posture in Canada's overwhelmingly largest international trading partner, the United States.

As time went by, what did become increasingly clear was that federal-provincial First Ministers' Conferences were distinctly not an effective arena for the development of Canadian national economic policy. Some specific problems between particular provinces and the federal government could be resolved. But, in any broader context, all the 11 first ministers could do was argue about what was being done and what ought to be done. They could not make the trade-offs and compromises among competing objectives, in a world of limited resources, that any effective policy would require. Responsible to their provincial electorates for provincial interests alone, they had no ultimate incentive to give up on any of their individual provincial objectives.

Besides, section 91 of the Constitution Act, 1867, made it clear that such fundamental public levers of national development as "The Regulation of Trade and Commerce," "Currency and Coinage," "Interest," and "Patents of Invention and Discovery" were the powers of the federal government at Ottawa, not the provinces. The Constitution Act, 1982, had done nothing to change this. Constitutionally, on this matter the provincial premiers could only offer advice to the federal prime minister, and his governing majority in the elected House of Commons.

For his part, Trudeau's ultimate response to the economic challenges facing the country was to appoint the Royal Commission on the Economic Union and Development Prospects for Canada, under the chairmanship of his former minister of finance, the Toronto corporate lawyer Donald Macdonald. The "Macdonald Commission" finally released its report in 1985, after Brian Mulroney had become prime minister and not long after the Alberta Select Special Committee on Upper House Reform had released its Triple E Senate proposal in *Strengthening Canada*.

The Macdonald Commission recommended that the new Confederation should start to make its way in the emerging new global economy of the twenty-first century, by doing what it could to secure its already highly developed and, broadly, quite profitable economic relationship with the United States. This meant abandoning the relatively few surviving vestiges of John A. Macdonald's old National Policy of tariff protection on Canadian industry with special reference to its American cousins, or, often enough, multi-national big brothers

This, in turn, pointed to a strand of Canadian economic development policy that had already begun under Mackenzie King, had evolved under the postwar international General Agreement on Tariffs and Trade, and had set down initial roots with the Canada-U.S. Auto Pact of 1965. Even the late Trudeau regime of the early 1980s had begun discussions with Washington on the prospects for extensions of the Auto Pact in other economic sectors. What's more, the Macdonald Commission urged, dismantling the last vestiges of the old tariff protection against the United States would have the great domestic political advantage of removing an ancient symbolic regional grievance harboured by both Western and Atlantic Canada.

With an eye on any future development of new national economic policies for the country, the Macdonald Commission also recommended that the Canadian "Economic Union" adopt an elected federal Senate that would effectively represent the less populous, and geographically largest extent of Canada in national economic decision-making.

In this recommendation the Commission no doubt had a particular eye on Alberta and Western Canada at large. But it also seemed to have paid special attention to the submission it had heard from Premier James Lee and the Government of Prince Edward Island in December 1983. "The challenge for Canada," Premier Lee had urged, "is two-fold; to establish truly national decision-making in the country, and to provide an environment in which economic activity can take place. The two are not unrelated."

It was especially notable that a royal commission chaired by a Toronto corporate lawyer had come to share such views. Once again, they reflected the advice that Harold Innis had offered in the wake of the Rowell-Sirois report some 45 years before: "The complex problems of regionalization in the recent development of Canada render the political structure obsolete ... the political scientist ... can best make a contribution to economic development by suggested modifications to political machinery." Like so much else in the old Dominion, the age of John A. Macdonald's late nineteenth century National Policy was at long last coming to a virtual end. Now, there were those who, in all parts of the Confederation, saw some credible version of Senate reform as a prerequisite to the development of any effective new national economic policy for the twenty-first century version of the Canada first crystallized by Cabot, Cartier, Champlain, and the Indians, several centuries before.

17
ALBERTA'S TRIPLE E SENATE: AN EVALUATION

The crystallizing virtues of Alberta's Triple E Senate reform concept lean on its stylistic affinities with the North American culture of boosterism. It is, to start with, a marketing formula that reduces the many inevitable complexities of major Senate reform to three general principles. And this gives the concept communication advantages in broad public debate.

At the same time, even if the Canadian federal government and all ten provincial governments finally agree in principle that the new Confederation must have an elected, equal, and effective Senate in Ottawa, there remains a great deal of room for quite fundamental debate and disagreement over the concrete details of how the concept is to be implemented.

Thus, even the most ardent and convinced supporter of the three Triple E principles might reasonably raise any number of questions about the necessarily somewhat sketchy detailed proposals advanced in Alberta's 1985 document, *Strengthening Canada*. And this document has remained the working basis both of Alberta's subsequent campaigning on the issue and, in a provisional way, of the wider endorsement in principle by all four western provinces in the May 1988 "Parksville Accord."

The complete text of *Strengthening Canada*'s recommendations is reproduced in Appendix B at the end of this book, along with excerpts from the much less radical 1984 Senate and House of Commons Special Joint Committee proposals for an elected Canadian Senate, in Appendix A. Two particular kinds of queries might be raised, however, by way of illustrating the more detailed national debate that has yet to be joined, to any significant degree.

Two Queries about Triple E Details

The first query concerns the "Method of Selection and Basis of Representation of New Senators."

Strengthening Canada recommends that the reformed Senate "consist of 64 Senators, six representing each province and two representing each territory." Senators "should represent constituencies whose boundaries are identical to provincial boundaries," and "be elected for the life of two provincial legislatures." In each province "three Senators should be elected during each provincial election, with each voter being able to vote for three candidates."

The understandable aim of the recommendations is to help ensure that the reformed Senate represents provincial interests in Ottawa, and does not become the captive of a national political life that cannot see beyond the banks of the Ottawa River.

Yet these particular proposals would also tie the election of members of a branch of the federal Parliament to the vagaries of ten different versions of provincial politics in a way that seems fraught with much potential for complexity and confusion. In larger provinces especially, province-wide constituencies for all senators would likely promote unusually high-cost election campaigns. And, to take just one specific case, if Ontario is going to have six elected senators, Northern Ontario, or even Eastern or Southwestern Ontario, might reasonably argue that it should have at least one of them.

The second query concerns "Senate Organization." Here *Strengthening Canada* recommends that members of the reformed Senate "should not be eligible for appointments to Cabinet" and "should be physically seated in provincial delegations, regardless of any party affiliations." Each provincial delegation "should select from its membership a chairman," and the "ten provincial chairmen, headed by the Speaker of the Senate, should constitute a 'Senate Executive Council'." This Senate Executive Council "should determine the order of business of the Senate," and its "members should receive remuneration and staff assistance in addition to that received by other Senators."

These proposals are designed to help ensure that the reformed Senate will not be co-opted and steered too far away from its regional representation objectives by the national political party system. They have been made with particular reference to experience in Australia, where, as the Canadian political scientist Alexander Brady reported in the late 1940s, "senators are inevitably more loyal to their parties than their states."

Yet to remove senators in Canada from eligibility for the federal Cabinet would do considerable violence to the logic of the national parliamentary democracy at large, and would arguably drastically reduce the reformed Senate's potential effectiveness as a regional voice in national institutions. To try to compensate for this by establishing a "Senate Executive Council" could amount to establishing a second rival cabinet at Ottawa, with considerable potential for, as C.E.S. Franks has complained, making "Canada more, not less, ungovernable" than it is now.

Because they relate to implementing details and not general principles, queries of this sort do not attack the fundamental integrity of the Triple E concept. But they do suggest that its implementing details are still open to much discussion and debate.

More broadly, it is eminently arguable that both queries ultimately relate to residual province-building impulses in Alberta's nation-building conception of an elected Senate. From a perspective concerned to stress more rigorous nationalizing impulses, an elected, equal, and effective Senate with elections keyed either to elections for the federal House of Commons in Ottawa or to some fixed national date, and with senators who continued to sit in the federal Cabinet, as they have recurrently since 1867, might strike some citizens as a more credible approach to reforms genuinely meant to strengthen Canada.

Put another way, C.E.S. Franks's "ungovernability" criticism acquires a heightened plausibility in connection with a few of Alberta's more detailed Triple E proposals. At the very least, even the most virulent regional protests are no good reason for implementing national reforms that seem all too likely to increase and exacerbate regional conflict.

Dilemmas of Provincial Equality

Quite apart from questions about the implementing details of general principles, even among friendly commentators in the wider arena of Canadian national politics there are still some strong reservations about at least two of the three Triple E principles.

Opinion polls, the proposals of the 1984 Joint Special Committee of the Senate and House of Commons in Ottawa, public statements by provincial premiers in both Western and Atlantic Canada, and similar musings by the prime minister of Canada himself all suggest some rising though still unclear consensus for an elected Senate in Canada. Gallup Polls indicate that some 51% of the national population favoured an elected Senate in 1989, compared with 41% in 1985, and 31% in 1954 (though 46% apparently supported the concept as long ago as 1961, and support fell from 46 to 44% between 1987 and 1988).

Similarly, on at least one technical detail, both the 1984 Joint Special Committee in Ottawa and the 1985 Alberta Select Special Committee agree: election should be via the same "first past the post" system already used in federal and provincial elections in Canada, and not by some more complicated "proportional representation" system, similar to any of those used in Western Europe or Australia. (As a technical aside, Donald Smiley has noted that this could tend to produce upper house party standings virtually identical to those of the lower house for Senate elections in province-wide constituencies keyed to House of Commons contests — a combination of assumptions that does not apply to either the Ottawa or Alberta proposals.)

Yet in the specific historical circumstances of Canada, it has been argued, the concepts of both an equal and effective Senate, in the specific senses used by the authors of *Strengthening Canada*, raise some unique difficulties. The principle of equal representation for each province is a case in point.

One objection concerns the particular number and demographic configuration of the provinces and territories in the Canadian Confederation. The issue has been put succinctly by the 1984 report of the Special Joint Committee:

> In Canada, the application of the equality principle would enable the five least populous provinces — that is, those accounting for 13.4 per cent of the Canadian population — to have a majority in the Senate if they had the support of the territorial representatives, whatever their number.

ALTERNATIVE PROPOSALS FOR PROVINCIAL REPRESENTATION IN A REFORMED CANADIAN SENATE

Number of Seats in Senate

Province/ Territory	Existing Senate	1984 Ottawa Joint Committee	1985 Alberta Triple E	%Canadian Population 1986
Ontario	24	24	6	35.9
Quebec	24	24	6	25.8
British Columbia	6	12	6	11.4
Alberta	6	12	6	9.4
Manitoba	6	12	6	4.2
Saskatchewan	6	12	6	4.0
Nova Scotia	10	12	6	3.5
New Brunswick	10	12	6	2.8
Newfoundland	6	12	6	2.2
P.E.I.	4	6	6	0.5
N.W.T.	1	4	2	0.2
Yukon	1	2	2	0.1
TOTAL	104	144	64	100.0

A somewhat related and still more thorny objection can be traced back to the original debates on provincial vs. sectional representation in the Confederation era of the 1860s and 1870s.

As George Brown explained, one crucial reason for equal sectional representation in the Senate was to reassure "our Lower Canadian friends" in French-speaking Quebec. As the P.E.I. delegate to the 1864 Quebec Conference, Edward Whelan, explained still further, "The French Canadians seem to apprehend that they will be swamped in the Upper House, and desire a larger representation than the Maritime Provinces ask for, so that they may not be overpowered by the British element."

Both the 1984 Ottawa Joint Committee and the 1985 Alberta Triple E elected-Senate documents respond to the French fact in Canada by proposing that, in the Joint Committee's language, "legislation of linguistic significance should be approved by a double majority" of both English- and French-speaking senators (though even in this context there are some significant differences of implementing detail between the Ottawa and Alberta schemes).

The 1984 Ottawa proposals, however, also respond by preferring an updated version of the old equal sectional representation over equal provincial representation. In effect, they envision three new 48-member Senate sections: one for Western Canada, one for Central Canada, and one for what might be called "Atlantic and Northern Canada."

Strategic Links with Distinct Societies

The best argument against merely updating the old sectional representation principle in this or any other way is that, no matter how it is done, it will still seem too much a part of some old Central Canadian imperialism to pass for a genuinely credible reform in the eight provinces of Atlantic and Western Canada.

As *Strengthening Canada* has urged, the best evidence for this is the ultimate resolution of the early 1980s debate over a constitutional amending formula. The principle of equal provincial representation in a reformed Senate flows from the logic of the 1964 Fulton-Favreau Formula — approval by any seven provinces that represent at least 50% of the national population. And this was the amending formula that nine out of ten provinces, and the federal government, finally proved able to agree on in 1981.

By itself, however, this evidence ignores the plain truth, that the 1981 amending formula, which enshrines the principle of provincial equality, was not in fact agreed to by the province of Quebec. Moreover, it can be argued that the special geographic provisions for representation of Quebec's old English Protestant minority in the original Canadian Senate of 1867 cannot be changed without Quebec's assent. Lowell Murray, Brian Mulroney's point man in the contemporary debate, has maintained that this may give Quebec an effective veto over Senate reform in the late twentieth century (quite apart from some particular provisions in the 1987 Meech Lake Accord).

Among at least those Triple E reformers who have thought the issue through, the implicit political position on this problem seems to be that, either under the 1987 Meech Lake Accord or as an unwritten element in the new Constitution, or in some different future version of a Meech Lake Accord, Quebec has now been or will soon be constitutionally recognized as a distinct society within Canada. Because of this, the French fact in Quebec no longer requires special protection in the federal Senate.

Thus, as most recently explained by Gordon Gibson, Vancouver businessman and co-author of the Canada West Foundation's *Regional Representation* report of 1981, the "only successful solution" to Canada's constitutional dilemmas in the 1990s "will surely retain a full 'distinct society' for Quebec, and a new central institution like the 'triple E' Senate for outer Canada."

In the same spirit (but on the opposite side of the argument), Trudeau's half-and-half appointed version of Senate reform, which, like the unreformed Senate of 1867, did not recognize the principle of provincial equality, flowed logically enough from his fundamental reservations about granting the distinct society in Quebec special constitutional recognition. Canada being what it is, in one way or another there must be some form of special

Don Getty, Progressive Conservative premier of Alberta since November 1985 and leader of the provincial government that has invented and ardently promoted the concept of a "Triple E" Senate for Canada. Getty was born in Montreal, and his Alberta government has taken a somewhat different approach to Senate reform than the Alberta government led by his predecessor, Peter Lougheed. Like Lougheed, however, Getty played football for the Edmonton Eskimos before he became a politician.

protection for Quebec.

(From a related angle, the fundamental difference between the kind of "special status" Quebec already enjoys within the present unreformed Senate of Canada and the kind it would enjoy as a "full" and constitutionally recognized distinct society is that, within the present Senate, Quebec shares its special status with Ontario. And, to complete the picture, on Trudeau's logic, Ontario ought to become officially bilingual, and Quebec ought not to be officially recognized as a distinct society.)

Trudeau and his supporters notwithstanding, all this highlights the extent to which an unambiguous and friendly recognition of Quebec as a distinct society is a pragmatic prerequisite for any kind of Senate reform that approximates the principle of equal provincial representation. At the same time, to embark on a provincially equal elected Senate, strictly on the argument that Quebec is or will soon be constitutionally recognized as a distinct society, would amount to saying that Canada is going to dispense altogether with Trudeau's vision of varying degrees of bilingualism in all parts of the country.

Like René Lévesque and the Parti Québécois, this would ignore French Canada outside Quebec — in officially bilingual New Brunswick, in "unofficially bilingual" Ontario or even Manitoba, and in virtually every other province as well. Put another way, it would amount to redefining the French fact in Canada not as a compromise, somewhere in between the competing visions of Lévesque and Trudeau, but merely as a lukewarm version of Lévesque's vision by itself. And it seems likely enough that at the end of this road some version of sovereignty-association or worse is lying in wait.

In a country with a less deeply rooted national political tradition of moderation and compromise than Canada, concerns of this sort could be enough to defeat the principle of a provincially equal elected Senate altogether, and much else besides. Yet beneath the northern lights of the diverse destiny, there does seem room for taking the principle as a fundamental point of departure, and then modifying it only slightly in ways that accommodate the strongest objections against it.

The Trudeau regime's 1983 discussion paper *Reform of the Senate*, for instance, noted that "the French-speaking Fathers of Confederation" saw the "representation and protection of minorities" as an important function of the original Senate of Canada. It noted as well that a case can be made for the "representation of aboriginal peoples in a reformed Senate." "A special aboriginal voters' list could be prepared and votes could be aggregated on a national basis to determine who would be assigned the seats."

In this context, adding an extra 12 to 18 seats, or two to three province-sized delegations, to Alberta's Triple E model, and pragmatically distributing them among various French, Indian, Inuit, and Métis constituencies, could answer the most compelling objections that the principle of equal provincial representation in its most ideologically rigorous expression typically calls forth.

This arrangement could include giving an extra Senate seat to Quebec, in recognition of its status as a distinct society, and an extra seat to New Brunswick, with respect to its status as Canada's only officially bilingual province. Other seats could be distributed so as to represent the officially bilingual population outside Quebec, which anyone could join simply by learning French to some not overly rigorous degree. Still other seats could be assigned to Indian, Inuit, and Métis constituencies, ultimately in conjunction with whatever bargains are finally struck on aboriginal self-government.

The logic of Quebec's, or New Brunswick's, extra Senate seat would be strictly symbolic. The argument that Quebec ought to be prepared to accept an arrangement of this kind still hinges fundamentally on its unambiguous recognition as a "full" distinct society. In a secondary way, it hinges on assumptions about Quebec's commitment to French Canada outside Quebec, and to the strength that English-speaking Canada can bring to the task of preserving a French-speaking society within Quebec's own borders, in the inhospitable continental environment of English-speaking North America. (And if it is naive in terms of politics inside Quebec to imagine that any of this could ever appeal to a Quebec provincial government, it is equally naive in terms of politics in other parts of the country to imagine that it could not.)

Like so much else in the evolving Canadian constitutionalism of the late twentieth century (the notwithstanding clause in the Charter of Rights, for example), approaches of this sort do involve a willingness to forego the psychological attractions of simple conceptions of citizenship. As the American writer Miriam Chapin observed in the late 1950s, "Canada is a nation which has been forced to put up with diversity, indeed forced to cherish it."

Nonetheless, to think about the problem in this way at least suggests that there are practical approaches to accommodating both the particular number and demographic configuration of Canada's ten provinces and its ancient and modern French fact without abandoning the fundamental principle of equal provincial representation in a new elected Senate. There does seem to be at least logical room for compromises that result in a scheme of essentially provincial representation, much closer to Alberta's 1985 Triple E proposals than to the 1984 proposals of the Senate and House of Commons Special Joint Committee in Ottawa.

The Parliamentary Problems of an "Effective" Senate

In one sense, of course, there is no point at all in taking on the arduous complexities of reforming the unreformed Senate of Canada in a major way if the "totally new second chamber" that results is not going to be effective, in one respect or another.

In the Canadian political arena of the late twentieth century, however, there are some quite deeply rooted reservations about just what the effective principle might mean for an elected Senate, given Canada's particular political heritage of "parliamentary democracy" as opposed to the presidential/

237

congressional variation on the theme that prevails in the United States.

The background to this concern draws on the peculiar mingling of, and even conflict among, influences from the British Empire and the American Republic in Canadian political history. In the early twentieth century, for instance, the French writer André Siegfried ("French" from Europe, not French Canadian) observed that Canadian politics puts "American actors on an English stage." Institutionally, it is a "curious mixture of English traditions and American customs which gives the keynote to Canadian political life."

In the late twentieth century, even English-speaking Canada is no longer a "British" culture overseas. And when an only recently retired president of the United States takes genuine delight in being knighted by the Queen of the United Kingdom, the external points of reference for the ancient "British" vs. "American" cultural debate in English-speaking Canada have changed fundamentally. But, as in Australia and New Zealand, or the modern Republic of India for that matter, the institutional logic of Canadian politics continues to flow from the assumptions of parliamentary democracy on an essentially British model.

In this context, it is said with great regularity, the greatest problem with an elected Canadian Senate that retained the quite vast theoretical powers of the current unreformed Senate, equal to those of the Commons except with regard to money bills and constitutional amendments, would be the potential for conflict between it and the elected Canadian House of Commons.

The operative convention of British parliamentary democracy is that the executive of the government — the prime minister and Cabinet — is responsible to the majority of the members in the lower house of Parliament: the House of Commons in both Canada and the United Kingdom; or the House of Representatives, following the American nomenclature, in Australia; or, following another nomenclature altogether, the *Lok Sabha* in India. And, as John A. Macdonald himself wondered aloud in the 1860s, what happens if an elected Senate and an elected House of Commons disagree on some fundamental piece of legislation?

The rebuttal to this argument is that the Commonwealth of Australia has shown how an elected, equal, and effective federal Senate can operate within the assumptions of parliamentary democracy since its creation in 1901. The response to this, in turn, is that, as recently as the mid-1970s, the Australian system in fact bred a major "constitutional crisis." This crisis turned around the very issue of a conflict between rival majorities in the Senate and House of Representatives, and a federal prime minister who strove to uphold, as a quite extensive discussion of the matter in *Strengthening Canada* puts it, "the Westminster convention that a government which retains the confidence of the House of Representatives stays in office."

The counter-argument here is that Australia's mid-1970s constitutional crisis was eventually resolved, using a device in the Australian Constitution known as a "double dissolution." This amounts to the calling of simultaneous new elections for both the Senate and the House of Representatives by the federal executive. It has now been used five times in Australian history: in 1914, 1951, 1974, 1975, and 1983.

A related argument, which seems implicit in the very principle of double dissolution, challenges "the Westminster convention" of the supremacy of the lower house of Parliament altogether.

In the history of the small islands of the United Kingdom, not merely was the upper house not elected, but it was filled with hereditary representatives of a landed aristocracy, created by the feudal society of the European Middle Ages. It is easy enough to see how here "democracy" had to come to mean the supremacy of the popularly elected lower house of Parliament. Yet it is not at all so easy to see why this convention must continue to apply, without at least some substantial modification, in independent countries where the upper house is composed of elected representatives of the democratic regional electorates in a transcontinental federal system. As the chief justice of Australia explained in the 1970s,

> There is no analogy in respect of a Prime Minister's duty between the situation of the Parliament under the federal Constitution of Australia and the relationship between the House of Commons, a popularly elected body, and the House of Lords, a non-elected body, in the unitary form of government functioning in the United Kingdom.

The history of Australia's double dissolutions in the 1970s and 1980s, it can be argued yet again, suggests that post-colonial Australian federalism actually is moving toward some recognition of at least a degree of joint accountability, on the part of the federal prime minister and Cabinet, to both the lower and upper houses of the federal Parliament.

No doubt, the road ahead has some rocky and still unclear parts, as did the historic road that marked the gradual evolution of parliamentary democracy in the United Kingdom and its colonies overseas, as recently as the nineteenth century. But Australia has yet to erupt into perpetual constitutional chaos, and it is unlikely to do so in any foreseeable future.

"American actors on an English stage"

In Canada the report of the 1984 Special Joint Committee of the federal Parliament in Ottawa was distinctly not impressed by arguments of this sort. Neither, for that matter, was the 1985 report of the Royal Commission on the Economic Union.

As the Special Joint Committee explained, an elected Canadian Senate should "not be able to overturn a government .... In a parliamentary system, a government cannot serve two masters, whose wills might on occasion be diametrically opposed." A reformed Senate for Canada should be

> designed in such a way that it would not be vying continually for supremacy with the House of Commons .... We

239

therefore propose that the new Senate be given only a suspensive veto, which would allow time for national debate and reflection, but which the Commons could, after a suitable lapse of time, override by re-passing the legislation in question.

In Alberta's 1985 Triple E model in *Strengthening Canada* this kind of merely suspensive veto is firmly "rejected because of a fundamental belief that a reformed Senate must have power to be effective."

Nonetheless, in recognition of the specific historical circumstances of Canada, Alberta's Triple E model pays some obeisance to the principle of the ultimate supremacy of the House of Commons, where the national electorate is represented fundamentally on the basis of population. (This may in fact have less to do with the older British "Westminster convention," and more with the newer North American principle that the highest expression of the national democracy is "one person, one vote.")

To start with, *Strengthening Canada* proposes that the new Senate should not be able to veto House of Commons "supply bills." This would mean that it could not "overturn" a prime minister and Cabinet with a working majority in the House, in at least the most fundamental sense of precipitating the federal government's bankruptcy — and this was in fact the issue at the bottom of Australia's constitutional crisis of the mid-1970s.

Alberta's Triple E model then proposes that the "House of Commons should have the power to override a Senate veto on money or taxation bills by a simple majority." Beyond this, the House "should be able to override" any other "amendment (veto) passed by the Senate" by "a vote that is greater in percentage terms than the Senate's vote to amend" (following a precedent from the German *Bundesrat*.) This "would ensure the supremacy of the House of Commons, but that supremacy could only be utilized when it was clear that representatives elected on a representation by population basis were very united."

Finally, in the midst of such characteristically Canadian compromising, Alberta's Triple E model also envisions bolstering the power of the totally new upper chamber with some particular American-style teeth: "Non-military treaties should be subject to ratification by the Senate."

What all this would amount to in practice would almost certainly depend a great deal on the particular configuration of political parties in both the new Senate and House of Commons at particular points in time, even in a world that took some extra trouble to try to dampen party influences in the Senate. Alberta's proposals may resolve some problems of rather broad principle in the quest for a workably effective reformed Senate of Canada. And they do highlight the essential futility of any design for credible Senate reform based on a merely suspensive veto.

What is the point of expending enormous energy and going to great expense to create an elected Senate that can only, in effect, delay legislation in the House of Commons for a period of several months? Why would anyone want to serve in such an assembly? How could it resolve any of the fundamental political problems of Canadian regionalism that lie at the root of the quest for major Senate reform?

At the same time, Alberta's particular Triple E proposals for ensuring an effective Senate might provide a more practical starting point, were they not also linked with proposals for tying Senate elections to the cycle of provincial election campaigns, and for disqualifying senators from sitting in the federal Cabinet (to say nothing of creating a separate Senate Executive Council).

In this setting, even in transcontinental federal systems, parliamentary institutions do have some logic of their own: you can have two elected legislatures, for instance, but not two Cabinets or executives. This logic probably can be escaped only at the price of inviting constitutional paralysis.

Thus — no matter what partial limitations may or may not be placed on the powers of the upper relative to the lower house of the federal Parliament —and it is not easy to see how Canada could have an effective reformed Senate without also making some emergency provision for some form of double dissolution initiated by the federal executive, in the Australian manner.

(On this model, the ultimate answer to the question of what happens when a government cannot command majority support for a measure it views as crucial to its legislative program in *both* an elected Senate and House of Commons is the same as the answer to the question of what a government does now when it loses the confidence of the elected Commons alone. It advises the governor general to call fresh elections — for both houses of Parliament. And, on the basis of Australia's experience, it may be more in keeping with parliamentary logic to safeguard provincial interests by having the Senate approve the prime minister's appointment of the governor general, whose role seems to be enhanced somewhat by the mechanics of a double dissolution system, than by tying federal Senate elections to the provincial election cycle.)

In the end, if the Canadian Confederation of the twenty-first century genuinely wants an elected, equal, *and effective* Senate, the people of Canada will most likely have to be prepared to take yet another leap of faith — and join Australia on the road to some more fundamental reassessment of the old "Westminster convention" about the absolute supremacy of the lower house of Parliament, in a federal parliamentary democracy. (In this context it is also worth noting that in the late twentieth century there is even serious talk about re-evaluating the role of the upper house, in the fabled mother of Parliaments in the United Kingdom.)

This is an issue that is never quite confronted head-on in Alberta's *Strengthening Canada*, though the supporting material for the document's actual recommendations does cast occasional provocative glances its way.

Jim Horsman, Alberta intergovernmental affairs minister in the late 1980s, point man in his province's campaign for an elected, equal, and effective Canadian Senate, and a Western Canadian realist about the nature of Canadian national politics. As he explained to the Canadian Club of Toronto in January 1989, "we must have Quebec at the table before any progress can be made."

Ultimately, moving away from the Westminster convention would indeed imply quite major changes in Canadian national politics. Yet the deepest premise of the long journey to Senate reform is that, in the late twentieth century, this is just what Canadian national politics needs.

*

18
A TALE OF TWO AGREEMENTS

Both the 1984 Ottawa Special Joint Committee report and Alberta's 1985 Triple E proposals wisely stressed that any "totally new second chamber" in Canadian national politics could not take shape overnight.

The Ottawa report noted that "putting in place an elected Senate will require constitutional amendment involving the consent of Parliament and of the specified number of legislative assemblies. All this will take time." The Alberta report observed that "radical reform to the Canadian Senate may take time because of the difficulty in reaching agreement necessary for the inevitable and complicated constitutional change which would be required."

Meanwhile, both reports dealt at least briefly with the importance of devising equitable retirement arrangements for the members of the existing Senate of Canada. Both also stressed that, in Alberta's language, some "Short and Medium Term Possibilities" for more modest reforms were worth considering, as initial steps along the path to the ultimate goal.

As it happened, two particular reforms of this sort (raised in Alberta's *Strengthening Canada*) were in fact taken up quite quickly by Brian Mulroney's new Progressive Conservative federal regime which continued with the late Trudeau era Canadian constitutional renewal process.

The first involved what Alberta called "Federal Appointments from Provincial Short Lists," taking a cue from the 1972 report of another joint Senate and House of Commons committee in Ottawa, or perhaps even from Jonathan McCully of Nova Scotia, at the Quebec Conference in 1864. The second involved "First Ministers' Conferences."

By June 1987 proposals dealing with both these issues had found their way into a tentative constitutional agreement among the federal prime minister and, astonishingly enough, all ten provincial premiers. This agreement was ultimately known as "the Meech Lake Accord."

Where Is Meech Lake, Anyway?

The initial purpose of the Meech Lake Accord was to have the provincial government of Quebec — now under the leadership of the second incarnation of the Liberal Robert Bourassa — at last give its assent to the Constitution Act, 1982, in return for certain concessions, culminating with the constitutional recognition "that Quebec constitutes within Canada a distinct society."

Yet in the process of the federal-provincial and interprovincial bargaining required to achieve this, room was opened up for meeting some of the continuing demands of the old English-speaking regionalist cause of the early 1980s: what Peter Lougheed had referred to just after the Quebec referendum, as important "aspirations of the people in the Atlantic and western regions."

The regionalist cause by now included some version of major Senate reform as one of its objectives, although outside Alberta and especially inside Atlantic Canada, not altogether the particular version embodied in the details of Alberta's Triple E proposals. Thus, the Meech Lake Accord included two items dealing with the Senate. These were intended as interim steps on a now increasingly shorter journey to major reform.

Other impulses on the English-speaking regionalist side of the Meech Lake Accord focused on strengthening First Ministers' Conferences and on the tradition of federal-provincial diplomacy more generally — which since the Second World War had become the alternative to Senate reform as a means of dealing with the abiding regionalism of Canada.

It was Brian Mulroney's claim that he was returning "civility" and effectiveness to the tradition, after the excessive conflict and confrontation of the late Trudeau era. The "Regina Accord" of 1985 actually made formal provision for an "Annual Conference of First Ministers" for the first time in Canadian history, even though up to this point there had already been five conferences in the 1980s, 16 in the 1970s, and 15 in the 1960s. Between February 1985 and November 1987, Mulroney himself would host an additional six First Ministers' Conferences, and one shorter and more informal "First Ministers' Meeting."

In the end, critics of the Meech Lake Accord would complain that it strengthened federal-provincial diplomacy to an inordinate degree. Trudeau urged from his thoughtful but still bristling retirement that the Accord "should be put out in the dust bin," and predicted that if it ever did bring true civil peace to Canada, it would be "the peace of the grave." On the other hand, the Accord itself would not become part of the written Constitution unless it was ratified by the federal Senate and House of Commons and the legislatures of all ten provinces by 23 June 1990.

At first blush, the Meech Lake Accord is a document of arcane complexity. To no small extent, it follows a Canadian constitutional tradition aptly characterized by the historian W.L. Morton when he noted how the original Confederation of the 1860s and 1870s leaned on "a failure to disagree for lack of understanding and clear definition." It took some time for the Canadian national democracy to grasp even the Accord's broader implications for the future of the new Confederation.

The most elemental query among the citizens of the democracy, however, is easy enough to answer. "Meech Lake" is the site of a Canadian federal government conference centre in the Gatineau Park area of Quebec, not far from Ottawa.

Meech Lake as a Revival of Federal-Provincial Diplomacy

The best approach to grasping the essential political substance of the 1987 Meech Lake Accord is to start with the understanding that its initial and most crucial purpose was to specify the constitutional role of Quebec in the new Confederation of the late twentieth century in a way that finally satisfied the duly elected government of the province of Quebec.

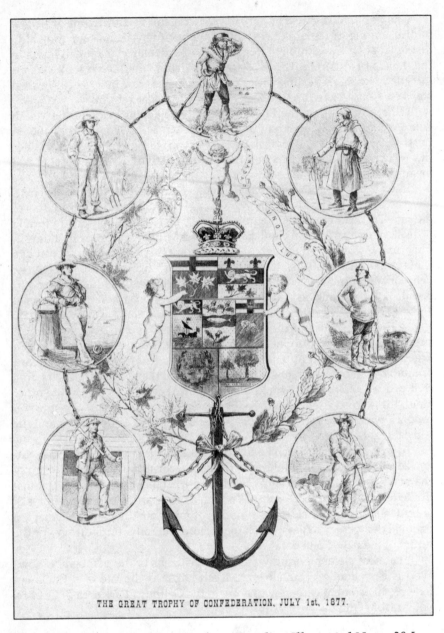

THE GREAT TROPHY OF CONFEDERATION, JULY 1st, 1877.

The Great Trophy of Confederation, from **Canadian Illustrated News**, *30 June 1877. The writing on the ribbon reads "The Confederated Provinces of Canada — Ex Uno Plures."*

John A. Macdonald's uncompromisingly centralist views of Canada have never gone unchallenged, especially when he himself was alive. And, whatever else, the Meech Lake Accord, negotiated some 110 years after this design was first published, can claim its own deep historical roots.

From here, it could be said without too much exaggeration, the key to Meech Lake is that the other nine provinces of Canada were persuaded to agree to recognize Quebec as an official distinct society by a commitment from the federal government, Quebec, and of course, themselves to recognize every other province in the Confederation as a kind of unofficial distinct society. The Quebec journalist Lysianne Gagnon put this succinctly — and again with only a degree of exaggeration: "Quebec didn't achieve even a shadow of special status ... the other provinces fought tooth and nail for the sacrosanct principle of equality. And they too will have everything Quebec asked for!"

The negotiations began with Robert Bourassa's "five demands" for at last "signing" the 1982 new Constitution. And the first demand was that Quebec should have a veto over constitutional amendments. The Meech Lake response was to double the length of a short list of highly entrenched subjects in the Constitution Act, 1982, amendments to which required unanimous approval from "each province," and not merely approval of any seven provinces with 50% of the national population. In this way Quebec acquired a veto over future changes in virtually all the major institutions of the Canadian federal system (governor general, provinces, House of Commons, Senate, and Supreme Court), and so did every other province.

In a similar fashion, under Meech Lake, Quebec and every other province acquired

- the constitutional right to opt out of federal-provincial shared-cost programs, and yet still receive federal funds for parallel exclusively provincial programs that are "compatible with the national objectives" (as in the Canada and Quebec pensions plans, for instance);

- a provincial role in appointments to the Supreme Court of Canada;

- the right to make agreements with the federal government "relating to immigration or the temporary admission of aliens into that province that is appropriate to the needs and circumstances of that province."

To all this — which dispensed with four of Robert Bourassa's five demands — were added the items from the English-speaking regionalist agenda regarding Senate reform and First Ministers' Conferences:

- interim federal Senate appointments from provincial short lists;

- entrenchment of an annual first ministers' constitutional conference, with Senate reform as its lead agenda item (and with "Roles and responsibilities in relation to fisheries" as another one);

- entrenchment of another annual First Ministers' Conference "to discuss the state of the Canadian economy and such other matters as may be appropriate."

The last two of these provisions reflected a continuing concern with strengthening the institution of First Ministers' Conferences, expressed earlier in Alberta's 1985 Senate reform document, *Strengthening Canada*. These conferences, the Alberta Select Special Committee had also recommended, "should assume a constitutionally entrenched place in our Parliamentary system," and "if no move is made to reform the Senate within a short period, First Ministers' Conferences should be given additional powers."

All that remained was Robert Bourassa's fifth demand. Here, Lysianne Gagnon notwithstanding, Quebec did achieve one fundamental thing that the other provinces did not: official constitutional recognition "that Quebec constitutes within Canada a distinct society." Exactly what this may or may not mean was left to be decided over time by the Supreme Court of Canada.

By 1989, however, one proposition that the distinct society clause had come to symbolize in English-speaking Canada — rightly or wrongly — was that Quebec had the right to be an officially unilingual French, not bilingual, province.

This did not mean that every other province acquired the right to be an officially unilingual English province, since New Brunswick was already officially bilingual. But did it mean that *some* other provinces might have acquired this right? By the late spring of 1989, for instance, both Alberta and Quebec seemed to be arguing, that it was acceptable for Alberta to be unilingually English, as Quebec was unilingually French.

The Two Faces of Senate Reform in Meech Lake

The distinct society clause in the Meech Lake Accord gave the side of English-speaking Canada that still did not accept the fundamental legitimacy of the modern French fact in the Canadian nation — or that still wanted to insist French Canadians were and should continue to behave as "a conquered people" — an opportunity to protest the progress of the new Confederation.

Yet Meech Lake was also vulnerable to attack from several quite different and distinctly post-colonial nation-building points of view. One was the rather utopian vision that Trudeau had come to stand for during his more than 15 years as federal prime minister. Another was the somewhat different Western (and Atlantic) vision that saw major Senate reform as the ultimate alternative answer to Trudeau's poignant question: "Who will speak for Canada?"

When it came to Senate reform, in fact, Meech Lake showed the profundity of its engagement with the venerable Canadian constitutional tradition of failing "to disagree for lack of understanding and clear definition." In some respects, it seemed to throw a big roadblock in the way of any kind of major and genuinely credible Canadian Senate reform. In others, it seemed to advance the cause, sometimes in essential ways. For instance:

(1) Under the original Constitution Act, 1982 changes to the Senate only required approval by seven provinces with 50% of the national population. Under the Meech Lake Accord, they would require unanimous provincial approval.

This would make achieving a workable federal-provincial consensus on major Senate reform extremely difficult, at best. The eminent constitutional authority at McGill University J.R. Mallory observed: "Meech Lake by imposing the unanimity rule on constitutional amendments affecting the Senate, will probably kill the prospect of all but very minor reforms in the foreseeable future."

(2) On the other hand, as the Alberta minister of federal and intergovernmental affairs, Jim Horsman, stressed in a January 1989 speech to the Canadian Club in Toronto, the Meech Lake Accord would "bring Quebec back as a full participant in future constitutional discussions — and we must have Quebec at the table before any progress can be made."

As Trudeau has quite correctly urged, this was in no sense necessary with regard to the fundamental legitimacy of the Constitution Act, 1982. Yet, as Horsman and others have pointed out with equal force, some formal assent to constitutional renewal from the provincial government of Quebec is a prerequisite for any continuing and expanded constitutional journeys on such matters as major Senate reform.

(3) The Accord itself would at least begin the political process of Senate reform, in two different ways:

First, it would require the federal prime minister to fill Senate vacancies on the basis of lists of "the names of persons who may be summoned," that were submitted by "the government of the province to which the vacancy relates." This directly reflected the "Federal Appointment from Provincial Short Lists" proposal from the "Short and Medium Term Possibilities" discussed in Alberta's *Strengthening Canada* in 1985.

Second, the Accord prescribed annual constitutional conferences of first ministers with, at the head of their agenda, "Senate reform, including the role and functions of the Senate, its powers, the method of selecting senators and representation in the Senate." In Jim Horsman's view, "section 13 of the Accord *requires* the prime minister to convene a constitutional conference at least once a year to discuss Senate reform until agreement is reached."

To complete the chain of paradoxes, there was another more diffuse way in which the Meech Lake Accord could be said to have increased the urgency of Senate reform.

Pierre Trudeau's uncompromising verdict that under the Canadian federal regime envisioned by the Accord the "possibility of building one Canada will be lost forever" may well be quite exaggerated, like a few other pronouncements from the side of his rigorous mind that never did actually move from philosopher king to Mackenzie King. But his comments had some sharp edges. Beyond the crucial recognition of the distinct society in Quebec, the Accord did amount to a quite dramatically decentralizing response to the abiding regionalism of the Confederation — a major new thrust of province building and federal-provincial diplomacy in national politics.

Without some countervailing new centralizing initiative, such as a bold nation-building version of major, radical Senate reform, it was extremely likely that the transcontinental Canadian destiny of the twenty-first century would be notably meek, mild, and very modest indeed.

By the summer of 1989, these were among the factors that had begun to cast a pall of gloom over the future of the Meech Lake Accord. As a result of provincial elections quite soon after its initial June 1987 negotiation, the provincial legislatures of New Brunswick and Manitoba had yet to ratify the document before the June 1990 deadline. Moreover, Newfoundland, following a provincial election that replaced a Conservative with a Liberal government, began to have some very serious second thoughts. Then the premier of British Columbia, who had already signed the original agreement, raised a few new reservations in public.

Many seasoned if not exactly jaded Canadian political observers came to view the document as a "dead letter," without at least some substantial renegotiation on several different fronts — or perhaps some parallel new accord covering additional matters. At the same time, a diverse assortment of pundits and commentators seemed to agree that some step not unlike the Meech Lake Accord was probably vital to the growth of the Confederation. Mackenzie King would have understood: Canada needed the Meech Lake Accord if necessary, but not necessarily the Meech Lake Accord.

The Canada-U.S. Free Trade Agreement

Less than six months after the negotiation of Meech Lake in the late spring of 1987, Brian Mulroney's new federal regime in Ottawa had also managed, to the surprise of many, to negotiate a historic free trade agreement with the United States.

This flowed from the advice offered by the 1985 report of the Royal Commission on the Economic Union and Development Prospects for Canada (which had also recommended an at least not too radical version of an elected Senate). More urgently, it flowed from rising concerns among the Canadian business community over signs of a new protectionist spirit in the late twentieth century American Republic.

By the end of 1988, a Canadian federal election centred around the "Canada-U.S. Free Trade Agreement" had returned Mulroney's Conservatives to power in Ottawa, with only 43% of the national popular vote but with a still quite workable majority of seats in the House of Commons. Not altogether unlike Trudeau, in one respect, Mulroney was another somewhat exotic national politician from the ancient St. Lawrence Valley: a thoroughly bilingual Quebec native of Irish descent. Whatever might happen to the Meech Lake Accord, with the 1988 election he had at least won himself some form of special and secure place in Canadian history.

Yet, like the Meech Lake Accord, the Canada-U.S. Free Trade Agreement, to be gradually implemented over a 10-year period and cancellable by either side, on six months' notice, only increased the urgency of some kind of major, nation-building Senate reform in the new Confederation. There were some notable subtleties, or even ironies, however, in exactly how the urgency was increased.

On the one hand, by at last abandoning the last vestiges of John A. Macdonald's old National Policy, the FTA could be said to have strengthened the forces of economic as well as political decentralization in Canada. Only the more distant future can tell just what this may finally mean for the evolution of Canadian economic geography, assuming that the Canada-U.S. Free Trade Agreement does endure for a significant length of time. There are some reasons for believing that it may not mean a great deal of change from the circumstances already prevailing in the late twentieth century.

In a rather different sense, however, the agreement did help demonstrate a need for new political means of strengthening Canada. In the ancient past of 1911 a Central Canadian business community, headquartered in Montreal and Toronto, had lobbied with enormous energy and conviction, and with ultimately enough success to count, against Wilfrid Laurier's earlier version of Canada-U.S. free trade. But in 1988 the Canadian business community, in all parts of the country — and in Toronto as much as in Montreal or Vancouver, or anywhere else — showed even more enthusiasm for "Mulroney's trade agreement" than Mulroney himself.

The world economy of the late twentieth century was different from the world economy of the late nineteenth and early twentieth centuries. Canada, like many other parts of the globe, could no longer depend on the crude private calculations of a national business class to help keep the nation together. Canadian "big business" was happy enough and in some or perhaps even many cases concerned to see Canada continue. But it no longer had the kind of raw self-interest in working hard to make this happen that it had in 1911.

On the other hand, in Canada the entire process of negotiating and ratifying the Free Trade Agreement showed how the federal government at Ottawa still had, in some crucial respects, a residual unilateral power in the new Confederation. The renewed Constitution of the early 1980s had not been altogether new. Its starting point was still the old Constitution of the 1860s. And power over such matters as "The Regulation of Trade and

Commerce," "Currency and Coinage," "Interest," and "Patents of Invention and Discovery" still lay unambiguously in the federal government's hands.

Mulroney found it politically helpful to solicit support from seven or eight premiers for the deal the federal government finally achieved. But the provinces did not and could not play any serious role in actually achieving the deal. In the final document, the federal governments in both Ottawa and Washington committed themselves to ensuring that their respective provinces and states would conform to the provisions of the agreement. First Ministers' Conferences could discuss such matters as much as they liked; only the federal government in Ottawa had the power to act.

Here was another kind of reason for the urgency of major Senate reform. It suggested that Atlantic and Western Canada could never fundamentally achieve more effective power over high economic policy in the nation at large through strengthening federal-provincial diplomacy, no matter how many First Ministers' Conferences were held. For this they needed new channels of influence within the institutions of the federal government itself — institutions such as Alberta's kind of reformed Senate, that would have the specific power to ratify, on behalf of all Canadians, from the Atlantic to the Pacific to the Arctic Ocean, any "Non-military treaties" signed by the Government of Canada.

19
PARTY POLITICS AND THE TROUBLED WATERS OF MEECH LAKE

From the standpoint of the trade deal between Canada and the United States that was finally struck in the late fall of 1987, it would have made more sense if the English-speaking regionalist side of the Meech Lake Accord had been tilted much more toward securing agreement from Quebec and Ontario on credible Senate reform, and much less toward abstract provincial equality, First Ministers' Conferences, and strengthening federal-provincial diplomacy.

Thus the political scientist Ted Morton explained in the fall of 1989: "As Canada enters the new era of free trade with the U.S., it needs a strong and effective national government to protect its interests." The key to achieving this kind of government was not more federal-provincial diplomacy; it was "Senate reform: elected, effective, and a more equal delegation from each province."

Yet the politics of Senate reform in Canada are complicated, and reflect in themselves the diversity of the Confederation. One reason that Meech Lake did not lean more logically toward Senate reform was a residual province builder's wariness about the centralizing, nation-building impulses implicit in an elected, equal, and effective Senate, even on the part of the concept's most ardent proponents among the provincial governments.

In the initial May 1985 debate on the Alberta Triple E proposals in the Alberta Legislative Assembly, for instance, Peter Lougheed had revealed why he had originally favoured a provincially appointed over an elected federal Senate for Canada.

"I've been puzzled," Lougheed allowed, "as to how we could establish an elected body that wouldn't be at odds with the provincial government and that wouldn't dominate intergovernmental negotiations," so that "the resource management responsibilities of an elected provincial government would still be the fundamental source of strength in a nation such as ours."

Even the 1984 elected-Senate proposals of the Joint Senate and House of Commons Committee in Ottawa had covered one side of these concerns. Like the Alberta Select Special Committee proposals of 1985, the Joint Committee rejected "the view that the principal, or even a secondary, function of the second chamber should be federal-provincial co-ordination. Such co-ordination is, we think, best left to the federal and provincial governments." Major Senate reform was not meant to replace the existing tradition of federal-provincial diplomacy, but only to do what it could not hope to do.

Canada would remain a notably decentralized federal system, with strong provincial governments, no matter what happened.

Alberta's concerns, however, went deeper than this. They were reflected in its detailed Triple E proposals to tie Senate elections to the provincial rather than the federal election cycle, and to create a separate Senate Executive Council, that could rival the federal Cabinet rooted in the House of Commons. Thus Premier Lougheed confessed that holding federal Senate elections at the same time as provincial elections was one of "some very innovative ideas" that enabled him "to change my view of concern" about "an elected Senate."

At the same time, these detailed proposals compromised the argument that Senate reform was a much-needed nation-building innovation in the wider national democracy. Despite the title *Strengthening Canada* and the maple leaf on the cover, it was still easy enough to picture the specific proposed version of reform as something that would, as C.E.S. Franks complained, "make Canada more, not less, ungovernable."

Regions and Nations in Canadian Political Parties

In fact, the authors of *Strengthening Canada* imply that Alberta's deeper concerns in this context do have a nation-building as well as a province-building dimension. And this, they explain, is illustrated by the Australian experience.

In the land of the kangaroo, as Alexander Brady reported in the late 1940s, "concerned with the industrial and social issues which enter into the partisan warfare of the nation, the senators are inevitably more loyal to their parties than to their states." Or, as *Strengthening Canada* put it in the mid-1980s: "Many individuals expressed concern regarding central party control of the Australian Upper House. It is the Committee's hope that the recommendations which are proposed for the internal organization of Canada's equal, elected, and effective Senate would not create similar concerns with party control in Canada."

On the other hand, even members of the Alberta Legislative Assembly have argued that, given the way democracy in Canada works, it would be impossible to shield a Triple E Senate from national party politics in any serious sense — no matter how many "very innovative ideas" are brought to bear on the details of its implementation. *Strengthening Canada* goes a considerable distance toward acknowledging the same point itself.

With regard to the Australian experience, still others will want to emphasize that Canada is not Australia. As Richard Simeon explained in the early 1970s, pointing to the work of the same Alexander Brady who published *Democracy in the Dominions* just after the Second World War, "Australia is a much less 'federal society' " than Canada.

In the same spirit, Western Canada already has a well-established regional history of strong suspicions about the national party system based in Ottawa. One result has been the growth of both the Social Credit and New

Democratic parties, which have formed provincial governments in the West, and spilled over into national politics to create what has sometimes been called a "two-and-a-half party system" at the federal level, and other times looked as if it might become a three or even multiparty system.

The New Democrats have also spilled over into Ontario provincial politics, and sometimes, to a much lesser extent, the provincial politics of Atlantic Canada. During the early Quiet Revolution, Social Credit spilled over into federal politics in Quebec as les Créditistes. What's more, Quebec, like Western Canada, has an established history of regionally based provincial parties in the Union Nationale and, of course, the late twentieth century Parti Québécois.

Even the two "mainstream" parties at the national level have evolved over time — and virtually reversed positions on major national and regional issues. Some Liberals still called themselves Reformers down to the early twentieth century. (And one of the meanings of the word "Grit" in the *Shorter Oxford English Dictionary* is: "In Canadian politics, a Radical or Liberal.") Macdonald's Liberal-Conservatives became the National Conservatives, and then the Progressive Conservatives, when the Progressive premier of Manitoba John Bracken became their federal leader in 1942.

With regard to the two visions of Canada that have clashed several times in the past generation, and will no doubt clash again in the next, in at least a few striking ways the Liberals of the late twentieth century tend to stand up for the vision that Macdonald's Conservatives stood for in the late nineteenth and early twentieth centuries. And the late twentieth century Conservatives tend to stand up for the early twentieth century vision of Laurier and the federal Liberals. From yet another angle, in the 1980s Donald Smiley stressed

> a growing tendency towards ... the "confederalization" of
> the Canadian political parties — a movement towards the
> organizational separation of the federal and provincial wings
> of the Liberals and Progressive Conservatives into elements
> directed to electoral success in the two political arenas.

The Canadian party system, nationally and provincially, has been far from monolithic. Like everything else in Canada, its history has been an exercise in pluralism, diversity, and change. As Smiley has also pointed out, this is quite different from the experience in Australia. There "the two major ... party groupings ... are important electoral contenders in every State whereas, as is well known, this is not so in Canada."

Potential Impact of Senate Reform on the National Party System

In this specific historical context, it could be that an equal, elected, and effective Canadian Senate — which the authors of *Strengthening Canada* themselves allow would amount to a notably "radical reform" in Canadian national politics — will have more impact on the Canadian national party system than the national party system will have on it.

A key unknown in party politics of the late twentieth century, for instance, is the future of the Parti Québécois. Its chances of surviving until a constitutional amendment that achieved some form of Triple E Senate seem good enough. And the chances that Quebec voters would put some PQ members in any new elected Senate seem not altogether negligible, even if Senate elections are tied to the federal rather than the provincial election cycle.

Similarly, Preston Manning's new regionally oriented Reform Party in Western Canada might well elect some senators in Alberta and British Columbia, and even Saskatchewan (proof of which, as will be discussed shortly, has in fact already been offered). It would also not be surprising if British Columbia were to elect some Social Credit senators. All four western provinces and Ontario are likely enough to elect some NDP senators.

Tendencies of this sort would almost certainly be enhanced by supplementary systems of representation for French Canadians outside Quebec and for the Indians, Inuit, and Métis. Moreover, in the same context who can say what strange and creative alliances an elected Canadian Senate might breed? George Woodcock, for instance, has noted that David Barrett, the mid-1970s NDP premier of British Columbia (and late 1980s unilingual candidate for the federal NDP leadership), once contemplated the prospects of an alliance with the Parti Québécois under René Lévesque. The New Democrats have more recently had experiences in Quebec themselves that could point in the same direction.

Given all this, it seems likely that even an elected, equal, and effective Senate with elections tied to the federal election cycle, and with senators who sat in the same federal Cabinet as members of the House of Commons, would move the national democracy still more toward some form of multiparty system at the federal level.

National governments at Ottawa may have to adapt by developing new skills in creating periodic multiparty governing coalitions, with support in both the Canadian House of Commons and the new elected Senate. But in the process, the national party system, the national mass media, and the federal bureaucracy must grow more sensitive to the great variety and diversity of regional interests in all parts of the new Confederation.

Similarly, the new elected Senate may increase the chances of periodic "minority governments" in Ottawa — or federal administrations that could not invariably count on instant majorities for all their policies and programs in Parliament, and that had to work at building national support for specific measures as a matter of routine. The American political scientist Joseph La Palombara has recently argued that a much more extreme version of such a system than Canada is ever likely to see has served late twentieth century Italian democracy remarkably well, despite popular stereotypes to the contrary. Moreover, to say that a system of this sort would inevitably make

Canada more, not less, ungovernable is to ignore Canada's own historical record.

The wizard Mackenzie King came to power in 1921 with slightly less than 50% of the seats in the House of Commons. He won less than 50% again in the election of 1925 that led to the King-Byng Affair, and only slightly more than 50% in two of his four subsequent electoral triumphs. Six of the 12 Canadian federal elections since 1957 have produced minority governments, with governing parties that could only count absolutely on less than 50% of the elected members of Parliament.

Paradoxically, the two overwhelming majority governments of the same era, produced by the elections of 1958 and 1984, were not widely regarded as strong national regimes. They were noted for a great variety of "political problems" — symbolized by low levels of popular support in inter-election opinion polls. On the other hand, it is highly arguable that the most energetic and successful nation-building regimes actually were either minority governments, or governments with only slim majorities.

Here, again, there is a contrast with Australia. To quote Donald Smiley once more: "Australians do not, like Canadians, elect minority governments." Abstract theorizing and ideology aside, on virtually all the available hard evidence there seems no overwhelming or even strong reason to fear that the regional impact of an elected Senate in Canada would quickly be blunted by "central party control" in Ottawa. In fact, drawing on an argument advanced by his colleague Alan Cairns, Smiley himself has said that in "the short run at least an elected Senate might have a provincializing effect," because "less than at present the federal executive would be able to speak for and commit the national government" in the vagaries of federal-provincial diplomacy. This could also be an advantage for a federal executive that wanted reasons for limiting the role of First Ministers' Conferences in setting national goals and objectives. But one of the fundamental arguments for an elected Senate is that setting national goals and objectives ought not to be a responsibility of provincial governments.

Alberta's Elected Senator

Some more particular evidence that an elected Senate in Canada would not be unusually susceptible to central party control had already appeared by the end of the 1980s. In February 1989, when it still looked as if the Meech Lake Accord probably was, as Prime Minister Mulroney had put it, a "done deal," the provincial government of Alberta took another step to enhance the prospects of "Senate reform, including the role and functions of the Senate, its powers, the method of selecting senators and representation in the Senate."

As part of the Meech Lake bargain, Mulroney's federal government had committed itself to fill new Senate vacancies on the basis of lists of names submitted by "the government of the province to which the vacancy relates," even before the constitutional amendments implementing the Accord actually came into force. Taking a leaf from the pages of the American history that had led to the Seventeenth Amendment of 1913, prescribing the election of senators in the United States, Alberta announced that it would hold elections to determine any names it might submit as part of this process.

A Senatorial Selection Act was tabled in the Alberta Legislative Assembly. The Alberta minister of federal and intergovernmental affairs, Jim Horsman, declared:

> When the first election is held under the Act, Albertans will be sending an important message to their fellow Canadians — that in a democracy, all citizens should be able to say who represents them. And that first Senate nominee, who I am confident will be chosen by the Prime Minister to sit in the Senate, will forever change the face of our second chamber.

In fact, Prime Minister Mulroney and his government leader in the Senate, Lowell Murray, were not altogether impressed. They noted that the Meech Lake bargain had referred to "the names of persons who may be summoned." This implied that a province would submit several candidates for the prime minister's consideration in respect to any particular Senate vacancy, not the single victor of an election. Other unofficial voices were raised elsewhere to the effect that the entire Alberta scheme was fundamentally "unconstitutional."

Momentum on this front flagged somewhat when the election of Liberal Clyde Wells as the new premier of Newfoundland in the spring of 1989 signalled new difficulties for the Meech Lake Accord itself, which the legislatures of New Brunswick and Manitoba still had to ratify before June 1990. Even so, one of Premier Wells's key objections to the Accord, a Toronto journalist reported, was "that it would make real Senate reform impossible. And ... Senate reform is the only hope for disadvantaged provinces, the only mechanism which can give provinces like Newfoundland a stronger role in federal policy-making."

In August 1989 the Senatorial Selection Act passed third reading in the Alberta Legislative Assembly, despite protests from the opposition Liberals and New Democrats. In October the first contest under the act was held, not in conjunction with a provincial campaign but as part of Alberta's municipal elections.

More than 610,000 Albertans cast votes in the contest for "Canada's first elected senator" — about half the number that had voted in the 1988 federal election. This could stand as a notably respectable showing, given the traditionally low turnout in municipal elections everywhere. And it confirmed the April 1989 Gallup Poll, which had indicated that almost two-thirds of Canadians in the Prairie provinces favoured an elected Senate.

The election was won not by a Liberal, a Conservative, or even a New Democrat, but by Stan Waters of Preston Manning's new Reform Party. Many felt that this was a distinct embarrassment for Alberta's Progressive

1989 BILL 1

Fourth Session, 21st Legislature, 38 Elizabeth II

THE LEGISLATIVE ASSEMBLY OF ALBERTA

BILL 1

SENATORIAL SELECTION ACT

THE PREMIER

First Reading ....

Second Reading ....

Committee of the Whole ....

Third Reading ....

Royal Assent ....

The Alberta government began the last year of the 1980s by tabling "Bill 1" — the Senatorial Selection Act — in the province's Legislative Assembly. By the fall the bill had been passed and a provincial "Senate election" had taken place. In the early 20th century United States, parallel tactics took a full decade to produce an elected federal Senate. But, despite much initial criticism and even some notable indifference, they worked in the end.

Conservative premier Don Getty. If it was, Getty took it in stride and duly submitted Waters's name to Brian Mulroney in Ottawa, along with the names of the defeated candidates in the election. It quickly became clear that Mulroney would be in no hurry to appoint Waters to the relevant Alberta Senate vacancy. At the same time, Mulroney's deputy prime minister, the native Albertan Don Mazankowski, observed that while the election of Stan Waters was not "an earth-shattering victory," it was "indicative of a mood that exists in Alberta and I think that in a democracy you have to accept those views and those decisions."

The Troubled Waters of Meech Lake

Logically enough, Stan Waters was a strong supporter of major Senate reform. Yet, as if to show that he did not grasp the constitutional political realities of the issue as well as the Progressive Conservative Government of Alberta (or the Progressive Conservative Government of Saskatchewan, or Gordon Gibson in Vancouver, B.C.), Waters was also a strong opponent of the Meech Lake Accord and its recognition of Quebec as a distinct society within Canada.

By this time, however, such aggressively negative opinions of Meech Lake had found many echoes throughout English-speaking Canada. The sentiment had been energized by Robert Bourassa's legislation mandating French-only signs in Quebec, and by a late September 1989 Quebec provincial election, which showed some resurgence of separatist strength under a Parti Québécois now led by the urbane and crafty Jacques Parizeau. What's more, though Bourassa in fact won the election handily enough, he himself finally suggested that remaining part of Canada was "not the only option" for Quebec's long-term future.

In this atmosphere the fate of the Meech Lake Accord, which still required ratification by the New Brunswick and Manitoba legislatures before 23 June 1990, became an unscheduled central issue at a First Ministers' Conference on the economy, held in the middle of November 1989.

Prior to the conference, both New Brunswick and Manitoba had issued reports suggesting modifications to the original Accord that would be required to win their support. At the same time, Bourassa made clear that Meech Lake represented Quebec's "minimum demands" for assenting to the 1982 Constitution, and could not be changed. (Though he did seem to leave room for some parallel "political agreement" about issues that could be addressed in a second round of constitutional discussions, after Meech Lake had been duly approved by all parties.)

Quebec had less trouble with New Brunswick's objections, which focused on the problems of Meech Lake for Canada's only officially bilingual province, than with Manitoba's, which raised more fundamental questions about the meaning of Quebec's distinct society. But the most dramatic performer at the November 1989 conference was the Liberal premier of Newfoundland, Clyde Wells, who combined a Trudeauesque critique of the original Accord, with demands for Senate reform that took at least some inspiration from Alberta's Triple E proposals. Under a different provincial government and a different premier, Newfoundland had already signed and ratified Meech Lake. But Wells now threatened to rescind this ratification if his concerns were not addressed.

By the end of the November 1989 conference, a final rather mysterious effort to salvage Meech Lake had begun. And the question of Senate reform played an equally rather mysterious part in the arrangements.

Clyde Wells had articulated a variation on Trudeau's theme that the particular recognition of Quebec's distinct society in the Accord amounted to "special status" for Quebec, with all the problems this raised for a genuine French and English Canadian unity, across the country. But he had also stressed the difficulties that the unanimous amending formula raised for Senate reform. While all the Western and Atlantic premiers had expressed good intentions in this direction, virtually no kind of reassurance had been heard from Ontario or Quebec.

This, it seemed, was also something of an issue for New Brunswick and Manitoba (and possibly British Columbia, and, in a more general sense, all the Western and Atlantic provinces). Behind closed doors, Ontario and Quebec apparently made some kind of appropriate noise. In public both seemed to agree that Senate reform was a worthy enough topic for discussion. (Bourassa stressed, however, that it was not something he would want to discuss with his Cabinet until after the Meech Lake Accord was secure.)

It was also announced that Lowell Murray, government leader in the federal Senate, would travel to the provincial capitals to discuss the future of Meech Lake, with particular reference to the future of Senate reform. Meanwhile, Clyde Wells would hold off with any plans to rescind Newfoundland's original endorsement of the deal.

If the Meech Lake Accord were in fact ratified by all ten provinces by the June 1990 deadline, a conference to begin discussions on Senate reform would be held in a Western province in November 1990. Finally, Brian Mulroney made clear, as Lowell Murray had already suggested early in 1989, that if Meech Lake did become part of the new Canadian Constitution, the federal government itself would bring forth proposals for the reform of the unreformed Senate of Canada.

This was not the first time that a Canadian prime minister had made public statements about reforming the muted voice of region bequeathed by the original Confederation of 1867. Mulroney revealed as well that at the original Meech Lake negotiations in 1987 he had offered to abolish the present Senate, supposedly as a start on creating some totally new second chamber "from the ground up." But other first ministers had not found the offer attractive. Virtually no pundits or commentators could see quite how discussions on Senate reform over the winter and spring of 1989–1990 could salvage the Meech Lake Accord by June 1990. (Bourassa was reported to have remarked in private, "Quelle game.") In October 1989 the editor of *The*

Financial Post in Toronto was only one among many Canadians to express "an ominous feeling that the country is falling apart."

All the same, the long journey to Senate reform in Canada had at last reached a point that it had never quite reached before. In one way or another, Senate reform had become an unavoidable element in the late twentieth century incarnation of "the Canadian question" that Goldwin Smith had first raised in 1891:

> Whether the four blocks of territory constituting the Dominion can for ever be kept by political agencies united among themselves and separate from their Continent, of which geographically, economically, and with the exception of Quebec ethnologically, they are parts ....

Robert Stanfield, premier of Nova Scotia, 1956-1967, leader of the federal Progressive Conservatives, 1967-1976, and after the November 1989 First Ministers' Conference in Ottawa, a more vocal and prominent friend of the Meech Lake Accord.

20
THE LONG ENOUGH JOURNEY
THAT REMAINS

For a brief period in the 1980s it seemed that the constitutional trials and tribulations of the new Confederation in Canada might have begun to subside into a somewhat more stable state, for the first time in a generation. By the end of the decade, it was clear that a still unsettled incarnation of the Canadian question remained on the agenda for the 1990s. Canada's constitutional dilemmas were possibly more acute than ever before.

Yet both historical and comparative perspectives can help put the challenge in a realistic context. Via the still rather recent technological miracle of television, many Canadians watched the people of the German Democratic Republic and the Federal Republic of Germany at last conquer the physical and psychological barriers of the Berlin Wall at about the same time that the first ministers of Canada were struggling to salvage the Meech Lake Accord. In this international setting, none of Canada's constitutional dilemmas, as urgent as they are, ought to be unusually overwhelming.

In historical perspective, the ways in which the most ancient Canada, crystallized by Cabot, Cartier, Champlain, and the Indians, came out of the political convulsions of the late eighteenth century and lived on into the nineteenth and twentieth centuries, were streaked with irony, defeats within victories, and victories within defeats. It should not be surprising if something similar accompanies the ways in which Canada comes out of the convulsions of the late twentieth century and lives on into the centuries ahead.

Similarly, for all its difficulties, disappointments, and harsh feelings, the most recent era of Canadian history has also been a time of at least some striking progress.

A Canada that had signed an unusually comprehensive free trade agreement with the United States at the start of the 1960s might well have been destined to become a perpetual satellite of the American Republic — merely to move from an old British to a new American Dominion. Yet both supporters and opponents of the Canada-U.S. Free Trade Agreement of the late 1980s have declared their determination to build a future in the most northern part of the North American continent, even if they disagree profoundly about how this is going to be done.

At the start of the 1960s the French fact troubled few people in Canada outside (or even, in some respects, inside) Quebec because it seemed little more than a historical relic, with no particularly notable future. Yet at the start of the 1990s what Canada's French fact means, or ought to mean, deeply agitates people in all parts of the country, because it is now so much more important than it has been at any time since la Conquête in the eighteenth century.

As recently as the end of the 1960s, the Canadian federal government proposed that the heirs of the seventeenth century Indians of Canada should simply be assimilated into the twentieth century mainstream of Canadian society once and for all. Métis were only "half-breeds" in history books, and most Canadians still called the Inuit "Eskimos." Yet late in November 1989 it was quietly announced that Lowell Murray's cross-country mission to salvage the Meech Lake Accord would also include "talks on ... expanded aboriginal rights," picking up on the failed discussions of the mid-1980s and the limited guarantees that were already in the renewed Constitution of 1982.

As recently as the end of the 1970s, or somewhat later, it was possible for even close students of the subject to doubt that there could ever be any genuinely major reform of the unreformed Senate of Canada. By the start of the 1990s, however, Senate reform had at least become an unavoidable element in Goldwin Smith's updated Canadian question. And, though the only genuinely ardent followers of Smith now live in the United States, Canada still has to come up with fresh answers to his question.

Who Supports Senate Reform?

The intellectual case for major Senate reform in Canada leans on historically rooted arguments about the logic and the justice of reorganizing the second chamber of the federal Parliament to accommodate the abiding regionalism of the Canadian Confederation. As a practical matter, however, Senate reform is part of the Canadian question in the 1990s because it has active political support.

There are several kinds of evidence about the character and depth of political support for Senate reform in Canada today. The most obvious kind is found in the positions that have been taken by a clear majority of Canada's provincial governments in the 1980s. Though it is sometimes said that only Alberta is deeply committed to the issue, it is also a plain fact that all four provinces of Western Canada endorsed the broad principle of an elected, equal, and effective Senate in the Parksville Accord of May 1988. All four Western premiers at the November 1989 First Ministers' Conference have also, on various occasions, voiced clear expressions of support for major Senate reform. After Alberta's October 1989 Senate election, the premier of Manitoba, Gary Filmon, indicated that his province might hold a similar contest.

All four Atlantic premiers present at the November 1989 First Ministers' Conference have made somewhat less bold gestures in favour of some kind of Senate reform. John Buchanan of Nova Scotia has indicated support for the principle of an elected Senate. New Brunswick's Frank McKenna has most recently been scrupulously diplomatic on the subject, but he did declare in 1987, before he became premier, that "an elected Senate" was the best way "for our National Institutions to incorporate the regional interests of our country." Until quite recently, Joe Ghiz of Prince Edward Island argued for a provincially-appointed rather than an elected Senate. On a television interview at the time of the November 1989 conference, however, he also allowed that something like Alberta's Triple E model had some attractions for his province. Clyde Wells from Newfoundland, though sounding a lot like Pierre Trudeau in some respects, has advanced Senate reform proposals that owe much more to the inspiration of the Government of Alberta.

Strictly popular support, even in Western and Atlantic Canada, is of course more difficult to judge. During the October 1989 campaign in Alberta, some ardent Senate reformers were disappointed that 100% of the provincial electorate did not turn out to vote for "Canada's first elected senator." They stressed how, even more than free trade with the United States, Senate reform is not an issue that lends itself to 15-second clips on the television news. Nonetheless, the April 1989 Gallup Poll on the subject suggests that majorities of the population in both Western and Atlantic Canada do support the principle of an elected Senate. Close to two-thirds apparently support the principle in the three Prairie provinces.

Finally, in 1989 Canada's federal prime minister, Brian Mulroney, at last made clear his own personal support for at least an elected and effective Senate in the federal Parliament. Cynics will note that Mulroney once opposed a comprehensive free trade agreement between Canada and the United States. But as matters stand at the edge of the 1990s, even the federal government in Canada is apparently committed to some version of major Senate reform.

What Is to Be Done?

It could be said that the political support that has been mobilized for Senate reform in Canada during the 1980s is more impressive than the institutional designs that have been advanced for breathing life into the concept. This reflects, however, the technical and political complexities of the issues involved more than the skills or commitments of the designers.

Technically, when Harold Innis urged political scientists to "escape from the hocus-pocus of the economist" and contribute to economic development by focusing on "modifications to political machinery," he was also urging the analyst of political machinery to "concentrate on the extremely difficult problems of his own field." The problems are rendered more difficult by popular suspicions that they are actually quite simple.

The political complexities of a specific workable design for major Senate reform in late twentieth century Canada owe much to conflicts between province-building and nation-building aspirations in the new Confederation.

Politically, it has been provincial governments that have given muscle to the Senate reform movement. The willingness of some provincial governments to press for an elected rather than a provincially appointed Senate signifies the depth of their nation-building concerns. Yet, as Roger Gibbins observed in the early 1980s, a genuinely effective and more equal elected federal Senate in Ottawa will ultimately constrain the role of provincial governments as national actors in Canadian federalism.

Thus, Alberta's proposals complicate the issue by urging Senate elections keyed to the provincial election cycle, senators who cannot sit in the federal Cabinet, and a Senate Executive Council that would probably compete with the Cabinet as the high policy arm of the federal executive.

Clyde Wells from Newfoundland raised strong national concerns at the November 1989 First Ministers' Conference. The Senate reform proposals he introduced (included in Appendix C of this book) do urge a fixed national date for Senate elections and make a rather unusual bow to both Quebec's distinct society and Trudeau's concerns for promoting official bilingualism in provinces outside Quebec. But they also envision excluding senators from the Cabinet, and they make provision for some form of "Senate executive council" in the Alberta manner. (Even the 1984 proposals of the Joint Senate and House of Commons Committee in Ottawa concluded "that senators should not be eligible for cabinet office." In Australia, on the other hand, senators do sit in the Cabinet, and this provincialist peculiarity of recent Canadian debate deserves at least much deeper thought.)

The upshot of both the technical and political complexities is that, at the edge of the 1990s, there is still no altogether convincing specific design for an elected, effective, and equal Canadian Senate, based on credible nation-building priorities.

This is not in any sense to denigrate what the Government of Alberta has accomplished through its staunch promotion of the Triple E model, which does pose the right general questions in a useful way. It is only to agree with the authors of *Strengthening Canada* themselves. Coming up with a workable specific design for an elected, equal, and effective Senate will "take time because of the difficulty in reaching agreement necessary for the inevitable and complicated constitutional change which would be required."

Similarly, some kind of informal federal-provincial political agreement about the general principles of Senate reform, and the appropriate processes for negotiating it, may somehow help salvage the Meech Lake Accord or bridge the gap between a failed Meech Lake Accord and some new agreement for winning Quebec's assent to the 1982 Constitution. But, given the time constraints involved, such an agreement would have to stop far short of any specific design for the actual "inevitable and complicated constitutional change" of Senate reform, in the short to mid-term future.

In the end, more public discussion and debate will be required to arrive at a workable design for major Senate reform in Canada, aided and abetted by more attention to the extremely difficult problems of constructing effective political machinery. In this process the federal government ought to be standing up boldly for broad national interests. While it certainly cannot arrive at a solution by itself, equally, it seems unlikely that a design for

Senate reform put together exclusively by provincial governments would ever completely address crucial nation-building priorities.

Two other somewhat more specific conclusions might be drawn about this part of the long enough journey that remains. First, coming at the end of almost a decade of rather muted preliminary debate in quite narrow circles, Alberta's 1985 Triple E model did focus attention in the right direction from the standpoint of comparative politics in the wider global village. Beyond the not altogether relevant example of the non-parliamentary United States, the right place for Canadians concerned about Senate reform to look for inspiration is not the Federal Republic of Germany or any other part of Western Europe. It is the Commonwealth of Australia.

Australia is a geographically vast, federal parliamentary democracy, with political institutions more like those of Canada than those of virtually any other country in the world. Its particular form of elected, equal, and effective Senate cannot be exactly suited to Canada's particular circumstances. It also has a few rather apparent problems of its own that designers of a Canadian Senate would be wise to avoid. But it almost certainly has more to teach us than we have digested so far. A student of comparative government must find it surprising that the Canadian debate of the 1980s has not paid more attention to the Australian example. The only good explanation may be that Canadians typically have too much of the same false disdain for the value of the Australian experience that Americans have for the value of the Canadian experience.

Second, while discussion is important and necessary, too much emphasis on debate can become a tactic for stalling on real action. Beyond the well-known impatience of Alberta, it is worth stressing the Government of Newfoundland's November 1989 declaration that it "shares the Manitoba Task Force's view of the urgency of Senate reform, and believes that Newfoundland and Labrador and all of the smaller provinces have little or no hope of ever achieving their rightful place in the Canadian federation until Canada has a Triple-E Senate."

Along with public discussion and debate on a specific workable design for Senate reform in Canada, there are good reasons for keeping up the pressure on the practical political front — through federal-provincial meetings, various broader forms of publicity and promotion, and even more "Senate elections" of the sort that Alberta held in October 1989. There are also good reasons for believing that, in one way or another, the pressure will be kept up.

What about Quebec?

If there is, at the edge of the 1990s, substantial evidence of a firming consensus about the urgency of major Senate reform among the eight provinces of Atlantic and especially Western Canada, there is still very little concrete indication of how the provincial governments of Ontario and Quebec might react, as the pressure for change in what Gordon Gibson has called "outer Canada" continues. And, however unfortunate, it is a stark political reality that it is here, in the old United Province of Canada which played a key role in beginning the modern Confederation in the 1860s and 1870s, that the fate of Senate reform in the late twentieth century will ultimately be decided.

Ontario and Quebec together had more than 75% of the Confederation's total population in the 1870s, and they still have more than 60% today. Under the Meech Lake Accord both provinces would have to agree to any changes in the Senate. Even under the less stringent general amending formula of the 1982 Constitution (any seven provinces with at least 50% of the national population), one or the other would have to agree.

Moreover, if Lowell Murray is right about the legacy of the old provisions for representing Quebec's English Protestant minority in the unreformed Senate of Canada, Quebec may have what amounts to a veto over Senate reform even without the Meech Lake Accord. These provisions, which are unique to Quebec, would have to be amended to accommodate some form of Triple E Senate, and under section 43 of the Constitution Act, 1982, amendments affecting "one or more, but not all, provinces" must be approved by "the legislative assembly of each province to which the amendment applies."

According to the April 1989 Gallup Poll, Quebec is also the only region in Canada today where even a bare majority of the population does not support the principle of an elected Senate. Quebec staunchly resisted the principle of equal provincial representation in the Senate during the original Confederation debates of the 1860s.

Still more crucially, the argument that Quebec in the late twentieth century no longer requires special representation in the federal Senate because it has become a constitutionally recognized distinct society under the Meech Lake Accord, must confront the near-death of Meech Lake late in 1989. It must equally confront a November 1989 Gallup Poll, which reported that Quebec is the only region of Canada where a majority of the population would approve "of the inclusion of Quebec in the Constitution as a 'distinct society' within Canada."

All this can be viewed as evidence in support of those Senate reformers who insist that, despite the apparent difficulties created by the unanimous amending formula, approval of the Meech Lake Accord is in fact an indispensable prerequisite for any serious reorganization of the unreformed Senate of Canada. The evidence suggests that, in terms of positions taken at the November 1989 First Ministers' Conference in Ottawa, the Alberta and Saskatchewan Senate reformers are right and those from Newfoundland and Manitoba are wrong.

Yet as Clyde Wells from Newfoundland has implied, the problem with this argument is that there is as yet virtually no concrete evidence to suggest that any provincial government of Quebec will itself be prepared to accept its constitutional recognition as a distinct society as a viable trade-off for even some workable version of an elected, equal, and effective federal Senate. At the beginning of the 1990s, the view in Quebec rather pointedly seems to be that its constitutional recognition as a distinct society is merely a trade-off for its continuing agreement to remain in the new Confederation.

All any English-speaking Canadian of good will can do at this stage in the debate is appeal to the underlying justice of the case.

Daniel Latouche, an earlier guru for the cause of sovereignty-association in Quebec, has articulated the crucial political logic (which, in an ironic way, owes much to the rigorous common sense of Pierre Trudeau). "The problem," Latouche wrote in the spring of 1989 in the Ottawa-based magazine *The New Federation*, "is that Quebec now insists on being an active player on the federal scene while retaining all that makes it different. And nowhere was this more evident than in the last federal election."

Put another way, late twentieth century Quebec has only just over one-quarter of the national population. According to the 1986 census, in Canada at large (including Quebec) some two-thirds of Canadians speak English, about 16% speak French, and almost 17% are bilingual. Outside Quebec, the bilingual proportion of the population ranges from a high of almost 30% in New Brunswick and just under 12% in Ontario, to a low of just under 5% in Saskatchewan and less than 3% in Newfoundland. In this setting, if Canada is going to have both an officially unilingual French Quebec and a bilingual federal government at Ottawa (to say nothing of an officially bilingual New Brunswick, and varying degrees of unofficial bilingualism in Ontario and Manitoba), then Quebec is going to incur a substantial political debt to the rest of its partners in the new Confederation. The best hope for major Senate reform is that, as the inevitable trials and tribulations of the 1990s unfold, at some decisive moment some provincial government of Quebec is going to recognize that the best way to discharge this debt is to agree to some workable version of an elected, equal, and effective federal Senate.

What about Ontario?

English-speaking Senate reformers cannot convincingly urge this kind of logic on Quebec if they are not themselves prepared to recognize Quebec as a distinct society — and to embrace with some conviction the crucial proposition that, under the 1982 Constitution, the federal government is now officially bilingual, such that the federal prime minister ought to be or become conversant in both English and French.

At the same time, according to Gallup Polls nothing that approaches a majority of the Canadian population is as yet willing to acknowledge the distinct society in Quebec, in any province except Quebec itself. The polls are not easy to interpret, and the regional breakdown of the numbers has been volatile in the most recent past. For the moment, however, Senate reformers who link their demands with Quebec's distinct society must be prepared to ignore the majority of current popular opinion on this subject in

English-speaking Canada. (There is as well no region of Canada, including Quebec, where a majority of the population supports the Meech Lake Accord. Yet equally, a clear national majority also confesses that it does not altogether understand the Meech Lake Accord.)

In Ontario, more than anywhere else, the issue is complicated by a continuing residual and rather fuzzy attraction to the somewhat utopian constitutional solutions of Pierre Trudeau, especially among various strategic political elites. Yet the side of Ontario that subscribes to Trudeau's bilingual national vision is still committed only in much more of a "let's pretend" sense than would satisfy Trudeau himself. The more the commitment is seriously tested —as any truly convincing version of it would require— the more the well over 85% of the present Ontario population that does not speak French will itself become alienated from the new Confederation.

Put another way, while it has some significance, Ontario's practical commitment to the legacy of Trudeau cannot be relied on to promote the vigorous survival of a French-language culture in English-speaking North America. And in the late 1980s Ontario began to discover that its own particular commitments to Trudeau's vision of Canada can never mean a great deal to those sections of Quebec most concerned about the survival of Canada's historic French-language culture.

This is the logic behind the position of David Peterson's Ontario provincial government of the late 1980s. With the support of both the opposition provincial New Democrats and Progressive Conservatives, Queen's Park has gone ahead with Bill 8, which extends French-language services in designated areas but stops well short of official bilingualism in the federal or New Brunswick sense. Meanwhile, in the spirit of what the late nineteenth century Ontario press dubbed "the Mowat-Mercier Concordat," Peterson's regime has stood staunchly beside Bourassa's regime in Quebec in support of the Meech Lake Accord.

In some quarters Peterson has been criticized for not trying to bridge the gap between Quebec and Western Canada — on Senate reform, Meech Lake, and much else — that had appeared in rather stark contours by the end of 1989. Yet until some version of a Meech Lake Accord is secure, for Ontario to reach out to Western or Atlantic Canada could risk isolating Quebec in some dangerous way.

At the same time, Ontario's strategy is essentially a pragmatic one, as implied by Peterson's frequently articulated distaste for some of the more extreme rhetoric in the Quebec of the late 1980s. On this sense of events, if and when some convincing version of a Meech Lake Accord is secure, the way could be open for Ontario itself to become a source of pressure on Quebec over Senate reform.

Some sides of Ontario opinion, it is clear enough, are stridently sceptical about trying to change what Keith Davey has called the "unreformable Senate." But Canada's most populous province also has sentimental and self-interested attachments to nation building in the new Confederation. The

April 1989 Gallup Poll suggested both that a majority of the Ontario population favours an elected Senate and that this majority is only slightly smaller than in British Columbia and actually somewhat larger than in Atlantic Canada.

As Roger Gibbins argued in the early 1980s, a workable specific design for an elected, equal, and effective Senate based on credible nation-building aspirations, could have significant popular appeal in Ontario. In the 1990s it might be especially appealing as a counterweight to the decentralizing impulses of some version of a successful Meech Lake Accord and the Canada-U.S. Free Trade Agreement. A version of Senate reform that made modest bows to a moderated approximation of Trudeau's national vision, and to the ancient rights of the Canadian Indians, Inuit, and Métis, might particularly appeal to some strategic elements in the Ontario regional imagination.

Will Canada Fail Anyway?

Canada is a complicated country, and it should not be surprising if those of us who live within its borders periodically become confused about national politics. Within the often acid rhetoric and multidimensional popular alienations of the late 1980s, it is easy enough to find much evidence of various lamentable regional and cultural chauvinisms from the Atlantic to the Pacific to the Arctic Ocean. Yet it is also possible to find some evidence that the 1990s will finally bring positive answers to Goldwin Smith's Canadian question, in its late twentieth century incarnation.

For better or for worse, the Québécois strategy of gaining ground inside the Confederation by threatening to leave it is burning out. English Canada used to say "What does Quebec want?". More and more, it is becoming willing to say that if Quebec really does want to leave Canada, it ought to go ahead. Part of the reason is sheer weariness with an issue that has now had a pointed edge for a full generation. Yet another part — all superficial appearances to the contrary notwithstanding — is a subtle new kind of confidence in English Canada itself.

It has been said, for instance, that Brian Mulroney's free trade agreement with the United States will make it easier for Quebec to separate. For obvious reasons, the argument can convince Quebec's surviving separatists. Yet it is equally arguable that, here as elsewhere, the historic ironies that have shaped Canada's past can also shape its future. Outside Quebec, the Free Trade Agreement can suggest another view of geopolitical realities in North America.

North of the Gulf of Mexico at least, unlike Western Europe, North America has not been a place hospitable to geographically smaller national states. There are regional tensions in the United States as well as in Canada. The American Union fought the bloodiest war in its history to suppress them. French was an official language in the Louisiana state legislature until the middle of the nineteenth century. The most generous but quite unserious response of American political culture to late twentieth century Quebec separatism has been the U.S. journalist Joel Garreau's *The Nine Nations of North America*, inspired by the 1980 referendum.

Especially in the context of the Canada-U.S. Free Trade Agreement, all this raises a fundamental question: Is a stable, independent Quebec at all a realistic prospect — outside a highly improbable continental political universe that also includes, say, an independent Texas and an independent California?

The late twentieth century American Republic is at last just barely prepared to have an "international" free trade agreement with a Canadian Confederation that has a smaller population than California, but commands a geographic territory larger than that of the United States itself. Yet would it be prepared to grant the same access to the U.S. market to an independent Quebec, which would have a population not too much larger than that of the state of Virginia, without also ultimately demanding that Quebec pay the same allegiance to Washington that Virginia does? After all, both Texas and California have substantial populations that do not speak English either. Both were once part of non-Anglo-Saxon political enterprises, rather more recently than Quebec. And both were once independent republics in North America.

Of course, in a democracy we are theoretically free to try to do anything we want. The Quebec that has still not signed the 1982 Constitution is quite apparently not at all happy with its place in the new Canadian Confederation. Under some new Parti Québécois government, or perhaps even under yet another incarnation of Robert Bourassa himself, Quebec could decide to separate, regardless of the consequences for itself or anyone else. The greatest irony in Canadian history could prove to be that the heartland of the first people who called themselves Canadians will at last decide to abandon Canada.

It seems clear as well, however, that there will be little inclination in the rest of Canada to accommodate such a decision in any generous spirit. At the edge of the 1990s Canada does seem to be approaching a point of no return. According to an October 1989 opinion poll sponsored by the *Globe and Mail* and the CBC, some 73% of English-speaking Canadians feel that either the right amount or too much "is being done to protect the language rights of French-speaking people outside Quebec," while 67% of French-speaking Canadians feel that too little is being done. Similarly, some 71% of French-speaking Canadians feel that either the right amount or too much "is being done to protect the language rights of English-speaking people within Quebec," while 72% of English-speaking Canadians feel too little is being done.

On the bottom line suggested by this kind of evidence, a Quebec which continues to insist that it will secede unless it is recognized as one version or another of a distinct society must in fact be prepared to secede, and risk being truly cast adrift in the sea of English-speaking North America. Conversely, an English-speaking Canada which continues to insist that Quebec cannot in any way express what makes it different in the Constitution of the Confederation must be prepared to see Quebec secede, and equally risk the gradual absorption of what remains of Canada into the regional history of the American Republic.

Northern Lights at the End of the Tunnel

At this point in the argument, the late twentieth century debate on Senate reform in Canada can be read as a sign that the new Confederation does have real instincts to move beyond survival and stake out a new place for itself in

Brian Mulroney and the provincial premiers at a press conference announcing the good news from Meech Lake, 30 April 1987. (The final agreement, subject to ratification by all federal and provincial legislatures before 23 June 1990, would be signed in Ottawa on 3 June 1987.)

Mulroney is seated at the table. Standing behind him, from left to right, are : Richard Hatfield, New Brunswick; Robert Bourassa, Quebec; David Peterson, Ontario; John Buchanan, Nova Scotia; Howard Pawley, Manitoba; Bill Vander Zalm, British Columbia; Joe Ghiz, Prince Edward Island; Grant Devine, Saskatchewan; Brian Peckford, Newfoundland; and Don Getty, Alberta.

In an imperfect world, and under the right conditions, it could be a beginning for carrying on with the forging of the renewed Canadian federalism, that Pierre Trudeau and nine provincial premiers began in 1981.

the global village of the twenty-first century. Whatever else, Canadian history is unfolding in a potentially workable way, following useful enough habits and instincts acquired over the past four centuries.

Thus, a Quebec that continues to try to negotiate its rightful place in the Confederation as a trade-off for merely agreeing to remain in the country cannot get what it wants — unless it really does want to abandon the Canada that it has done as much or even more to create than any other province. It can only destroy Canada.

If Canada is destroyed, Canadians in other provinces must clearly bear part of the blame. But so must Quebec. In the new Confederation Quebec is no longer the oppressed heartland of a conquered people that it was in the old Dominion — even if it has not yet quite come to understand this itself (or even if this has not yet come to be fully understood by all Canadians in other provinces).

If the Canadian federal government of the 1990s were not officially bilingual, such that federal prime ministers must speak both English and French, then Quebec might be blameless. If New Brunswick were not officially bilingual, if there were no Bill 8 in Ontario and other French-language services in Manitoba, and if "French immersion" (for all its obvious inadequacies) were not part of English-speaking provincial education systems, then Quebec might be blameless. If there had been in Ottawa no Pierre Trudeau from Quebec, and if there were now no Brian Mulroney from Quebec, no Lucien and Benoît Bouchard from Quebec, and no Marcel Masse from Quebec, then Quebec might be blameless.

If the old British Canadian merchants of Montreal still ruled the regional economy on the banks of the ancient River of Canada, then Quebec might be blameless. If Ottawa had sent in red-coated Mounties to prevent the enforcement of French-only signs in Quebec, notwithstanding the notwithstanding clause in the 1982 Constitution, then Quebec might be blameless. And Quebec might also be blameless were it not now, as Daniel Latouche has explained, so insistent "on being an active player on the federal scene while retaining all that makes it different."

Yet, as it happens, there actually have been some rather deep changes throughout the Confederation since the late 1960s. The Quebec of the 1990s must itself accept part of the blame if the rest of Canada denies its right to be a distinct society, strictly on the argument that if this right is not recognized Quebec will leave the country.

On the other hand, if Quebec negotiates its rightful place in Canada on the basis of trade-offs for the kind of reformed federal Senate that will also help Western and Atlantic Canada gain their rightful places in the country, then it can help build the new Confederation — at the same time that it perfects its own regional dreams of maîtres chez nous.

In an imperfect world the Meech Lake Accord, or something very much like it, is the right, if not the best, beginning for this kind of new national development strategy. But those who support the Accord ought to be prepared to show that it will be only a beginning, not an end: not "the peace of the grave" that still troubles Pierre Trudeau and his most ardent surviving supporters.

Similarly, this kind of strategy — along with parallel new national development strategies for implementing the Canada-U.S. Free Trade Agreement in ways that strengthen, not weaken, Canada, and for weaving the rights of the Indians, Inuit, and Métis into the constitutional fabric of the 1990s — will demand something extra from all regions of the country. To believe in the future of Canada is to believe that, in one subtle or ironic way or another, all regions will give something extra when the clock strikes at last.

Some urge, for instance, that there is nothing for Ontario in Gordon Gibson's constitutional formula of a full distinct society for Quebec and some variety of elected, equal, and effective federal Senate for Western and Atlantic Canada. In the mid-1980s Donald Smiley alluded to a similar point. He speculated that especially the specific version of an elected Senate that excludes senators from the federal Cabinet

> might well have prevented the NEP from being put in effect
> or at least would have caused certain changes to be made to
> conform with Western interests. Yet this kind of obstruction
> might well have resulted in a consequent decline in Ottawa's
> legitimacy among residents of regions which benefitted
> from NEP.

This makes particular sense if Goldwin Smith was fundamentally correct about what Canada is and has been — if the Confederation actually is no more than an accidental and artificial collection of regions in the most northern part of North America, with no latent or inherent common interests and sympathies. What's more, no sensible observer of the elected, equal, and effective senates that already exist in the transcontinental federations of the United States and Australia would claim that there is anything inherently noble in these kinds of institutions.

Yet the argument that the long journey to Senate reform in Canada must soon enough come to a successful conclusion assumes that Harold Innis (who said La Vérendrye, not the British Empire, laid down the western border of Canada) has more apt and interesting things to tell us about the future of the country than Goldwin Smith. It assumes that the Canada which looks ahead to the twenty-first century actually is a place with some underlying political and geographic logic. It assumes that Canada today is a place where people in all regions and from all cultural groups have developed some authentic common interests and attachments in the course of a now not altogether inconsiderable history together. If this is true, then a new kind of federal Senate in Ottawa will at last give these interests and attachments a national forum for coalescing into new national policies that can command support from all parts of the Confederation.

The Quebec entertainer Yvon Deschamp's words are worth repeating when he claims that what Quebec really wants, in case anyone in English-speaking Canada is still listening, is "an independent Quebec in a united Canada." To some, this only reflects the improbability of carrying Canada's diverse destiny on into the twenty-first century. But the idea is also incredibly Canadian, in either official language. In many respects it is Quebec's own regional version of what the other regions and provinces of Canada want as well. In fact, an independent Quebec in a united Canada sounds very much like something that the wizard Mackenzie King might have been proud to invent. And it could easily enough be translated politically into a distinct society in Quebec and an elected, equal, and effective federal Senate in an at last truly united Canada.

In the same spirit, it is appropriate to propose at least one kind of answer to the general question set by Gordon Gibson, and noted in the first chapter of the book: "What is the usefulness of Canada anyway?" For someone who lives in the place and looks out at the ferment of the global village in the early 1990s, Canada has now achieved — from any sensible comparative perspective — a respectable enough, rather intriguing, and still happily youthful past, that has some authentic instincts about the challenges of the difficult but interesting new century of global history before us.

It is, of course, an extremely important part of the usefulness of Canada that Canadians are not meant to take their country with quite the kind of seriousness that finally leads to political prisoners, torture, and death camps (or even committees on "un-Canadian" activities). Canada will surely lean hard on its historic tradition of moderation and compromise as it moves on into the twenty-first century. Yet we have equally reached a point where, in both official languages, we ought to be taking our transcontinental confederation in a more serious and steely way than we did in the days of the now vanished Empire, on which the sun never set. And this is the deepest message of the late twentieth century political movement to at last reform the unreformed Senate of Canada, while opportunity is still knocking. Whatever else it may or may not be wrong on, Alberta is unmistakably right about the objective of *Strengthening Canada*.

APPENDICES

Three Proposals for a Reformed Senate

What follows summarizes three of the most prominent official proposals for an elected Canadian Senate advanced in the 1980s — one from the legislative branch of the federal government and two from provincial governments (one in Western and one in Atlantic Canada).

Appendix A. The first proposal was put forward by a joint committee of the federal Senate and House of Commons in Ottawa in 1984. Appendix A reproduces an abridged version of the chapter of the committee's report that outlines its specific recommendations. Everything that appears is taken directly from the report, but subsidiary parts of the original text have been omitted, to achieve a degree of brevity broadly comparable to the other proposals.

Appendix B. This reproduces the specific recommendations of the 1985 "Triple E" proposal developed by a committee of the Alberta Legislative Assembly and published in *Strengthening Canada*. Everything that appears is taken directly from the original document, with no omissions. For the sake of clarity one footnote has been added, taken from background material in the original document.

Appendix C. This reproduces a proposal tabled by the Government of Newfoundland and Labrador at the November 1989 First Ministers' Conference in Ottawa. Unlike the other proposals, it is cast in the form of a potential constitutional amendment. Again, everything that appears is taken directly from the original document, the only omissions being material dealing with matters other than Senate reform. Two footnotes have been added, taken from background material in the original document.

The proposals have been reproduced with the kind permission of responsible authorities in Ottawa, Edmonton, and St. John's.

APPENDIX A

EXCERPTS FROM *REPORT OF THE SPECIAL JOINT COMMITTEE OF THE SENATE AND OF THE HOUSE OF COMMONS ON SENATE REFORM.* Ottawa, January 1984. Chapter 6. An Elected Senate: The Committee's Proposal.

Having concluded that an elected Senate would best meet our objectives for reform, the Committee faced a wide range of choices on questions such as the method of election, the distribution of seats among the provinces, and the powers of the Senate. The choices ranged from a Senate with powers equal to those of the House of Commons and with an equal number of seats for each province, to an advisory rather than a legislative body, with a distribution of seats proportionate to the population of each province.

We tried to strike a balance between these extremes ....

The electoral system

The Committee had to choose between a majority system and proportional representation ....

Proportional representation is the system used to elect the Australian Senate and most western European legislatures. Essentially it gives each political party a number of parliamentary seats corresponding roughly to the percentage of votes cast for it ....

Opponents of proportional representation argue that if the system were used for Senate elections ... it would facilitate the emergence of purely regional parties ....

We have been impressed by this argument and have concluded that Senate reform should not stray from its true objectives ....

... the Committee found the present single-member plurality system simple and satisfactory. Voters are familiar with the system, having used it for generations to elect representatives to all levels of government ....

We should not conclude these comments ... without noting that we were urged by a number of witnesses to take a first-hand look at how proportional representation works in practice for Australian Senate elections .... We do recognize ... that a comprehensive review of alternative electoral systems for the Canadian Senate should ideally include an on-the-spot examination of the system used in Australia.

Constituency boundaries

... voters in each senatorial constituency would elect only one representative, as is the case in House of Commons elections .... Although population should be one criterion in determining the boundaries of Senate electoral districts, greater importance should be attached to geographic, community, linguistic and cultural factors than is the case for House of Commons constituencies .... At present Quebec is divided into 24 senatorial districts, the boundaries of which were delineated in 1856. They no longer have much relation to contemporary realities and should be abolished ....

The senatorial term and the timing of elections

We recognized that in choosing single-member constituencies we had to ensure that the role of elected senators would be quite clearly different from that of members of the House of Commons. Our proposal to restrict senators to a single term of office does this ....

It was difficult to decide how long the single term should be .... We ... decided to recommend a nine-year term, with one-third of the senators being elected every three years ....

These triennial elections should be held separately from Commons elections and on fixed dates — for example, on the second Monday of March in every third year. A number of witnesses recommended that Commons and Senate elections be held simultaneously, with half the Senate being elected at each Commons election ... we had ... objections ... the power to dissolve Parliament would give the government a certain measure of control over the Senate. We believe that senators would have more independence, and more authority as regional representatives, if their elections were separate....

Legal provisions governing Senate elections

Legal provisions will be needed governing such matters as who is eligible to vote or to stand as a candidate for election. These provisions should be set out in a new statute designed specifically to govern all aspects of Senate elections, including election expenses ....

The distribution of seats between the provinces and territories

At present, Senate seats are divided according to the principle of four equal geographic regions — Ontario, Quebec, the Western provinces and the Atlantic provinces. The principle of equality is not followed strictly, because the four Atlantic provinces have a total of 30 seats in the Senate, compared with 24 for each of the other regions ....

A number of witnesses argued strongly that each province should have equal representation in the Senate ....

... In Canada the application of the equality principle would enable the five least populous provinces — that is, those accounting for 13.4% of the Canadian population — to have a majority in the Senate if they had the support of the territorial representatives, whatever their number .... Moreover, if this system were adopted, the only province with a francophone majority would see its relative weight in the Senate, which stood at 33 per cent of the seats in 1867 and today stands at 23 per cent, plummet to less than 10 per cent.

We therefore concluded that, while providing for substantial over-representation of the less populous provinces and territories, we should propose a distribution that reflects the Canadian reality more accurately than simple numerical equality can do ....

... most members of the Committee favoured the following distribution: Ontario and Quebec would retain the same number of seats that they have now (24), and the other provinces would be given 12 seats each, with the exception of Prince Edward Island, which would be given 6. Yukon and the Northwest Territories would both have increased representation. This formula would produce a Senate with 144 members ....

The Senate's powers

Almost all the witnesses who spoke in favour of an elected Senate recommended that the Senate not be able to overturn a government. We agree fully. In a parliamentary system, a government cannot serve two masters, whose wills might on occasion be diametrically opposed.

A number of witnesses maintained that an elected Senate ought to have the same legislative powers as the House of Commons or, more accurately, that it should continue to have the powers assigned to it by the Constitution Act, 1867 .... If there were persistent disagreement between the two chambers, the disputed bill might be left in abeyance, or a joint committee composed of members from each house could try to agree on a mutually satisfactory redrafting. Some people proposed that if the disagreement persisted, a joint session of the two chambers could be held to resolve it by a majority vote; and if that failed, both houses could be dissolved and an election called.

... if the Senate enjoyed an absolute veto, the parliamentary process would become considerably more unwieldy than if it had just a suspensive veto. The government would have to be responsible to both houses. Double dissolution could mean a proliferation of elections, and the threat of dissolution could become an instrument of government control over senators. But the principal factor in our decision not to accord the Senate an absolute veto was the possibility, if not the probability, of our parliamentary institutions continually becoming deadlocked ....

We therefore decided that it was wiser and more in keeping with the character of parliamentary government to give the Senate the power to delay but not altogether prevent the adoption of measures voted by the House of Commons. The Senate would therefore have a suspensive veto of a maximum of 120 sitting days, divided into two equal periods of 60 days. Supply bills would not be subject to any delay ....

The double majority

To ensure additional protection for the French language and culture, we accept the argument of a number of witnesses that legislation of linguistic significance should be approved by a double majority in the Senate. Two methods for calculating such a majority were proposed to the Committee. One called for a majority of both francophone and anglophone senators. The other called for a majority of all senators that would have to include a majority of the francophone senators ....

Such a voting procedure would achieve its purpose only if the Senate veto on these matters were absolute ...

We propose that, at the time of swearing in, senators would be asked to declare whether they consider themselves francophone for purposes of the double majority.

Ratification of appointments

We believe that order in council appointments to federal agencies whose decisions have important regional implications should be subject to Senate ratification within a period of perhaps 30 sitting days. If the Senate did not reject an appointment within that period, it would be deemed to have ratified it.

Internal organization of the Senate

Under section 34 of the *Constitution Act, 1867*, the Speaker of the Senate is appointed and removed by the Governor General, on the recommendation of the Prime Minister .... We feel that the independence of the Senate would be increased if it would elect its own Speaker after each triennial election....

... we believe that the government and opposition supporters in the Senate should elect their own officers.

We considered the question of whether senators should be eligible for membership in the Cabinet .... The majority of Committee members ... believes that if ministers are drawn from the Senate, cabinet solidarity would prevail over their responsibility as regional representatives .... We conclude therefore that senators should not be eligible for cabinet office or for a position as parliamentary secretary ....

Witnesses have suggested that regional caucuses should be created, grouping senators from a given region regardless of their party affiliation, in order to emphasize their role as regional representatives. Such a practice would accord with the spirit and general intent of our report ....

APPENDIX B

REPORT OF THE ALBERTA SELECT SPECIAL COMMITTEE ON SENATE REFORM. Edmonton, March 1985.
Recommendations.

THE PURPOSE OF THE CANADIAN SENATE

IT IS RECOMMENDED THAT

The Senate of Canada should maintain as its primary purpose the objective established by the Fathers of Confederation, namely to represent the regions in the federal decision-making process.

In addition,

a) the Senate should continue to act as a body of "sober second thought";

b) another original purpose of the Senate, that is, to represent property owners, should be abandoned immediately;

c) the Senate should not be a forum for inter-governmental negotiations.

METHOD OF SELECTION

1. Current Membership

IT IS RECOMMENDED THAT

a) The tenure of current Senators should be terminated through an equitable severance process.

b) The termination of tenure should be accomplished as quickly as possible to facilitate an immediate move to the new system.

2. Method of Selection and Basis of Representation of New Senators

IT IS RECOMMENDED THAT

a) The Senate should consist of 64 Senators, six representing each province and two representing each territory;

b) Senators should be elected on a first-past-the-post basis, a system now in use in federal and provincial elections;

c) Senators should represent constituencies whose boundaries are identical to provincial boundaries;

d) Senators should be elected for the life of two provincial legislatures;

e) In each province, three Senators should be elected during each provincial election, with each voter being able to vote for three candidates;

f) The qualifications for candidates to the Senate should be the same as those for Members of Parliament;

g) Upon winning an election, Senators should be required to resign from any provincial or civic elected office they hold.

POWERS OF THE SENATE

IT IS RECOMMENDED THAT

a) The Senate should have the power to initiate any legislation except a money or taxation bill;

b) Notwithstanding (a), the Senate should have the power to initiate supply resolutions relating to the Senate's own operational budget;

c) The Senate should have the power to amend any bill, after which the House of Commons would consider the amendment;

d) The Senate should have the power to veto any bill except a supply bill;

e) The Senate should retain the existing 180 day suspensive veto over constitutional issues;

f) The House of Commons should have the power to override a Senate veto on money or taxation bills by a simple majority;

g) The Senate should vote on a money or taxation bill within 90 days and on other bills within 180 days after it is sent to the House of Commons;

h) The House of Commons should be able to override any amendment (veto) passed by the Senate on a bill other than a money or taxation bill, by a vote that is greater in percentage terms than the Senate's vote to amend;

i) Non-military treaties should be subject to ratification by the Senate;

j) All changes affecting the French and English languages in Canada should be subject to a "Double Majority" veto, that is, a majority of all Senators combined with a majority of French-speaking Senators or English-speaking Senators, depending on the issue. *

SENATE ORGANIZATION

IT IS RECOMMENDED THAT

a) The traditional opposition and government roles in the current Senate be abolished, including the positions of Government Leader and Opposition Leader;

b) Senators should be physically seated in provincial delegations, regardless of any party affiliations;

c) Each provincial delegation should select from its membership a chairman; chairmen should sit at the pleasure of the provincial delegation;

d) A Speaker should be elected by a majority of the Senate at a specified time every four years, and the Senate may, at any time, initiate an election for Speaker by a two-thirds vote;

e) The ten provincial chairmen, headed by the Speaker of the Senate, should constitute a "Senate Executive Council";

f) The Senate Executive Council should determine the order of business of the Senate, appointment of committee chairmen and membership of committees;

g) The characterization of legislation, that is, the determination of whether a bill is or is not a money or taxation bill, should be carried out by joint agreement of the Speakers of the House of Commons and the Senate, in accordance with the British definition of a supply bill;

h) Senate Executive Council members should receive remuneration and staff assistance in addition to that received by other Senators;

i) Senators should not be eligible for appointments to Cabinet.

---

* Candidates to the Senate would declare themselves French or English-speaking at the time of being nominated and would be judged in that way by the electorate.

OTHER RECOMMENDATIONS

IT IS RECOMMENDED THAT

a) The requirement that First Ministers' Conferences meet on a regular basis should be entrenched in the Constitution;

b) First Ministers should have the power to ratify Supreme Court appointments by a majority vote;

c) The use of emergency powers by the federal government should require ratification by a majority vote of First Ministers except in war time;

d) Federal powers of reservation and disallowance are antiquated and unnecessary and therefore should be abolished.

APPENDIX C

CONSTITUTIONAL AMENDMENTS ON SENATE REFORM PROPOSED BY THE GOVERNMENT OF NEWFOUNDLAND AND LABRADOR.
First Ministers' Conference, Ottawa, November 1989.

The *Constitution Act, 1867* is amended ... by adding thereto immediately after section 1 thereof, the following section:

2. (1) In order to uphold the fundamental characteristic of Canada and preserve the distinct society of Quebec ... the Senate of Canada shall, solely for the purposes set out in paragraph (2), be divided into linguistic divisions in which all senators from every province in which English is the provincial official language shall constitute the English Division and all provinces in which French is the provincial official language shall constitute the French Division and each province where, by constitutional provision, English and French are provincial official languages shall constitute a separate Division.

(2) Every constitutional amendment affecting linguistic or cultural rights or the civil law system including the proportion of civil law judges on the Supreme Court of Canada shall be submitted to a separate vote in each linguistic division of the Senate and no such constitutional amendment shall be deemed to have been approved by the Senate unless it shall have been approved by the majority of the whole Senate and the majority in each division of the Senate ....

Sections 21 to 36 inclusive and Sections 51A and 53 of the *Constitution Act, 1867* are repealed and the following substituted therefore:

The Senate

21. The Upper House, styled the Senate, constituted by Section 17 of this Act, shall be composed of members called Senators who shall be drawn from throughout Canada in accordance with the provisions of sections 22 and 23.

22. (1) Each of the Provinces of Canada is at all times entitled to be represented in the Senate by 6 Senators.

(2) Any province which may be created pursuant to the provisions of the Constitution, after this section comes into force, shall on and after its creation be entitled to be represented in the Senate by 6 Senators.

23. (1) Senators shall be chosen by the people of Canada through popular election in accordance with the provisions of this section.

(2) Except as otherwise provided in sub-section 5, Senators shall be elected for a term of 6 years and Senators shall be eligible for re-election.

(3) Senate elections shall be held throughout Canada on the last Monday of October every three years.

(4) The first election, hereinafter referred to as "the initial election" will be held on the last Monday of October not less than one year nor more than two years after this provision comes into force.

(5) One half of the Senators elected from each Province at the initial election shall be elected for a term of 3 years and the balance of the Senators elected at the initial election shall be elected for a term of 6 years.

(6) The Parliament of Canada may make laws in relation to the method of election, the creation of senatorial districts, and procedures for the election of Senators, including laws in relation to the financing of elections, the funding of election campaigns, and the nomination of candidates.

24. Any person is eligible to be elected as a Senator for a Province if that person:
    (a)   Is a Canadian citizen;
    (b)   Is of the full age of 18 years as at the date of the election;
    (c)   Has been ordinarily resident within that province for an aggregate period of at least five years during the ten years immediately preceding the election and is resident within that province at the date of the election; and
    (d)   Is not a member of the House of Commons or a Legislative Assembly at the date of the election.

25. A Senator shall not be eligible to be a Minister.

26. If a vacancy occurs in the Senate through the death or resignation of a Senator at any time before the final year of the term, then such a vacancy shall be filled by a by-election to be held within 90 days. The Senator to be elected to fill the vacancy shall be elected for the balance of the term of the Senator who vacated the seat.

27. The Senate is empowered to establish its own procedures for the election of the Speaker of the Senate and the conduct of its business.*

28. (1) Bills proposed to Parliament, other than bills for appropriating money solely for the ordinary annual essential services of the government or for imposing any tax or impost, may originate in the Senate equally as in the House of Commons.

(2) A Bill shall not be taken to impose taxation, by reason only of its containing provisions for the imposition or appropriation of fines or other pecuniary penalties, or for the demand or payment or appropriation of fees for licences or services.

29. (1) A Bill certified by the Speaker of the House of Commons as being a Bill to appropriate money solely for the ordinary annual essential services of the government shall not be required to be passed by the Senate, if the Senate has not within 45

---

* This section would permit, for example, the establishment of a non-partisan Senate executive council made up of the chairpersons of the 10 provincial delegations, as proposed by the Alberta Task Force on Senate Reform.

sitting days either passed the Bill as presented or amended it in a manner agreeable to the House of Commons.

(2) A Bill which appropriates revenue or money for the ordinary annual essential services of the government shall deal only with such appropriation.

30. Neither a defeat of a government sponsored Bill, motion, or resolution in the Senate nor a specific confidence motion in the Senate shall constitute a vote of non-confidence in the government so as to require the government's resignation.

31. (1) A joint standing committee known as the Reconciliation Committee which shall be composed of ten Senators and ten members of the House of Commons is hereby established for the purpose of this section.

(2) The Senate and the House of Commons shall elect from among its members persons to be appointed to the Reconciliation Committee established pursuant to this section.

(3) Where any Bill that has been passed by one House and presented to the second House
(a) has been refused passage by the second House;
(b) has not been finally dealt with by the second House and not less than 45 sitting days have elapsed since the Bill was presented to the second House; or
(c) has been duly amended by the second House and the first House has duly advised the second House that it does not concur in all or some of the amendments made by the second House, the Bill in the form in which it was presented to the second House but with such amendments made by the second House as may be concurred in by the first House in the case of a Bill to which clause (c) applies, may be referred by the Speaker of either House to the Reconciliation Committee for the purpose of seeking to reconcile the differences and seek a mutually acceptable compromise.

32. (1) No appointment of a person to be a chairman, president, chief executive officer or director of any of the Crown Corporations, Boards or Commissions subject to the application of the federal Financial Administration Act shall have effect until such time as the appointment of that person has been affirmed by the Senate.

(2) If no decision is taken by the Senate within 60 sitting days of a nomination being referred to it, then the appointment shall be deemed to have been affirmed by the Senate.

Section 47 of the Constitution Act, 1982 is repealed.*

---

* This repeals a section of the current constitutional amending formula which allows the Senate to be by-passed on certain constitutional amendments. Its repeal is essential in order to ensure an effective vote by the linguistic divisions. Otherwise such votes could be overridden by the House of Commons after six months.

SELECT BIBLIOGRAPHY

Where appropriate, the date of first publication for an item is inserted before the date of the edition cited.

Speeches and Addresses

Ghiz, Joseph. "Text of Speech to the Canadian Club of Montreal." Montreal, 19 January 1987.

Horsman, Jim. "Notes for an Address to the Canadian Club of Toronto." Toronto, 30 January 1989.

Kent, Tom. "Notes for an Address." Atlantic Provinces Economic Council, Atlantic Conference '69. Halifax, 27 October 1969.

Lee, James. "Statement by the Hon. James M. Lee to the Royal Commission on the Economic Union and Development Prospects for Canada." Toronto, 9 December 1983.

MacKinnon, Stuart. "First Ministers' Conferences." Presentation at the Fifth Conference on Public Policy and Administrative Studies, University of Guelph, 22 April 1988.

MacTavish, W.L. "A Western Viewpoint of the Imperial Conference." Toronto, 31 October 1932. Reprinted in *Addresses Delivered before the Canadian Club of Toronto. Season of 1932–33.* Toronto: Warwick Bros. & Rutter, 1933, 130-143.

McKenna, Frank. "Presentation to the Special Joint Committee on the Constitution." Ottawa, 25 August 1987.

Murray, Lowell. "Keynote Speech to the National Conference on Senate Reform." Edmonton, 5 May 1988.

Books First Published before 1945

Bryce, James. *Canada: An Actual Democracy.* Toronto: Macmillan of Canada, 1921.

Creighton, Donald. *The Empire of the St. Lawrence.* Toronto: Macmillan of Canada, 1937, 1956.

Grant, George M. *Ocean to Ocean: Sanford Fleming's Expedition through Canada in 1872.* Edmonton: Hurtig, 1873, 1967.

Haliburton, Thomas Chandler. *The Bubbles of Canada.* London: Richard Bentley, 1839.

Innis, Harold. *The Fur Trade in Canada: An Introduction to Canadian Economic History.* Toronto: University of Toronto Press, 1930, 1970.

Jenness, Diamond. *The Indians of Canada.* Toronto: University of Toronto Press, 1932, 1977.

Parkman, Francis. *The Conspiracy of Pontiac and the Indian War after the Conquest of Canada.* Toronto: George N. Morang, 1851, 1899.

Siegfried, André. *La Canada, les deux races: problèmes politiques contemporains.* Paris: Librairie Armand Colin, 1906.

Smith, Goldwin. *Canada and the Canadian Question.* Toronto: University of Toronto Press, 1891, 1971.

Wrong, George M., et al. *The Federation of Canada 1867–1917.* Toronto: Oxford University Press, 1917.

More Recent General Literature

Berger, Carl. *The Writing of Canadian History, Aspects of English-Canadian Historical Writing: 1900 to 1970.* Toronto: Oxford University Press, 1976.

Bernard, André. *La Politique au Canada et au Québec.* Montreal: Les Presses de l'Université du Québec, 1976.

Brady, Alexander. *Democracy in the Dominions: A Comparative Study in Institutions.* Toronto: University of Toronto Press, 1947, 1958.

Chapin, Miriam. *Contemporary Canada*. New York: Oxford University Press, 1959.

Creighton, Donald. *Harold Adams Innis: Portrait of a Scholar*. Toronto: University of Toronto Press, 1957, 1978.

Easterbrook, W.T., and Hugh G.J. Aitken. *Canadian Economic History*. Toronto: Macmillan of Canada, 1956.

Franks, C.E.S. *The Parliament of Canada*. Toronto: University of Toronto Press, 1987.

Grant, George P. *Lament for a Nation: The Defeat of Canadian Nationalism*. Toronto: McClelland and Stewart, 1965.

Innis, Harold. *The Bias of Communication*. Toronto: University of Toronto Press, 1951.

_____, *Essays in Canadian Economic History*. Edited by Mary Q. Innis. Toronto: University of Toronto Press, 1956.

Peckham, Howard. *Pontiac and the Indian Uprising*. Princeton: Princeton University Press, 1947.

Wallace, Elisabeth. *Goldwin Smith: Victorian Liberal*. Toronto: University of Toronto Press, 1957.

The Canadian Centenary Series History of Canada

Brown, Robert Craig, and Ramsay Cook. *Canada 1896–1921: A Nation Transformed*. Toronto: McClelland and Stewart, 1974.

Creighton, Donald. *The Forked Road: Canada 1939–1957*. Toronto: McClelland and Stewart, 1976.

Granatstein, J.L. *Canada 1957–1967: The Years of Uncertainty and Innovation*. Toronto: McClelland and Stewart, 1986.

Morton, W.L. *The Critical Years: The Union of British North America 1857–1873*. Toronto: McClelland and Stewart, 1964.

Thompson, John Herd, and Allen Seager. *Canada 1922–1939: Decades of Discord*. Toronto: McClelland and Stewart, 1985.

Waite, P.B. *Canada 1874–1896: Arduous Destiny*. Toronto: McClelland and Stewart, 1971.

Western Canada

Brown, Brian A. *The New Confederation: Five Sovereign Provinces*. Saanichton and Seattle: Hancock House, 1977.

Canada. *Western Economic Opportunities Conference, Calgary, Alberta, July 24 to 26, 1973.* Verbatim record and documents. Ottawa: Minister of Supply and Services Canada, 1977.

Conway, J.F. *The West: The History of a Region in Confederation*. Toronto: James Lorimer, 1983.

Cook, Ramsay. *The Politics of John W. Dafoe and the Free Press*. Toronto: University of Toronto Press, 1963.

Doern, G. Bruce, and Glen Toner. *The Politics of Energy: The Development and Implementation of the NEP*. Toronto: Methuen, 1985.

Fetherling, Doug, ed. *A George Woodcock Reader*. Ottawa: Deneau & Greenberg, 1980.

Fisher, Robin. *Contact and Conflict: Indian-European Relations in British Columbia, 1774–1890*. Vancouver: University of British Columbia Press, 1977.

Fowke, Vernon. *The National Policy and the Wheat Economy*. Toronto: University of Toronto Press, 1957.

Gibbins, Roger. *Prairie Politics: Regionalism in Decline*. Toronto: Butterworths, 1980.

Howay, F.W., W.N. Sage, and H.F. Angus. *British Columbia and the United States: The North Pacific Slope from Fur Trade to Aviation*. Toronto: The Ryerson Press, 1942.

Kilgour, David. *Uneasy Patriots: Western Canadians in Confederation*. Edmonton: Lone Pine Publishing, 1988.

Lipset, Seymour Martin. *Agrarian Socialism: The Cooperative Commonwealth Federation in Saskatchewan*. New York: Doubleday, 1950, 1968.

Macpherson, C.B. *Democracy in Alberta: Social Credit and the Party System*. Toronto: University of Toronto Press, 1953, 1962.

Milloy, John S. *The Plains Cree: Trade, Diplomacy and War, 1790 to 1870*. Winnipeg: University of Manitoba Press, 1988.

Mitchell, David J. *W.A.C. Bennett and the Rise of British Columbia*. Vancouver: Douglas and McIntyre, 1983.

Morton, W.L. *The Progressive Party in Canada.* Toronto: University of Toronto Press, 1950, 1967.

Pratt, Larry, and Garth Stevenson, eds. *Western Separatism: The Myths, Realities and Dangers.* Edmonton: Hurtig, 1981.

Rasporich, A.W., ed. *The Making of the Modern West: Western Canada Since 1945.* Calgary: University of Calgary Press, 1984.

Stanley, George F.G. *The Birth of Western Canada: A History of the Riel Rebellions.* Toronto: University of Toronto Press, 1936, 1960.

Tyre, Robert. *Douglas in Saskatchewan: The Story of a Socialist Experiment.* Vancouver: Mitchell Press, 1962.

Wild, Roland. *Amor De Cosmos.* Toronto: The Ryerson Press, 1958.

Atlantic Canada

Acheson, T.W., et al. *Industrialization and Underdevelopment in the Maritimes 1880–1930.* Toronto: Garamond Press, 1985.

Alexander, David G. *Atlantic Canada and Confederation: Essays in Canadian Political Economy.* Compiled by Eric W. Sager et al. Toronto: University of Toronto Press in association with Memorial University of Newfoundland, 1983.

Atlantic Development Council. *A Strategy for the Economic Development of the Atlantic Region, 1971–1981.* Fredericton: The Council, 1971.

Bird, Will R. *These are the Maritimes.* Toronto: The Ryerson Press, 1959.

Chadwick, St John. *Newfoundland: Island into Province.* Cambridge: Cambridge University Press, 1967.

Chapin, Miriam. *Atlantic Canada.* Toronto: The Ryerson Press, 1956.

Clark, Andrew Hill. *Acadia: The Early Geography of Nova Scotia to 1760.* Madison: University of Wisconsin Press, 1968.

Innis, Harold. *The Cod Fisheries: The History of an International Economy.* Toronto: University of Toronto Press. 1940, 1954.

Mackenzie, David. *Inside the Atlantic Triangle: Canada and the Entrance of Newfoundland into Confederation, 1939–1949.* Toronto: University of Toronto Press, 1986.

Rawlyk, G.A., ed. *Historical Essays on the Atlantic Provinces.* Toronto: McClelland and Stewart, 1967.

_____., ed. *The Atlantic Provinces and the Problems of Confederation.* St. John's: Breakwater, 1979.

Stanley, Della M.M. *Louis Robichaud: A Decade of Power.* Halifax: Nimbus Publishing, 1984.

Tricoche, George Nestler. *Rambles through the Maritime Provinces of Canada: A Neglected Part of the British Empire.* London: Arthur H. Stockwell, 1931.

Whitelaw, William Menzies. *The Maritimes and Canada before Confederation.* Toronto: Oxford University Press, 1934.

Ontario and Quebec

Behiels, Michael D. *Prelude to Quebec's Quiet Revolution: Liberalism vs. Neo-Nationalism, 1945–1960.* Montreal: McGill-Queen's University Press, 1985.

_____., ed. *Quebec Since 1945: Selected Readings.* Toronto: Copp Clark Pitman, 1987.

Biggar, C.R.W. *Sir Oliver Mowat: A Biographical Sketch.* 2 vols. Toronto: Warwick Bros. & Rutter, 1905.

Hall, Roger, et al., eds. *Patterns of the Past: Interpreting Ontario's History.* Toronto: Dundurn Press, 1988.

Lévesque, René. *La Solution: Le Programme du Parti Québécois.* Montreal: Editions du Jour, 1970.

McRoberts, Kenneth. *Quebec: Social Change and Political Crisis.* Toronto: McClelland and Stewart, 1976, 1980, 1988.

Piva, Michael J., ed. *A History of Ontario: Selected Readings.* Toronto: Copp Clark Pitman, 1988.

Ryerson, Stanley B. *Unequal Union: Roots of Crisis in the Canadas, 1815–1873.* Toronto: Progress Books, 1968, 1983.

Silver, A.I. *The French-Canadian Idea of Confederation, 1864-1900.* Toronto: University of Toronto Press, 1982.

Spelt, Jacob. *Urban Development in South-Central Ontario.* Toronto: McClelland and Stewart, 1955, 1972.

Trigger, Bruce G. *The Huron: Farmers of the North.* New York: Holt, Rinehart and Winston, 1969.

Yeates, Maurice. *Main Street: Windsor to Quebec City.* Toronto: Macmillan of Canada, 1975.

Books By and About Politicians

Borden, Robert. *Robert Laird Borden: His Memoirs.* 2 vols. Toronto: McClelland and Stewart, 1938, 1969.

Bothwell, Robert, and William Kilbourn. *C.D. Howe: A Biography.* Toronto: McClelland and Stewart, 1979.

Brown, Robert Craig. *Robert Laird Borden: A Biography.* Vol. 1, 1854–1914. Toronto: Macmillan of Canada, 1975.

Camp, Dalton. *Gentlemen, Players and Politicians.* Toronto: McClelland and Stewart, 1970.

_____,*The Rainmaker: A Passion for Politics.* Toronto: Stoddart, 1986.

Gordon, Walter. *A Political Memoir.* Toronto: McClelland and Stewart, 1977.

Hutchison, Bruce. *The Incredible Canadian.* Toronto: Longmans Canada, 1952.

Neatby, H. Blair. *William Lyon Mackenzie King 1924–1932: The Lonely Heights.* Toronto: University of Toronto Press, 1963.

_____,*William Lyon Mackenzie King 1942–1939: The Prism of Unity.* Toronto: University of Toroto Press, 1976.

Pelletier, Gérard. *The October Crisis.* Translated by Joyce Marshall. Toronto: McClelland and Stewart, 1971.

_____, *Years of Impatience 1950–1960.* Translated by Alan Brown. Toronto: Methuen, 1984.

Pickersgill, J.W. *The Mackenzie King Record.* Vol. 1, 1939–1944. Toronto: University of Toronto Press, 1960.

Sweeny, Alastair. *George-Etienne Cartier: A Biography.* Toronto: McClelland and Stewart, 1976.

Trudeau, Pierre. *Le Fédéralisme et la société canadienne française.* Montreal: Editions HMH, 1967.

_____, *With a Bang, Not a Whimper.* Edited by Donald Johnston. Toronto: Stoddart, 1988.

Confederation and the Constitution

Banting, Keith, and Richard Simeon, eds. *And No One Cheered: Federalism, Democracy and the Constitution Act.* Toronto: Methuen, 1983.

Canadian Intergovernmental Conference Secretariat. *The Constitutional Review 1968–1971: Secretary's Report.* Ottawa: Information Canada, 1974.

_____, *Proposals on the Constitution 1971–1978.* Ottawa: The Secretariat, 1978.

Forsey, Eugene. *Freedom and Order: Collected Essays.* Toronto: McClelland and Stewart, 1974.

Hogg, Peter. *Meech Lake Constitutional Accord Annotated.* Toronto: Carswell, 1988.

Lederman, W.R. *Continuing Canadian Constitutional Dilemmas: Essays on the Constitutional History, Public Law and Federal System of Canada.* Toronto: Butterworths, 1981.

McWhinney, Edward. *Canada and the Constitution, 1979–1982: Patriation of the Charter of Rights.* Toronto: University of Toronto Press, 1982.

Nicholson, Norman L. *The Boundaries of the Canadian Confederation.* Toronto: Macmillan of Canada, 1954, 1979.

Romanow, Roy et al. *Canada ... Notwithstanding: The Making of the Constitution 1976–1982.* Toronto: Carswell/Methuen, 1984.

Smith, Jennifer. "Canadian Confederation and the Influence of American Federalism." *Canadian Journal of Political Science,* 21,3 (September 1988): 443–463.

Waite, P.B. *The Life and Times of Confederation 1864-1867: Politics, Newspapers, and the Union of British North America.* Toronto: University of Toronto Press, 1961, 1962.

White, W.L., et al. *Canadian Confederation: A Decision-Making Analysis.* Toronto: McClelland and Stewart, 1979.

Regionalism and Regional Development

Aucoin, Peter, ed. *Party Government and Regional Representation in Canada.* Toronto: University of Toronto Press for Supply and Services Canada, 1985.

Bradfield, Michael. *Regional Economics: Analysis and Policies in Canada.* Toronto: McGraw-Hill Ryerson, 1988.

Brewis, T.N. *Regional Economic Policies in Canada.* Toronto: Macmillan of Canada, 1969.

Careless, Anthony G.S. *Initiative and Response: The Adaptation of Canadian Federalism to Regional Economic Development.* Montreal: McGill-Queen's University Press, 1977.

Elkins, David J., and Richard Simeon. *Small Worlds: Provinces and Parties in Canadian Political Life.* Toronto: Methuen, 1980.

Gibbins, Roger. *Regionalism: Territorial Politics in Canada and the United States.* Toronto: Butterworths, 1982.

Harris, R. Cole, and John Warkentin. *Canada before Confederation: A Study in Historical Geography.* New York: Oxford University Press, 1974.

Long, J. Anthony, and Menno Boldt, eds. *Governments in Conflict? Provinces and Indian Nations in Canada.* Toronto: University of Toronto Press, 1988.

Norrie, Kenneth, ed. *Disparities and Interregional Adjustment.* Toronto: University of Toronto Press for Minister of Supply and Services Canada, 1986.

Savoie, Donald J. *Federal-Provincial Collaboration: The Canada–New Brunswick General Development Agreement.* Montreal: McGill-Queen's University Press, 1981.

_____,*Regional Economic Development: Canada's Search for Solutions.* Toronto: University of Toronto Press, 1986.

Weaver, Sally M. *Making Canadian Indian Policy: The Hidden Agenda, 1968–1970.* Toronto: University of Toronto Press, 1981.

Federalism and Federal-Provincial Relations

Armstrong, Christopher. *The Politics of Federalism: Ontario's Relations with the Federal Government, 1867–1942.* Toronto: University of Toronto Press, 1981.

Canada. *Report of the Royal Commission on Dominion-Provincial Relations. Book I.* Ottawa: The Commission, 1940.

Canadian Intergovernmental Conference Secretariat. *Federal-Provincial First Ministers' Conferences 1906–1985.* Ottawa: The Secretariat, 1986.

Crepeau, P.-A., and C.B. Macpherson, eds. *The Future of Canadian Federalism/L'Avenir du fédéralisme canadien.* Toronto: University of Toronto Press, 1965.

Milne, David. *Tug of War: Ottawa and the Provinces Under Trudeau and Mulroney.* Toronto: James Lorimer, 1986.

Quantrell, James. *Canada, Federal Provincial Conferences of First Ministers, 1887–1976: Guide to Microfiche Edition.* Toronto: Micromedia Limited, 1977.

Saunders, S.A., and Eleanor Back. *The Rowell-Sirois Commission. Parts I and II.* Toronto: The Ryerson Press, 1940.

Simeon, Richard. *Federal-Provincial Diplomacy: The Making of Recent Policy in Canada.* Toronto: University of Toronto Press, 1972, 1973.

Smiley, Donald V. *Canada in Question.* Toronto: McGraw-Hill Ryerson, 1972, 1976, 1980.

_____, *The Federal Condition in Canada.* Scarborough: McGraw-Hill Ryerson, 1987.

Stevenson, Garth. *Unfulfilled Union: Canadian Federalism and National Unity.* Toronto: Macmillan of Canada, 1979.

Wiltshire, Kenneth. *Planning and Federalism: Australian and Canadian Experience.* St. Lucia, Queensland: University of Queensland Press, 1986.

Alberta. *A Provincially-Appointed Senate: A New Federalism for Canada.* Edmonton: Government of Alberta, 1982.

_____. Select Special Committee on Upper House Reform. *Strengthening Canada: Reform of Canada's Senate.* Edmonton: Plains Publishing, 1985, 1988.

Campbell, Colin. *The Canadian Senate: A Lobby from Within.* Toronto: Macmillan of Canada, 1978.

Canada. The Honourable Mark MacGuigan, Minister of Justice. *Reform of the Senate: A Discussion Paper.* Ottawa: Publications Canada, 1983.

_____, Special Joint Committee of the Senate and House of Commons on Senate Reform. *Report.* Ottawa: The Senate of Canada, 1984.

Dempsey, Hugh A. *The Gentle Persuader: A Biography of James Gladstone, Indian Senator.* Saskatoon: Western Producer Prairie Books, 1986.

Engelmann, Frederick C. "A Prologue to Structural Reform of the Government of Canada." *Canadian Journal of Political Science,* 14, 4 (December, 1986): 667-678.

Gibbins, Roger. *Senate Reform: Moving towards the Slippery Slope.* Kingston: Institute of Intergovernmental Relations, Queen's University, 1983.

Knowles, Valerie. *First Person: A Biography of Cairine Wilson, Canada's First Woman Senator.* Toronto: Dundurn Press, 1988.

Kunz, F.A. *The Modern Senate of Canada 1925–1963: A Re-appraisal.* Toronto: University of Toronto Press, 1965.

MacKay, R.A. *The Unreformed Senate of Canada.* Toronto: McClelland and Stewart, 1926, 1963.

McCauley, Janet Marie. "The Senate of Canada: Maintenance of a Second Chamber through Functional Adaptability." Ph.D. dissertation, Pennsylvania State University, 1983.

McCormick, Peter, et al. *Regional Representation: The Canadian Partnership.* Calgary: The Canada West Foundation, 1981.

Robertson, Gordon. *A House Divided: Meech Lake, Senate Reform and the Canadian Union.* Ottawa: Institute for Research on Public Policy, 1989.

Rosen, Philip. "Major Proposals for Reform of the Senate and the Supreme Court of Canada Since the 1971 Victoria Charter." Ottawa: Library of Parliament, 1980.

Ross, George. *The Senate of Canada: Its Constitution, Powers and Duties Historically Considered.* Toronto: Copp Clark, 1914.

Smiley, Donald V. *An Elected Senate for Canada? Clues from the Australian Experience.* Kingston: Institute of Intergovernmental Relations, Queen's University, 1985.

LIST OF ILLUSTRATIONS

Page. Illustration and Credit

INDEX

Page numbers in bold type indicate an illustration.

CURRENT ISSUES IN HISTORICAL PERSPECTIVE SERIES

1. *Fur Trade to Free Trade:*
   Putting the Canada-U.S. Trade Agreement in Historical Perspective
   by Randall White

   Fur Trade to Free Trade:
   Putting the Canada-U.S. Trade Agreement in Historical Perspective,
   Second Edition by Randall White
   (Revised and enlarged after the Canada-U.S.
   Trade Agreement came into effect)

2. *Voice of Region:*
   The Long Journey to Senate Reform in Canada
   by Randall White

3. *The History of Immigration in Canada*
   by Valerie Knowles (publication date: 1991)

For further information on these and forthcoming titles, please contact:
DUNDURN PRESS, 2181 Queen Street East, Suite 301, Toronto, Ontario, M4E 1E5
Tel: (416) 698-0454 Fax: (416) 698-1102